W9-BRS-921

DISCARDED
Northbrook Public Library
3 1123 00762 0449

ALSO BY GEORGE STELLA

Livin' Low Carb: Family Recipes Stella Style

Eating Stella Style

Low-Carb Recipes for Healthy Living

George Stella

with Christian Stella

SIMON & SCHUSTER

NEW YORK • LONDON • TORONTO • SYDNEY

SIMON & SCHUSTER
Rockefeller Center
1230 Avenue of the Americas
New York, NY 10020

First Simon & Schuster paperback edition 2006

SIMON & SCHUSTER and colophon are registered trademarks of Simon & Schuster, Inc.

For information about special discounts for bulk purchases, please contact Simon & Schuster Special Sales: 1-800-456-6798 or business@simonandschuster.com.

Designed by Charles Kreloff

Manufactured in the United States of America

10 9 8 7 6 5 4 3 2 1

Library of Congress Cataloging-in-Publication Data
Stella, George.
Eating Stella style : low-carb recipes for healthy living / George Stella with Christian Stella.
p. cm.
Includes index.
1. Low-carbohydrate diet—Recipes. 2. Weight loss. I. Stella, Christian. II. Title.

RM237.73.S74 2006
613.2'5—dc22 2005054196

ISBN-13: 978-0-7432-8521-6
ISBN-10: 0-7432-8521-2

Acknowledgments

This book is a combined family effort with the pages bound by our individual strengths and achievements.

I count my blessings every day for my amazing, supportive, and loving family. I can never thank my wife, Rachel, enough, for not only keeping the house running but for shopping and tirelessly testing all of the recipes in this book and still finding the time and energy to be at my side after twenty-five years.

Proud thanks to my son, Anthony, who devoted months toward creating our supportive Web site stellastyle.com and then researching to ensure detailed, accurate nutritional information for every recipe.

To Christian, who I have learned is quite the polished writer, I send gleaming thanks for helping me get this book together, working day and night and making my stacks of notes into something legible!

My family will always be grateful to our friends Dr. Timothy O'Leary and his wife, Kathleen. From the start they have unselfishly sacrificed and *paid it forward* by helping us continue to share our story to help others.

Warmest thanks to my wonderful friends at Simon and Schuster: to Amanda Murray, our editor, who I love like a sister. She has made writing books a pleasurable experience, allowing us to often forget that it is actually hard work. Thanks to Sandra Bark, who worked hand in hand with Christian to make this the best book it could be, and to take out some of my nonsense before you would think I was crazy or something! (Bet they take out that last line, too!)

Many thanks to my friends in the marketing department: Elizabeth Hayes and Deirdre Mueller for always being there to help whenever I need it, especially free books! (I have a lot of relatives, you know.)

Continued thanks go to my literary agent, Susan Barry of the Barry-Swayne Literary Agency, for her continued support.

It was our sincere pleasure to have our food so deliciously caught on film by Mark Thomas of Mark Thomas Studios once again. Big thanks to Nancy Micklin Thomas, prop stylist, and Anne Disrude, food stylist extraordinaire, for making our food look fit for a king!

Thank you to a true great and a truly great guy, Frank Veronsky, for the amazing cover photograph. Frank made it easy, fun, and real; we had a blast!

Speaking of the cover photograph, very special thanks go to two new friends here in Norwalk, Connecticut. First thanks goes to Tess Abalos and Wild Oats Market for supplying all the outrageous food in the picture. Wild Oats is by far the best and most up and coming whole foods market in the country. If you are lucky enough to have one nearby, you will love it! Neighborly thanks to Meredith Miller and CLARKE Distribution Corporation, New England's luxury kitchen and bath resource, for unselfishly and freely opening your kitchen wonderland to us to take photographs!

Most of all, I am thankful to be here. I have been given another chance to enjoy my family—my life—and I will never let it go again.

Contents

Eating Stella Style

Introduction: Getting Started

Where to start, where to start?

Let's start fresh.

I'm George Stella, professional chef and champion of fresh, healthy foods that taste great! I call it *Stella Style.*

It seems like only yesterday that I tipped the scales at a whopping 467 pounds. That's right, 467 pounds!

Now, I'm healthier than I've ever been!

What do *you* have to lose?

Over the past seven years, my family and I have dropped a combined total of 560 pounds. We've exchanged our old habits for new, healthier ones, and we've never felt better! I'm traveling in airplanes without having to ask for a seatbelt extender. I'm fitting into smaller and smaller clothes, and no longer have to shop from specialty "big men's" catalogs.

I feel like I'm finally living the life I always should have had.

Even now, after losing more than 260 pounds and keeping the weight off for years, it's still painful for me to think back to what my life was like then. When my whole family was overweight, we couldn't do anything without attracting attention—the stares of strangers were something we came to expect! Now, when I'm spotted in the fresh produce section of my local grocery store, I'm not getting glaring looks, and children aren't hiding behind their mother's legs. When people point at me, it isn't because I'm fat; it's because I'm the *low-carb chef from TV.*

Sometimes, when I need a few ingredients for my newest recipe, a trip to the store can take hours! Seems everyone knows my name! Seems everyone has been inspired by my family's weight loss and are *hungry* for more. More often than not, they'll ask—

Where should I start? Or . . .

How do I get started? Or . . .

How did you *start?*

Stella Style . . . A Fresh Start

Stella Style is, quite simply, how we did it. It is our recipe for weight-loss success.

My family's fresh start began the moment my wife and I decided to give the low-carb lifestyle a try. We swapped our sugar-filled highly processed packaged foods for wholesome fresh foods that were naturally low in carbohydrates. We rethought the way we cooked, shopped, and ate. We rethought the way we lived.

Over the years, our eating philosophy evolved into something we call *Stella Style.* What began as a strict low-carb "diet" has grown into a flexible lifestyle that allows us to eat a broad range of healthy and fresh foods that taste great.

For me, *Stella Style* means preparing simple meals using the best kind of food—*fresh* food. There's no reason to sentence yourself to tasteless, monotonous menus: With *Stella Style,* you'll eat low-carb meals, snacks, and desserts that are delicious and satisfying. Most important, you'll eat food that you love, without pinching on the portions!

With *Stella Style,* you'll learn to:

- Eliminate all the "white stuff" from your diet. This means refined sugars, white flour, and potatoes.
- Replace processed foods with fresh, healthy choices.

- Shop the outer aisles of your grocery store for fresh, healthy foods.
- Select the right, high-fiber veggies.
- Get into your kitchen and COOK!
- Reinvent your high-carb favorites with low-carb alternatives.
- Eat well-rounded meals.
- Surround yourself with a strong support system.
- Identify the right foods without obsessing over each and every carb.
- Keep menus simple while still staying creative.
- Eat until you're satisfied.

Living by these simple guidelines gave my family and me a fresh start and a new lease on life. I want this book to do the same for you. I want to give *you* your fresh start toward success. Hey, I feel so great, I'm eating such delicious food, how could I *not* tell the world?

This book is put together for anyone who's trying to lose weight.

In *Stella Style*, I'll give you all the information you need to make each and every recipe your own. I'll show you how to reinvent old favorites and create a few new ones along the way, so you'll never get bored or hungry. I think you'll find *Stella Style* to be simple, satisfying, and extremely flexible. I wouldn't have it any other way! What I *know* works for everyone is food that just tastes *good*.

I've included not only carb counts for each and every recipe, but the calories, fat, protein, and fiber content as well, so whether you're just starting out or heading into the home stretch, you can tune the recipes to your liking. My sons have stepped in to offer some *Healthful Hints*, so you can lower some of those calorie and fat counts without sacrificing flavor.

The recipes in this book are for everyone. They all make the most of fresh, wholesome ingredients. Once you give them a try, I'll bet you never go back to your old eating habits again.

I sure didn't.

How to Get a Fresh Start *Stella Style*

Step One: Welcome Change

Seven years ago, I experienced the unforgettable indignity of being wheeled outside a hospital—down to the back dock—so that I could be weighed on a flatbed laundry scale.

I was sick yet again. It was pneumonia, for the third time in a little more than a year. But this time felt different. *I* felt different. By the time I made it to the emergency room, I felt lifeless.

They wheeled me out to that laundry scale and I was way too sick to care.

I remember sitting in the wheelchair in a hospital gown that didn't fit. There were several laundry room workers gathered around, and one of them announced, "He weighs **four hundred and sixty-seven pounds!**"

That's when my doctor sat down and told me that I had congestive heart failure. He told me that I had to take this medication, and that medication, and this medication over here. I had no idea really what these medications were, or how I could possibly afford them.

That was when he said it.

My doctor looked me in the eyes and laid it out plain and simple. He said, "You are going to die."

I had too much body for my heart to supply with blood, and that was going to be the end of me.

I was sent home with a lecture and many, many pages of dieting instructions. Menus, recipes, everything, but I was more demoralized than ever. I was dwelling on the fact that I was going to die. In fact, I had accepted it.

But the worst thing, worse than my own health problems, lack of direction, and hopeless feelings, was that my family was following in my footsteps. Making the same bad decisions. Feeling that same hopelessness.

Somewhere along the line we had become . . . a fat family.

My sons had tried this diet and that diet and had always failed. Anthony weighed in at 225 pounds, my wife at 200, and my youngest son, Christian, was well on his way to a future like mine. At fifteen years old, he was already over 300 pounds and growing. Christian had even been pulled out of public schools and was now being home schooled, because he couldn't fit in with the other kids.

My wife, Rachel, tried to make better choices at the grocery store, but it was too little too late, and it didn't keep us from ordering out for pizza. We all seemed to be resigned to the way things were, to the way we were.

But with that doctor's words always in the back of my head, I realized our life together wasn't going to last long if things didn't change.

Soon after, my father died. I didn't attend his funeral because I couldn't afford the two plane tickets I was required to purchase because of my size.

Things finally became clear. I needed help. We needed help.

But as I sat in that wheelchair, all 467 pounds of me, I didn't know where to start. I didn't know what to do. I was living off disability, so a dietician was out of the question. Most commercial diet plans seemed confusing and ultimately unsatisfying. As a chef that had his start in some of Florida's best restaurants, for me, the idea of eating prepackaged frozen dinners that I counted out on a calculator was just another kind of death sentence. My health was failing and my wife and sons were bigger than they'd ever been.

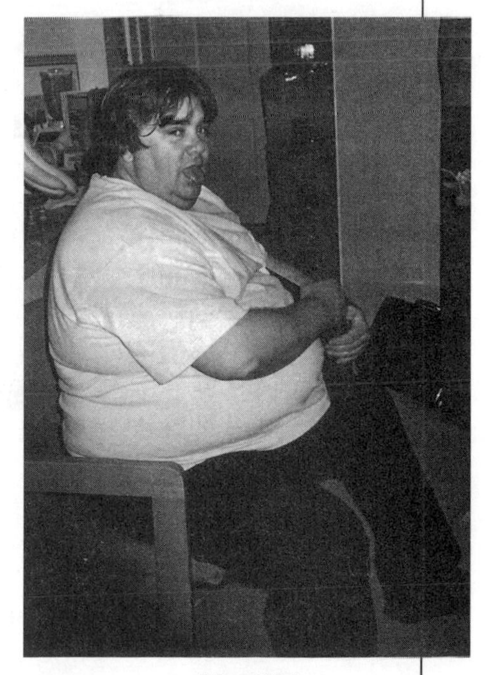

Me, 1998

We were at the bottom and we were ready to listen to anything.

They say that you have to hit the bottom before you can work your way back, and I am living proof of this. Sometimes, my weight loss is so sweet—the only sugar I really need—that I *almost* forget just how hard getting started really was.

When I heard of low carb, everything clicked. Here was a diet that said, the way we understood it at the time, that you could eat all the meat and cheese and butter you wanted and still lose weight. Rachel always says that she thought low carb was a joke, and that she only gave it a chance because—what other choice did we have? We laughed, and we thought it would never work, but we still gave it our all.

If anything, running across an Atkins book was fate. Low carb came into my life when I was at my lowest, and I was ready to do anything. I finally had that courage to *start,* but even more important, I finally had something that I thought I *could* start. Even though we thought it was a joke.

So nowadays, when people ask us how we started, I like to tell them . . .

We started laughing.

Step Two: Choose Your Best Approach

The basic concept behind all low-carb diets is this: Carbohydrates are the simplest, most accessible fuel your body can burn for energy. So what happens when those carbs are taken away? Your body burns fat instead. First the fat you eat, and then your own stored fat.

There are many low-carb diet plans out there, but for the most part they can all be boiled down to two basic approaches. One is the well-known Atkins approach, which is how we began. I call this one the "Fat Burner." With Atkins, your body takes in so few carbohydrates that it burns your fat for energy instead, helping you to shed pounds. With the other approach, the "Calorie Burner," carbohydrates are limited to small quantities of high-quality carbs only, cutting down on calories in the process, so you can lose weight.

Of course, both approaches ultimately help you to burn fat and calories. For our purposes, think of the Fat Burner as the approach that keeps empty carbs from being stored as fat, and the Calorie Burner as the approach that cuts down on calories so you can enjoy those tasty whole grains.

How do *you* want to lose?

Approach 1: Fat Burner

Carb counters know something that people who live by the USDA's food pyramid don't: Our bodies were not designed to eat so many carbohydrates. When your body has too many carbs, it kicks up insulin production, and stores the excess energy as body fat. On the other hand, when you're eating few carbs, your body goes into an accelerated fat-burning state. For your body to stay in this fat-burning state, you'll need to watch the types of food that you eat, making sure that they are naturally low in carbohydrates all around. A bad-carb indulgence like real sugar can knock you out of the fat-burning state for as long as a few days and you'll once again be storing fat! I recommend sticking to under thirty to forty carbs a day, and make sure that most of those are coming from good sources like high fiber veggies.

This approach to *Stella Style* is how my whole family began their journey; with this method, you won't have to obsess over portion sizes. When we first started, we ate to our hearts' content and *still* lost weight rapidly.

All of the recipes in this book are perfect for this approach, just as they are.

Approach 2: Calorie Burner

My son Christian lost his first eighty pounds eating low carb before adding a more controlled calorie and fat approach to lose the rest—another eighty pounds!

Christian had realized that adjusting and lowering his calorie and fat intake allowed him the luxury of enjoying wholesome whole grains, such as brown rice or oatmeal (not the instant kind!). Eating a low-carb diet that included any kind of grain was unheard of at that time, when low carb was synonymous with bacon fat and pork rinds. But halfway through their weight loss, Christian and Anthony starting paying more attention to their portion sizes and saturated fat intake with dramatic results. They were still losing weight *and* able to eat more and more good carbs like whole grains and fruit.

Choosing lean cuts of meat and low-fat dairy products instead of the full-fat versions used for the Fat Burner also cuts calories and fat so you can incorporate

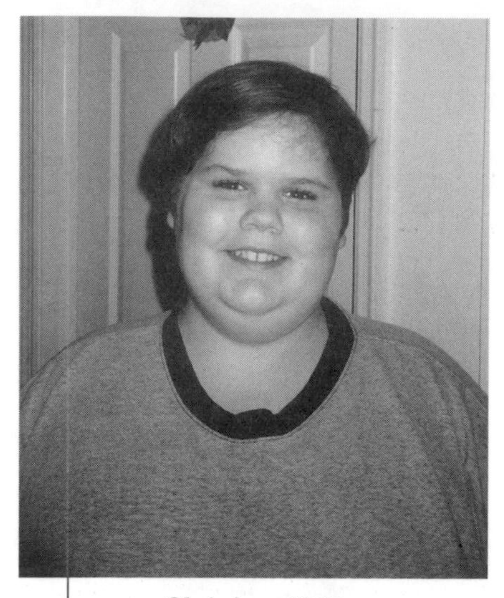

Christian, 1998

more of the *healthy,* high-fiber carbs such as whole grains. The lack of processed or "empty" calories keeps your calorie count low—and *you* keep losing weight, slow and steady.

Keeping a close eye on the "Healthful Hints" at the bottom of the recipes in this book will help lighten the load on this approach.

I'm not a dietician and I'm not trying to invent a new miracle diet here. I'm just trying to put the focus on becoming independent in the kitchen and independent of a long list of eating rules and regulations that may or may not suit your particular body. Hey, we're not all the same! So why not embrace our differences?

The traditional low-carb diet worked for me, and it still works for me. It's easy and it honestly doesn't leave me asking for more. But my solution isn't the solution for everyone! I've been around long enough—as a husband, father, and chef—to know that it isn't *my* particular way or the highway. While we started with this approach, my family found it too restrictive for the long term. So each of us stepped back to look at the big picture, modifying our eating plans to better suit and better motivate us.

This is how *Stella Style* was born.

Stella Style is so flexible that you can approach it the way *you* want and still eat the same great food. The main principles of *Stella Style* listed earlier apply either way. Breaking your dependence on processed foods and going *fresh* is the key, no matter what.

Eating Outside the Box

Not all carbs are considered equal!

When I was 467 pounds and eating processed junk, I'd sit on the couch for hours, getting up only to grab more boxed foods from the pantry. What I didn't know then is that when you eat high-carb processed foods, you create a roller coaster of up and down blood sugar that leaves you in a constant state of hunger. Insulin stores excess energy as fat, like I said, and it works by getting sugar—the stuff that gives you an initial "high" when you've had a sweet treat—out of the blood. Once the insulin has done its job, the sugar is packed away, and you're tired again—and stuck in a vicious cycle of being hungry, eating and feeling guilty for having eaten. By the time that guilt sets in, the carbs have metabolized and been stored as fat, your blood sugar is low, and you're ready to comfort yourself with . . . more processed food.

This is why *Stella Style* puts such an emphasis on *fresh* foods. They're alive with vitamins, fiber, and what they were intended to have! In fact, no matter how you choose to lose weight, fresh foods are fundamental! They metabolize slowly and give you energy over a longer period of time. Most important, they leave you satisfied and full, so even if you're eating higher-calorie foods, you end up eating less of them. Whether you're making a snack or giving your girlfriend a diamond ring, any path you follow will run smoother if you just choose the real over the fake. Fresh over processed. It's what nature intended!

Besides, isn't that why they invented the refrigerator? So that we wouldn't *have* to eat from boxes and cans anymore?

Most of the things that people eat these days have been so overprocessed, boxed, canned, chemically preserved, artificially flavored, hydrogenated, and soaked in corn syrup that it's barely even food anymore. In fact, think about how many "foods" you associate with their packaging instead of their contents. Highly processed breakfast cereals are a perfect example. Could you tell what they were made from if they were outside of their colorful boxes? They're so processed, artificially colored, and flavored that they bear no resemblance to natural foods.

When I talk about "eating outside the box," I mean eating fresh foods, not processed. I'm talking about getting into your kitchen and actually cooking your own meals instead of thawing or microwaving. Giving shopping and cooking their due respect. Taking pride in the delicious food that *you* can make for yourself and your family.

Recently, there have been a lot of news stories about low-carb eating going the way of the dinosaur. I've noticed that articles are always quick to cite the dwindling sales of low-carb products. But it's not the low-carb lifestyle that's going away; it's that the people doing low carb know better than to buy *any* processed foods. It's what low carb has taught us! Just because it says low carb on a package of cookies or candy doesn't mean that it's healthy, and we now know it.

Think about a pantry full of boxed and canned foods or a freezer full of frozen dinners—the food that is just sitting there, preserved. You could leave them for months and return to find them in the exact same state. You can depend on them to stay exactly as you left them, because they're loaded with chemicals! All the vitamins and fiber are left in the factory, and you're left with "food" that serves only to raise your blood sugar and convert to fat. It's food you can't use. It's barely even food at all.

You deserve better.

Step Three: Get Organized

To give *Stella Style* your all, you'll need a carb-proofed kitchen filled with a variety of fresh foods and the right tools to prepare them with. The less you have to worry about, the better, so it's important to get organized early.

Start on the right foot and you'll be prepared for anything. Start strong and you'll be sure to succeed!

Creating a Temptation-Free Environment

I put a lot of emphasis on carb proofing your pantry—your whole home, for that matter—and there's a good reason. You can't eat what isn't there! So get that white stuff out! Throw away those bags of sugar! Do this at your strongest moment. You can do this *right now.* (Go ahead. I'll wait for you.)

For you to see success, you have to see the foods of successful, healthy eating all around you, whichever cabinet you open. You have to nurture yourself with an environment that makes your new lifestyle easier. Before starting *fresh,* you'll have to fill a garbage bag or two. Don't be afraid to get rid of everything that isn't designed for *Stella Style success.*

If you don't want to waste the food, give it to a neighbor or friend. You can box any packaged food that's unopened and drop it off at your local food bank. Others may not have a choice about the foods they eat, but you *do.*

Remove the Refined

Refined flours, grains, rice, and everything made from them are processed by your body in almost the same way that sugar is, which is to say, quickly and with few benefits. Removing them should be your very first order of business.

Clear your pantry of any white flour, bread, pasta, rice, crackers, salty snacks, cereals, cakes, pies, muffins, and any other processed grains.

Watch Out for High-Carb Produce

I love my fruits and veggies and who doesn't? But not all of them are naturally low in carbs, making them better left for maintaining your weight (maintenance).

If you're just starting out, you'll want to avoid potatoes and all of the products made from them, as well as peas, carrots, corn, beans and legumes, raisins or most any dried fruit, pears, plums, bananas, apricots, oranges, and watermelon.

Don't worry, though. Many of these can be reintroduced as you near your desired goal.

Always Read the Ingredients

When I weighed 467 pounds, those nutritional labels may as well have been written in Latin. At first, they truly were daunting, but then I learned the language. I started recognizing the code words for the added fillers and sugars in the packaged food I *did* purchase. You have to *always, always, always* read the ingredients. It's important to watch for carby fillers like:

- maltodextrin
- dextrose
- modified food starch
- cornstarch

Almost as prevalent as hidden fillers in processed foods are hidden sugars, so toss anything made with these often overlooked forms of sugar:

- high-fructose corn syrup or most any "syrup"
- fructose
- glucose
- sucrose
- evaporated cane juice

It goes without saying that you should always keep a watchful eye out for the simplest to spot, just plain "sugar."

In the beginning, we had some missteps, but we quickly learned from them. We learned to watch out for bacon cured with sugar. We learned that even vanilla extract can have added sugar. We learned that the only way you can truly know what is going into your body is to turn over a package and see what it is made with. You have to look! Checking the carb count alone won't help. Small portions or trace amounts of sugars and fillers that are under the regulated marks can be omitted from the nutritional label—which is why you need to read the ingredients!

What was at first daunting became quite simple in a relatively short amount of time. Personally, I can now look at a product and tell you what's in it—even before I glance at the ingredients! I've read so many labels that I can just anticipate which foods will have corn syrup solids or modified food starch. Sadly, these are the staples of most food manufacturers today. The only way we can get that to change is to just stop purchasing the stuff!

So be diligent and read those labels! Even a little added sugar here and there is counterproductive, especially when you're just getting started.

Make Your Life Trans-Fat Free

You've probably heard about "trans-fats" in the news. Fats like shortening and margarine are made by hardening liquid vegetable oil through a process called hydrogenation. There's a reason you won't find any hydrogenated oil in fresh foods—hydrogenated oil isn't natural! Hydrogenated oils raise LDL, or bad, cholesterol, and decrease HDL, the good cholesterol. They've been linked to an increased risk of heart disease and are now considered worse than saturated fat!

Since there aren't always enough trans-fats in a product to be listed in the

Nutrition Facts, always check the ingredients for hydrogenated or "partially" hydrogenated oils of all kinds.

What to Do with Whole Grains

When you're just getting started, you should keep your distance from whole grains for at least the first two weeks. That said, whole grains are far more wholesome than their refined cousins, and a suitable addition to the Calorie Burner approach outlined earlier. Just be sure to check the ingredients to see if what you're eating truly is "whole" grain, with the bran and germ still intact, because many breads and cereals make the claim but only use *some* whole grains in the product.

If you're a Fat Burner, you should be able to bring all whole grains back into your life as soon as you've reached your goal!

Once you've tossed the temptation from your cabinets, you'll have plenty of room for fresh, healthy food. You'll have taken your very first step toward success and you should feel proud. But teary good-byes? Who needs 'em? What's to come will be far more satisfying than a cardboard box full of processed foods.

Now, you're ready for action!

Grocery Shopping *Stella Style* . . . Infinite Possibilities!

If the kitchen is your castle, then let the grocery store be your playground.

My saying is—**shop the outer aisles first,** because that's where all the great, fresh, naturally low-carb foods can be found. Hey, it's where they've *always* been! Grocery stores go through great trouble to keep them fresh for a reason—they're **worth** it!

The Produce Department

When I walk into a grocery store, the first place I head for is the fresh produce section. Call me crazy, but I can never say enough about my veggies! How can you go wrong when so many of them are naturally low in carbohydrates?

Just some of the vegetables that are lowest in carbs and great every single day are:

- all lettuces
- artichokes
- asparagus
- bean sprouts
- bell peppers
- broccoli
- brussels sprouts
- cabbage
- cauliflower
- celery
- cucumbers
- eggplant
- fresh garlic and herbs
- green beans
- leeks
- mushrooms
- onions and tomatoes—great, but only in moderation because of their high sugar content (natural sugar, that is)!
- snow peas
- spaghetti squash—my favorite alternative to pasta!
- spinach
- yellow squash
- zucchini

You may find great deals in bulk on your produce department's reduced rack. A package of assorted vegetables can be taken home and turned into a stir-fry in minutes! Eating fresh foods, *Stella Style,* doesn't mean breaking the bank! In fact, when we first started, we noticed that our grocery bills actually went *down.*

You can also save time, money, and effort by purchasing chopped veggies right off your grocer's salad bar. If you're planning a small meal, why buy a whole bunch of broccoli, a whole head of cauliflower, and a whole package of green beans? Prechopped ingredients mean a quick, easy vegetable medley for one or two.

Canned and frozen vegetables are just fine if you're in a hurry, as long as they don't have any added sugars or sauces. But remember that fresh is always best!

These days, I love shopping—and it's only now that I can see how grueling a trip to the grocery store used to be for me! Just shopping for all the junk that I ate was exhausting, never mind that at my weight, trips anywhere were few and far between. I could never decide between a box of this or a box of that, and so I always got both. We had no idea how quickly all of that processed stuff added up, especially when it never left us full or satisfied.

When it comes to fruit, you should stay away from the ones that are high in sugar, such as bananas, watermelon, grapes, and oranges. Over time, you'll be able to add apples, pears, peaches, plums, and more as you get closer to your goal—or, if you're watching your calories and fats, even sooner! Fresh fruit is so delicious that it's important to remember not to overdo it, especially if you're just starting out.

Great low-carb fruits we use all the time are:

- blackberries
- blueberries
- cantaloupe
- cranberries
- honeydew
- lemons and limes
- raspberries
- strawberries

The Deli Counter

Though I usually slice my own lunch meats from fresh roasts and turkey breasts, I still can't escape the deli counter! If you're in a pinch, or if you're in the mood for some Italian favorites like mortadella, capicola, and salami—always check the labels for added sugar, even if you have to ask to see the package before they start slicing! Usually, it's the better brands that are your best bet. Get a little of this and a little of that, and you'll have a last-minute antipasto platter in no time!

If I'm running late, I'll also grab one of their rotisserie chickens for dinner that night. It's quick and the closest I'll get to "fast" food.

Meats, Poultry, and Seafood

The sky's the limit in the fresh meats, poultry, and seafood departments. You'd be hard pressed to find carbs there! Plus, protein stimulates your body to turn fat into energy *and* it stabilizes blood sugar levels. You can't ask for more than that!

Be on the lookout for sugar added to sausage, hams, or anything store-bought that is pre-marinated.

If you're controlling carbs *and* watching your fat, you can't go wrong with:

- beef tenderloin
- fresh fish
- lean ground turkey or chicken
- lean pork
- lean veal
- shellfish
- shrimp
- skinless chicken breasts
- turkey breast

Dairy

Making the correct dairy choices can get a little bit tricky. If you're on the Fat Burner, you'll want to look for the full-fat forms of dairy (which tend to be lower in carbs) and stay away from milk until maintenance. If you're a Calorie Burner, you'll want to do the opposite because low-fat dairy isn't *that* much higher in carbs. But remember to make sure that any lower fat cheese, sour cream, or cream cheese isn't full of an abundance of added sugars!

Good full-fat dairy choices/low-fat alternatives:

- butter / light or fat-free trans-fat free margarine
- cheese / low-fat or fat-free cheese
- cream cheese / low-fat or fat-free cream cheese
- eggs / egg whites or Eggbeaters
- half-and-half / skim milk (in moderation)
- heavy cream / unsweetened soy milk
- sour cream / low-fat or fat-free sour cream, plain yogurt
- whole milk ricotta cheese / part-skim ricotta or cottage cheese

Wholesome Whole Grains

As I said, when it comes to processed foods, the bran and germ are removed from the grain in the refining process, taking away nutrients and fiber. Once ingested, the processed, refined carbs turn right to sugar in the body, raising insulin levels and slowing down the calorie burning. On the other hand, whole grains are starches that still contain their natural bran, germ, and loads of fiber. What that means is that whole grains are still intact and that's what makes them so good for you! Fiber is crucial when it comes to starches, and the more the better. Remember that fiber helps you digest more slowly, giving you more time to burn the calories of the food.

Start small when introducing whole grains into your diet, because while they are *better* carbs, they're still carbs! The less fat and calories you eat, the more whole grains your body will be able to handle while still losing weight. There *is* a trade-off and it's up to you to decide. Remember that moderation is key if you do go for those grains!

Some smart whole grain choices are:

- 100% whole wheat bread
- brown or wild rice
- hominy
- oatmeal (not instant)
- spelt
- whole grain, sugar-free cereals (hard to find!)
- whole wheat pasta

I can wander the supermarket for hours, but it's your turn to take a look around. So visit your supermarket in a *Stella Style* frame of mind. And shop those outer aisles!

Prepping Your Kitchen

Falling in love with your kitchen is the first step toward falling in love with food all over again. That is to say, the *right* kinds of food.

There's no reason to be afraid of your kitchen. It won't bite. It doesn't have to be a place where bad decisions are made. When properly equipped with the fresh healthy foods that we all love, your kitchen will be the place where life-changing choices are made.

One meal at a time.

Nothing happens overnight, you know.

To eat *Stella Style,* you *have* to *cook.* There is no way around that! To cook, you'll have to enter that kitchen. The kitchen is more than a place where you toss a frozen dinner in the microwave during a commercial break. In fact, my microwave stopped working last year and nobody noticed until one of my son's friends pointed it out! Who knows how long it had been that way? And who cares?! With *Stella Style,* a fresh healthy dinner *can* be as easy as pressing "Start."

You are the most important ingredient in every meal you cook. But life sure is easier when you have the right tools!

Arming Your Spice Rack

Is your spice rack in disarray? Are your spices up to code? If you haven't used that thyme in years, I think it's fair to say that it can be laid to rest. Cooking without good spices is like painting without paints: Before you can get creative with your cooking, you'll have to have the tools of the trade—and I'm not talking pots and pans . . . yet. Fresh spices add richer flavors, and that's what we're after!

While you're shopping the outer aisles for the fresh and low-carb foods to fill that cleared-out refrigerator and pantry, it's a good idea to venture into the *inner* aisles to fill in those spice rack blanks. They're relatively inexpensive and invaluable.

You don't need to collect them all, but you'll certainly need the essentials. No spice rack should be without:

basil	ground cinnamon	pepper
bay leaves	Italian seasoning	poultry seasoning
cayenne pepper	nutmeg	sage
chili powder	onion powder	salt
cumin	oregano	thyme
garlic powder	paprika	

If you like to use all-in-one seasonings, make sure that there's no added sugar in the ingredients.

Your Arsenal of Cookware

It's important to remember that fancy kitchen gadgets and top of the line pans don't make the meal—you do! But just like you have to fill your house with the right foods, you have to have *something* to cook them in.

Every kitchen should have:

at least 1 good nonstick pan
1 good chef's knife
stockpot
saucepan
sheet pans for baking
broiler pan

Where it came from, how much it cost you—those worries won't put dinner on the table! (Your kitchen isn't the set of *Iron Chef,* right?)

When my family first started low carb, everything in our kitchen was in disrepair. Our "nonstick" pans were dollar store purchases. Our low-carb whipped cream was whipped by hand. I went to Wal-Mart and bought my first new chef's knife in years.

It was under twenty dollars and it was great! I used the one knife for everything because that's how we did things in my early days at Café Max, Sausalito Restaurant, and Windows on the Green—some of Florida's finest restaurants. And this one knife is all I needed for years, until one Christmas when my sons surprised me with a far nicer one. The bottom line is, we didn't have much, but we had our determination and that's the most important thing of all!

If you can afford a few cool gadgets—anything beyond the essential—hey, that's great, too. I can't deny that that's even *more* fun! I'm not going to pretend that I don't sometimes salivate at all the possibilities! Food processor, mixer, and an easy-to-clean hand blender will certainly make your life easier. A good wok is perfect for making big family-style meals all in one pan, a nice indoor grill/griddle can save you a ton of time, and a good outdoor grill is *almost* indispensable in my life.

Step Four: Find Emotional Support

I don't know what I'd do without my family.

It was a horrible feeling to wake up one morning and realize that they had followed my lead, making the same bad choices and inheriting the same bad habits. But when it came to losing the weight, they were indispensable to my success. We were all in it together and we were all the support we had. Apparently, it was more than enough!

You can't expect all of the members of your family to jump on board your new lifestyle immediately, but anyone who cares for you should support you all the way. Since you can't force others to change their eating habits, you may want to designate a separate cabinet for family members' high-carb foods. Keep them out of sight and out of mind. (And remember, they'll notice if their food goes missing!)

Support doesn't stop at your family. It's best to find *someone* that's ready to do this with you, but if you're going it alone, speak up! Your friends—everyone, really!—should know about your new plans. Your friends will start watching what you eat almost as closely as you do! Don't be the only person in your life that wants to see yourself succeed. Find the right circle of friends, because they will really help you get past the rough patches. And don't forget to feed them! Make a few meals *Stella Style* and the reluctant may be joining you sooner than you think.

Gather in the Kitchen

With a family as busy as mine, it seems the only place that we *can* get together is the kitchen. We're in it *all the time* and I can't think of *anything* healthier than that togetherness. Some families sit and talk around the dinner table, but we do most of our talking while I'm cooking up my latest recipe—we're all crowded around the counter for the first taste!

The family that eats together stays together, I say. Growing up in an Italian family, there was always something going on at our house and it always revolved around food. There was a small Cessna airport with a grass runway across the street from my house, and every weekend a skydiving club would make good use of it. My relatives would come to watch and my mother would always make a gigantic family-style buffet. All from scratch. All made with wonderful fresh foods, too! Tomato sauce cooking on the stove and roasts in the oven. Meat and cheese platters, olive assortments, and fresh veggies on the table. The whole family would gather around the kitchen and help, eating all the while. A little of this and a little of that.

The funny thing is, I didn't run into the worst of my weight problems until later on in life when I was—seemingly—not eating enough. I was working in a kitchen all day long, but I never had the time to stop and eat something. But by the time I made it home from the restaurant, usually late into the night, I would be starving, and would eat anything I could get my hands on. Then it was off to bed to do it all again. By then I was waking up in the middle of the night to snack even more.

It was this bad habit that got the ball rolling, and without the kitchen traditions and rituals that I grew up with, my family's weight and health spiraled out of control. We would never sit down around the table for meals; we had all day eating binges. We never celebrated special occasions in the kitchen, but around the television amidst bowls and bowls of processed foods. It wasn't that we were eating too much; it's that we were eating too much junk.

It's funny that I had to regain my own mother's values and kitchen traditions in order to save my family. I may have lost focus for a while, but I had known the answer all along!

To be successful with your weight loss, you'll have to create new rituals and traditions while modifying your old ones. Every aspect of your life should be set up for success, and celebrating should be no different. There's no reason to dread holidays or get-togethers as inevitable temptations. Instead, make them your own by gathering around the kitchen for fresh, healthy cooking.

I put out an antipasto platter that spreads the entire counter as I'm cooking up some of my favorite *Stella Style* appetizers and entreés. Even guests that aren't on a low-carb lifestyle will welcome the great food. Home cooked meals are something that we can all use a little more of!

Me, Rachel, Anthony, and Christian—2005

Going Down: The Keys to Ongoing Weight Loss

Now that you have a good sense of *Stella Style* and the path you plan to follow, it's time to put it into practice. Now that your cupboards are sugar-free and your refrigerator is full of fresh foods, all that's left to do is lose—

Lose weight, that is!

Venturing into the land of the low-carb living may be overwhelming at first, but it doesn't have to be for long. In the pages ahead, I'll share my personal experience and advice to make your weight loss the best kind: simple *and* sustaining. Whether it's keeping yourself motivated or moving past a pesky stall, I'll give *you* the keys to carry on. All that's left is to take the wheel and go, go, go!

Nothing Succeeds Like Success

When I was overweight, it wasn't just that I couldn't walk. It was that I couldn't walk, sleep, or breathe.

I had terrible sleep apnea that made it nearly impossible to sleep for more than an hour at a time. I'd wake up feeling like I was suffocating, and the only way to relieve the pressure of my own body weight against my lungs would be to run a bath. Often, I'd fall asleep and wake up hours later in what was by then a freezing cold tub.

That was before I reached the first real milestone in my weight loss. With so much to lose, it was at fifty pounds down that I first began to notice the changes in my appearance *and* health.

I was out of the wheelchair, for starters.

It was barely three months after starting and already my clothes were falling off! Even my old size 68 pants, once secured by safety pins because they were too small to button, were several sizes too big! When I went to purchase new clothing, the ones that actually fit me looked far too small when I saw them hanging on the rack. They were *so* much smaller than my old clothes—already—that it hit me.

It was working!

Losing that first fifty pounds was proof. After many years of our family's weight, health, and prosperity spiraling out of control, it was now obvious to all of us that things were turning around.

You may have heard that a car will not run if you put sugar into its gas tank. Well, once I got rid of the sugar in *my* tank, I was finally up and running again—with plenty of fuel to make it to the finish line!

Eat to Lose

Don't ever forget that with *Stella Style* you have to *eat* to *lose.* Eat healthy, naturally low-carb fresh foods. Eat well-balanced meals with high-fiber veggies. Eat at least three meals a day. Think of your stomach as a furnace, burning everything you eat to make energy. If you stop feeding the fire—your metabolism—it goes out and your body begins storing fat. They say that breakfast is the most important meal of the day, and they're right, because a well-balanced breakfast starts that fire. This is why you always hear that it's better to eat *more* smaller meals throughout the day than *one* big one. You keep the fire going strong. Your body keeps burning fat and you stay alert and energized.

Make Things Up

If you don't think you can eat this—you can! If you don't think you can eat that—yes, you can!

My wife, Rachel, was an artist even before she was a commercial baker. She's been creative her whole life, and her paintings adorn all of our walls. I'd like to see anyone tell someone with her imagination that you can't eat Coconut Macaroon Muffins on low carb. Or that low carb doesn't include Pumpkin Pound Cake.

As I worked my way up as a chef in fine dining restaurants, I majored in music education. I was even a founding member of the Boca Pops Symphony Orchestra in Boca Raton! Before that I was percussion sergeant for one of the best high school marching bands in the world, no kidding. In competition, we'd have to think up newer, more creative, more innovative ways to catch the judges' attention. So when my son said to his friend that he *couldn't* eat macaroni and cheese (his old favorite) on low carb, I got into the kitchen and cooked up my recipe for Cauliflower "Mac" and Cheese Casserole. Even *he* was surprised!

To truly find success, you'll have to be happy and stay happy. And happiness means *comfort foods. Stella Style* is all about reinvention! Turn your old favorite into your new *healthy* favorite.

The substitutions throughout this book should give you a good idea of where to start; after that, it's all yours!

Don't Focus on the Numbers

When my family first started eating low carb, we admittedly did not have a full understanding of the concept. The one thing we knew for sure was, having just started, that we should keep our carbs under twenty grams a day, the recommendation for the first two weeks on the Atkin's program. What we didn't know was that we were on our way to replacing our gaggle of old bad habits with a few new good ones.

I had heard that cheeseburgers without the bun were great for low carb and McDonald's would always have their Quarter Pounders two for two dollars. That it was easy to hit the drive-thru and that it was so darn cheap were a dangerous combination. I "drove thru" constantly—I had replaced my fast food habit with a new low-carb fast food habit! The fact that a hamburger without the bun has no carbs meant it was a free food to me. That I could eat three, four, or five of the things! I didn't stop to think that five bun-less fast food burgers may be low carb, but they certainly weren't a balanced meal!

I soon learned that I was too focused on the numbers. Instead of obsessing about counting carbs, we should truly care about the *quality of the food* that we are putting into our bodies. If you get into the habit of stocking your house only with healthy, naturally low-carb fresh foods, you'll find that you won't *need* to count carbs!

Because all carbs are not created equal, counting carbs is not an exact science. Back then, I knew I could eat tons of great veggies and still lose weight, but I didn't know why. It hadn't come out then that fiber (and only fiber) can be subtracted from the total carb count.

The truth is, thirty carbs from ice cream isn't comparable to thirty carbs from green beans, because your body processes the foods differently. Some carbs—the processed, refined, simple carbs—are turned straight into glucose, while others, such as fiber, are not. Carbs such as fiber are not digested, and move through your body without being absorbed. When fiber is part of your meal, it keeps your body from metabolizing the food too quickly. The food takes longer to digest, and your body can use the energy before it is stored as fat.

In the beginning, I couldn't understand how a green vegetable such as broccoli could have any carbs at all. I'd flip a frozen bag over to check the carb count to see if I was eating too much. (This is reason enough to purchase your veggies instead from the fresh produce section. You don't have to see that carb count.) I wondered, how could eating something so healthy ever be a bad thing? The fact is, it's not. Broccoli is one of the most perfect foods on this planet! It's full of vitamins and essential fiber and, best of all, it has only one ingredient . . . broccoli.

Eventually, I stopped counting each and every carb, learning instead which foods would keep me on track, and which would slow me down. The foods that had the most beneficial bang for their buck became staples on Rachel's grocery list. And *that's* a great habit to have!

Weighing In

Once I got going, I couldn't wait to weigh myself every day. I expected to see a *loss* every day, too! But was I expecting too much? Of course I was. After all, it took twenty years of wrong choices to top four hundred pounds, so why should I think the weight might disappear at more than ten times that rate?

On the days that I was sure I should have lost more pounds, but didn't, the numbers on the scale starting weighing heavily on my mind. I would step on that scale again and again and again. Several times throughout the day and night. Several times in one single day! It was addictive at first, but it was also an unnecessary stress. You should never focus on the negative!

It is always important to keep close track of your progress, but obsessing over the numbers will only drive you batty! I've heard stories of people literally throwing their scale out the window. Think about it: Say you've had a successful month of weight loss but today you're retaining fluids, and the scale will *say* you've gained two pounds. There are two possible reactions. One is to reassess your habits and hype yourself up for your next wave of weight loss. The other is to beat yourself up over it, and maybe even fall completely off the wagon. I've heard time and time again of both scenarios happening.

My tug-of-war with the scale ended when I accepted that, for me, weight comes off sporadically. I would lose four pounds all at once and then nothing for the next five days. So, in time, I curbed my "appetite" for that scale. I started limiting myself to only a few visits a month. I weighed myself only at the same time of day: First thing, before breakfast, because my weight would fluctuate any time after that.

But most important, I learned that one of the best ways to keep track of your progress—to know if you are losing, maintaining or, dare I say, gaining—is your clothes. When something started feeling tight, I used to ask Rachel if she used the dryer on high heat and shrunk my clothes (because *that's* happened more than once)! But now I've learned to stop asking Rachel about the dryer altogether, and simply evaluate my eating habits for the week and adjust.

I don't *mind* dropping a few more pounds while still keeping the peace!

Stalled Out

Your body on the fresh foods of *Stella Style* is like a well-oiled machine. The weight starts falling off and your body is running like a sports car, but what happens if that car stalls? If your weight loss goal is closer than it has ever been, but you hit your very first plateau?

When your weight just won't budge—what then?

Well, then it's time for a tune-up. There's no need to panic. Just think long and hard about the foods that you have been eating and pinpoint where you made a wrong turn.

Everyone is different, but when I am asked for help in these situations I rattle off the following list of possible culprits, starting with the one that I hear about most:

- Sugar alcohols. Many low-carb products, especially sugar-free candy and ice creams are made from these corn syrup alternatives such as maltitol, sorbitol, and most anything ending in -tol that they *claim* can be subtracted from the total carb count. These same low-carb products just didn't exist when my family started losing weight, and when a few popped up on the market, they stalled my son, Christian, immediately. Me, I've never touched the stuff!

- Low-carb products such as breads, bagels, muffins, snacks, etc.
- Low-carb baking mixes.
- Hidden sugars and starches in purchased food.
- Hidden sugars and starches in restaurant food if you eat out often.

In a handful of people, overindulgence in more specific things such as dairy, caffeine, sugar substitutes, diet sodas, soy flour, low-carb fruit, nuts, tomatoes, and onions can slow or halt weight loss, though my family never had a problem with any of them.

If you have no idea what's causing the plateau, the best thing for you to do is to strip your diet down to the bare bones of low carb—to all those healthy fresh foods. You may see plateaus as your worst enemy, but getting back to basics is never a bad thing. In fact, you may find yourself losing as fast or faster than ever before!

If your goal is near, you may want to pay closer attention to fats, especially saturated fats. If you haven't already, you might want to look into the Calorie Burner approach. Lowering fat while still controlling carbs is a one-two punch that can knock you out of anything! It's what my sons did to make it to their final goals. When all else is failing, it's so highly effective that you will probably find yourself able to add more and more fruit and fiber-rich whole grains back into your life while losing weight once again.

Start small, replacing high-fat dairy with lower fat choices when possible—trans-fat-free light margarine in place of butter, sugar-free soy milk in place of half-and-half or heavy cream. Take everything in baby steps. Shop for leaner cuts of meat, such as skinless chicken breasts or ground turkey instead of beef. When you have your eye on the prize, every little bit counts.

When it comes down to those last stubborn pounds standing in your way, calories can catch up with you. I don't advocate counting them, but eating more reasonable portions may be the boost you need to see that magic number.

Always keep in mind that maintenance is waiting for you at the finish line, and not *every* change you make has to be forever. Those same small steps you take to get to your goal can be taken in reverse toward a more satisfying, effortless maintenance—for life!

Putting Your Energy to Use

It all started with baby steps. It didn't happen overnight and, at first, I didn't even know it was happening at all. As I regained my health, my energy, my stamina, I started moving more. Not just because I *could* for the first time in years, but because I *had* to do something with all that energy!

When I was just out of the wheelchair, I started by walking from bench to bench at Orlando's Universal Studios where we had annual passes. As the months went by, I could skip one bench, then two, and finally—I was passing all of them without a breather! It may not be the most impressive thing to brag about, but for me it was like finally being able to run a marathon!

I didn't even realize that I was getting exercise for the first time in years!

It wasn't until the weight had all disappeared that I looked back, seeing that much of my success came from not only eating fresh, low-carb food but moving as I was doing it. When I had lost enough weight to get back to work in a restaurant kitchen, I had a brand new "exercise regimen"—one that I actually got paid for!

If you've ever seen my show on the Food Network, you know exactly how much energy I burn when I'm working.

I have always been proud of the speed at which I work, a valuable asset in the kitchen, as there is never enough help or hours in the day to get all the work done. And no sooner does the day end than the next one begins. Working those long hours in a hot kitchen can be a workout and a half! That, combined with healthy eating, was *my* secret to success.

Exercise can be invaluable to your own success. Start with baby steps. Find something that you love to whip you into shape and you'll never have to dread visits to a gym. Just find a way to get active, and you'll be supercharging the *Stella Style* way of life!

Battling Boredom

To be successful on any eating plan, with any lifestyle—to be *Stella Style* successful like my family and me, you have to stick with it. That can feel like an uphill battle if you become bored or start to feel like your food choices are limited.

Variety is the spice of life, you know. It's a cliché, but when it comes to eating, it's worth mentioning. Boredom can stop you right in your tracks! We should all know by now that the best way to keep life interesting is to always, always, always keep a variety of fresh foods at your disposal. My family also found that staving off boredom is all in the details. There are plenty of low-carb fresh foods that are surprisingly easy to find and anything but ordinary. Spaghetti squash, jicama, avocado, eggplant, artichokes, and pumpkin are just a few. Using a great assortment of naturally low-carb spices and condiments will give you all the creative room in the world to prepare them.

If you think of every meal as an adventure, your journey toward success will be just that—adventurous. If you think of every meal as a work of art, you'll take even more pride in what you are accomplishing—in the kitchen *and* in your body. Making an elaborate meal can be quite a rewarding experience.

At least once a week, go all-out with dinner. Be extravagant! While you're making that masterpiece meal, why not invite your friends over to enjoy it with you? Entertaining can be a great way to show off your new cooking chops, but, more important, a great way to show your friends just how *well* you're eating. If you've forgotten that yourself, they'll surely remind you!

The Stella family, 2005

Once your meal is on the table, eat until you're full. Eating *Stella Style* with the recipes in this book should always leave you satisfied. And when you've cleared your plate, there are plenty of low-carb desserts waiting for you at the end! Still, the sweetest thing of all is success, and I truly hope you find it. Rachel, Anthony, Christian, and I will be waiting for you at the finish line. We did it and so can you!

So what are you waiting for? Make *yourself* the next *Stella Style* success story. Run to the kitchen and get started on a mouthwatering dinner—*Stella Style!*

Breakfast Best Bets

Some families fight over the shower in the morning, but for mine, it's the kitchen! The first to rise has to fend off the others with a spatula, because we know how important breakfast is! Breakfast is the most important meal of the day (I can't say that enough!) because it kick-starts your metabolism and gets those calories burning early!

We all have our morning routine, but that doesn't mean your breakfast has to *be* routine. I think you'll find that my **Strawberry and Mascarpone Cream Crêpes** are anything but the everyday! And if you think eggs come only two ways, over easy or scrambled, think again! I've scoured the world (okay, maybe just the world's cuisines) to bring you a **Riviera Omelet,** my awesome **Asparagus and Cheese Soufflé,** a great **Greek Frittata,** and a *Stella Style* twist on **Baked Eggs Benedict**.

If you're always on the grab and go, why not keep a batch of delicious **Cranberry Pumpkin Muffins** handy? Make a pan of **Christian's Banana Bread Muffins** and you'll have breakfast covered for days, if they can last that long! Every day is another step toward success, and each day's success starts at the breakfast table. So make breakfast your habit, and always remember that the early bird gets the burn!

Savories

Riviera Omelet

We know that breakfast can be the hardest meal of the day to plan or keep interesting. Yet, breakfast gets your system going so you can effectively burn the food you eat all day long. Since *Stella Style* means never getting bored, at *any* meal, this omelet of French and Italian influence, or Riviera style, fits the bill perfectly! (Especially for me, because I'm Italian *and* a French-trained chef!)

Yield:	**2 servings**
Prep Time:	**10 minutes**
Cook Time:	**10 minutes**
Calories:	**350**
Total Fat:	**31 grams**
Saturated Fat:	**14 grams**
Carbohydrates:	**3 grams**
Net Carbohydrates:	**2 grams**
Fiber:	**1 gram**
Protein:	**27 grams**

4 large eggs
2 tablespoons water
⅛ teaspoon salt
⅛ teaspoon freshly ground black pepper
1 tablespoon unsalted butter
1 tablespoon canola oil
2 ounces crimini or "Baby Bella" mushrooms, thinly sliced (about 1 cup; may use any mushroom)
2 ounces Brie cheese, rind trimmed off and cut into small bits
2 ounces prosciutto or Parma ham, fat trimmed and diced (may use bacon or ham; see Note)
1 tablespoon thinly sliced scallion top
4 fresh strawberries, optional, as garnish

SPECIAL EQUIPMENT: 8-inch seasoned omelet skillet (black steel or cast iron)

1. Arrange the oven rack in the highest position and preheat the broiler.

2. Put the eggs, water, salt, and pepper in a bowl and whisk until frothy.

3. Melt the butter and oil together in the skillet over medium-high heat, add the mushrooms and cook for about 2 minutes, just until slightly tender.

4. Pour in the egg mixture and let sit until the bottom starts to cook. Using a rubber spatula, slowly push the cooked egg from one side of the skillet to the other, allowing the raw egg to reach the bottom and cook; this creates fluffiness and keeps the bottom from burning.

5. When the omelet is cooked on the bottom and the top is still runny, place the skillet just under the broiler with the oven door open and the handle sticking out. Broil until the omelet rises and browns lightly, just about 1 minute. (Alternatively, flip the omelet in the skillet and cook briefly, to finish.)

6. Scatter the Brie cheese and diced prosciutto over the omelet, then sprinkle with the scallion. Broil again to warm the topping, about 30 seconds.

7. Cut the omelet in half and place on 2 plates garnished with a couple of fresh strawberries, if desired.

NOTE: If you cannot find diced prosciutto or Parma ham in a small plastic package as it sometimes can be found, simply order one ¼-inch-thick slice of prosciutto at the deli and dice it yourself. (Ask the clerk to set the meat slicer to #10 on the dial.)

MAKE IT MEMORABLE

This omelet is great for lunch, or sliced into 6 wedges and served as a quick and easy appetizer garnished with fresh berries.

HEALTHFUL HINTS

Eggbeaters or egg whites may be used in place of whole eggs, and low-fat cream cheese may be used in place of the Brie. The Parma ham can be replaced with any lean protein, such as Canadian bacon, sliced or shredded leftover cooked chicken breast, or even shrimp or fish.

Hot Ham and Cheese Egg Roll

You don't need chop sticks to eat this breakfast *egg* roll! But if you like hot ham and cheese sandwiches, this rolled omelet can curb the urge. Some might say it's nothing more than a ham and cheese omelet, but it's a cool ham and cheese omelet; and that counts for something when you're trying to make food fun and interesting. Best of all, because of the way this omelet is made, it's only 1 egg per serving. Make it for someone you love—they'll never know it!

Yield:	2 servings; 1 egg each
Prep Time:	10 minutes
Cook Time:	10 minutes
Calories:	170
Total Fat:	13 grams
Saturated Fat:	7 grams
Carbohydrates:	1 gram
Net Carbohydrates:	1 gram
Fiber:	0 gram
Protein:	12 grams

2 large eggs
2 tablespoons water
⅛ teaspoon salt
⅛ teaspoon freshly ground black pepper
1 tablespoon unsalted butter or trans-fat-free margarine
1 ounce boiled or baked ham, about 2 slices from the deli
¼ cup shredded Cheddar cheese (may use 1 slice of Deluxe American Cheese)
1 tablespoon roasted red pepper strips, optional, for garnish
2 sprigs fresh parsley, optional, for garnish

SPECIAL EQUIPMENT: 8-inch seasoned omelet skillet (black steel or cast iron)

1. Arrange the oven rack in the highest position and preheat the broiler.

2. Put the eggs, water, salt, and pepper in a bowl and whisk until frothy.

3. Melt the butter in the skillet over medium heat, add the ham slices, and cook for about 1 minute, just until hot.

4. Remove the ham and pour in the egg mixture and let sit until the bottom starts to cook. (Do not move the eggs from side to side; the eggs should cook like a pancake on one side.)

5. When the omelet is cooked on the bottom and the top is still runny, place the skillet just under the broiler with the oven door open and the handle sticking out, and broil until the omelet rises and browns lightly, about 1 minute. (Alternatively, flip the omelet in the skillet and cook briefly, to finish.)

6. Remove from the oven and scatter the cheese over the omelet; then arrange a single layer of the ham slices on top. Broil again to melt the cheese and heat the ham just slightly, about 1 minute.

7. Remove and roll the omelet up like a jelly roll; cut into 2 slices and place on 2 plates spread with julienne roasted red peppers and garnished with a sprig of fresh parsley on each plate, if desired.

MAKE IT MEMORABLE

Since this *breakfast roll* already has eggs and ham, all you need to round out the meal are some wonderful healthy fresh berries, such as strawberries, blueberries, or raspberries. You can even serve this dish as lunch or dinner by adding a salad and a side of sautéed spinach!

HEALTHFUL HINTS

Eggbeaters or egg whites may be used in place of whole eggs and your favorite low-fat cheese may be used, with Swiss as a great alternative. The ham can be replaced with vegetables such as mushrooms, spinach, or peppers, and lean protein such as sliced or shredded leftover cooked chicken breast, steak, or pork may be used.

Asparagus and Cheese Soufflé

Real men don't eat quiche! So I gave this dish a fancy French name—soufflé. It's an entire gourmet meal packed into one slice of heaven! It's elegant, it's good, and most important, it's good for you! Try it as an anytime meal that can be made days ahead, or let it stand alone as the breakfast main event. It's also great as part of a healthy lunch or as an exciting side that's sure to make any dinner memorable! (Just don't tell the men it's quiche!)

Yield:	**8 servings**
Prep Time:	**15 minutes**
Cook Time:	**1 hour and 10 minutes**
Calories:	**150**
Total Fat:	**9 grams**
Saturated Fat:	**4.5 grams**
Carbohydrates:	**6 grams**
Net Carbohydrates:	**4 grams**
Fiber:	**2 grams**
Protein:	**12 grams**

1 tablespoon vegetable oil
¼ cup diced red onion
1 medium yellow squash, cut into ¼-inch-thick half-moon slices
1 pound thin asparagus, bottoms trimmed and cut into 1-inch pieces
½ cup roasted red pepper strips
2 tablespoons thinly sliced scallion greens
6 large eggs
½ teaspoon kosher salt
¼ teaspoon freshly ground black pepper
Pinch of freshly ground nutmeg
1 cup shredded Swiss cheese
½ cup grated Parmesan cheese
Vegetable oil spray, as needed
Fresh herb sprig, optional, for garnish

SPECIAL EQUIPMENT: 9-by-5-inch loaf pan; parchment paper

1. Preheat the oven to 400°F. Spray the loaf pan with vegetable oil spray and line the bottom with a piece of parchment paper, and spray again.

2. Heat the vegetable oil in a large skillet over medium-high heat. Add the onion, squash, and asparagus and cook, stirring, until crisp-tender, about 3 minutes.

3. Remove from the heat and stir in the pepper strips and scallions. Transfer to a bowl and let cool.

4. In a large bowl, whisk together the eggs, salt, pepper, and nutmeg. Stir in the cheeses and the cooled vegetables.

5. Pour the egg mixture into the prepared pan and top with another piece of vegetable oil–sprayed parchment paper.

6. Place the loaf pan in a larger baking dish and place on the center oven rack. Pour enough hot water into the larger baking dish to reach halfway up the loaf pan. Bake until the center is firm and a toothpick stuck in the center comes out clean, about 1 hour and 10 minutes.

7. Remove the soufflé from the oven and let cool for 10 minutes. Run a butter knife around the edges of the pan to release the soufflé. Turn the soufflé out onto a cutting board and remove the parchment paper. Cut the soufflé into 8 slices and serve hot or at room temperature garnished with a sprig of any fresh herb on hand, if desired.

MAKE IT MEMORABLE

Take a slice or two of this anytime treat with you for lunch and bring along some nuts and strawberries to round out the meal! You can even pack a salad in a zip-lock bag with a frozen bottle of water to keep everything cold.

HEALTHFUL HINTS

Low-fat Swiss cheese will lighten things up and Eggbeaters always make a great whole egg alternative!

Rachel's Birthday Omelet

Rachel's birthday is May 8 and it fell on Mother's Day this year. So I let Rachel sleep in while I took out our dogs, fed the cats, cleaned the kitchen, and decided to make breakfast in bed for her. I had been able to sneak around the day before to buy her presents, but we didn't go grocery shopping. So when I went to make breakfast, it was time to play Iron Chef! We always have eggs; and it *was* breakfast, so I started rummaging through the refrigerator drawers to find my other "secret" ingredients! Turned out that I had the makings of a pepperoni pizza omelet. Rachel was surprised by all I did that morning, but we both were surprised at just how good this omelet was.

Yield: 2 servings; 2 eggs each	
Prep Time:	10 minutes
Cook Time:	10 minutes
Calories:	360
Total Fat:	26 grams
Saturated Fat:	11 grams
Carbohydrates:	4 grams
Net Carbohydrates:	3 grams
Fiber:	1 gram
Protein:	24 grams

4 large eggs
2 tablespoons water
⅛ teaspoon salt
⅛ teaspoon freshly ground black pepper
1 tablespoon unsalted butter or trans-fat-free margarine
1 tablespoon small diced green bell pepper
1 tablespoon small diced red bell pepper
1 tablespoon small diced red onion
½ cup shredded mozzarella cheese
2 ounces pepperoni slices, about 12 slices
2 slices tomato, optional for garnish
2 sprigs fresh basil or parsley, optional, for garnish

SPECIAL EQUIPMENT: 8-inch seasoned omelet skillet (black steel or cast iron)

1. Arrange the oven rack in the highest position and preheat the broiler.

2. Put the eggs, water, salt, and pepper in a bowl and whisk until frothy.

3. Melt the butter in the skillet over medium-high heat, add the diced peppers and onion and cook for about 1 minute, just until slightly tender.

4. Pour in the egg mixture and let sit until the bottom starts to cook. Using a rubber spatula, slowly push the cooked egg from one side of the skillet to the other, allowing the raw egg to reach the bottom and cook; this creates fluffiness and keeps the bottom from burning.

5. When the omelet is cooked on the bottom and the top is still runny, place the skillet just under the broiler with the oven door open and the handle sticking out, and broil until the omelet rises and browns lightly, about 1 minute. (Alternatively, flip the omelet in the skillet and cook briefly, to finish.)

6. Scatter the mozzarella cheese over the omelet, then arrange a single layer of pepperoni slices on top. Broil again to melt the cheese and crisp the pepperoni just slightly, about 2 minutes. (The omelet should be well done on top.)

7. Cut the omelet in half and place on 2 plates garnished with a tomato slice and sprig of fresh basil or parsley, if desired.

MAKE IT MEMORABLE

You can add tomato sauce and your favorite pizza toppings to make this omelet something spectacular!

HEALTHFUL HINTS

Eggbeaters or egg whites may be used in place of whole eggs and low-fat mozzarella cheese may be used. The pepperoni can be replaced with vegetables such as mushrooms or lean protein such as sliced or shredded leftover cooked chicken breast, or even shrimp or fish.

Stella Style Baked Eggs Benedict

Eggs Benedict has been popular forever. I've made it a gazillion times in my lifetime and it remains a "comfort food" tradition on Sunday brunch buffet tables everywhere. At a recent brunch, I kept taking the Canadian bacon and egg and leaving the English muffin behind; I felt guilty as if I was wasting food. Then I started to "think outside the bun" (or muffin in this case) and found that portabella mushrooms make a perfect healthy alternative to the useless white flour muffin, while adding body, flavor, fiber, vitamins, and more to this recipe!

Yield:	**2 servings**
Prep Time:	**15 minutes**
Cook Time:	**6 minutes**
Calories:	**390**
Total Fat:	**34 grams**
Saturated Fat:	**16 grams**
Carbohydrates:	**3 grams**
Net Carbohydrates:	**2 grams**
Fiber:	**1 gram**
Protein:	**18 grams**

2 large or 4 small portabella mushrooms, stems removed
1 tablespoon olive oil
¼ teaspoon kosher salt
⅛ teaspoon freshly ground black pepper
2 ounces Canadian bacon, julienne cut (may use deli baked ham)
4 large eggs
4 tablespoons Foolproof Hollandaise Sauce (page 94)
1 tablespoon chopped fresh parsley
2 wedges fresh lemon, optional, for garnish

SPECIAL EQUIPMENT: 1 small sheet pan or pie tin, or sauté pan with all metal handle, no glass; one 6-cup muffin pan, sprayed with vegetable oil

1. Place the oven rack at least 6 inches below the heat and preheat the broiler.

2. Place the portabella caps on the small sheet pan, gills side up, and sprinkle with olive oil, salt, and pepper.

3. Fill the mushroom caps evenly with the julienne Canadian bacon and place the pan under the broiler just until the mushrooms are tender and the bacon is bubbly hot, 3 to 4 minutes.

4. While the mushrooms broil, crack 1 egg each into 4 of the 6 cups in the vegetable-sprayed muffin pan and place under the broiler next to the mushrooms. Cook for about 2 minutes, until the egg whites are mostly done but the yolks are still soft.

5. Remove the cooked eggs and mushrooms and finish by topping each cap with 2 cooked eggs and 2 tablespoons Hollandaise sauce. Sprinkle with fresh parsley and garnish with a lemon wedge to serve, if desired.

MAKE IT MEMORABLE

Skip the bacon or add to it—lump crabmeat, shrimp, or lobster! Not so extravagant? Try julienne leftover cooked chicken breast!

HEALTHFUL HINTS

Replacing the hollandaise with my Low-Fat Hollandaise Sauce (page 95) will lighten up this recipe considerably. Egg whites may be used to fill 2 cups of the muffin pan, and you can replace the bacon with a leaner protein such as chicken breast.

Greek Frittata

Rachel and I are both admitted "Greek Freaks," that is, we're crazy about Greek food! There may be no baklava on our plates (not yet anyway, give me time to reinvent that one . . .), but if it's Greek flavors and tastes you crave, this frittata is sooo delicious it will have you shouting from Mount Olympus!

Yield:	**6 servings**
Prep Time:	**10 minutes**
Cook Time:	**10 minutes**
Calories:	**240**
Total Fat:	**17 grams**
Saturated Fat:	**5 grams**
Carbohydrates:	**7 grams**
Net Carbohydrates:	**6 grams**
Fiber:	**1 gram**
Protein:	**11 grams**

8 large eggs
¼ cup water
2 tablespoons grated Parmesan cheese
2 tablespoons fresh basil leaves, cut chiffonade style, finely shredded
¼ teaspoon salt
⅛ teaspoon freshly ground black pepper
2 tablespoons extra virgin olive oil
½ cup diced red onion
1 fresh garlic clove, minced
½ cup roasted red peppers, julienne cut
½ cup crumbled feta cheese
½ cup kalamata olives, pitted (may use any pitted black olives)
¼ cup sliced pepperoncini (about 3 pieces)
6 whole pepperoncini, optional, for garnish
6 sprigs fresh basil, optional for garnish

SPECIAL EQUIPMENT: 10-inch seasoned omelet skillet (black steel or cast iron)

1. Arrange the oven rack in the highest position and preheat the broiler.

2. Put the eggs, water, Parmesan cheese, basil, salt, and pepper in a bowl and whisk until frothy.

3. Melt the oil in the skillet over medium-high heat, add the onion and garlic and cook for about 1 minute, just until slightly tender.

4. Pour in the egg mixture and let sit until the bottom starts to cook. Using a rubber spatula, slowly push the cooked egg from one side of the skillet to the other, allowing the raw egg to reach the bottom and cook; this creates fluffiness and keeps the bottom from burning.

5. When the frittata is cooked on the bottom and the top is still runny, place the skillet just under the broiler with the oven door open and the handle sticking out, and broil until it rises and browns lightly, about 2 minutes.

6. Remove from the oven and scatter the roasted red pepper, feta cheese, olives, and sliced pepperoncini over the frittata and broil again to warm the toppings, about 30 seconds.

7. To serve, cut the frittata into 6 wedges and garnish each piece with a whole pepperoncini and a sprig of fresh basil, if desired.

MAKE IT MEMORABLE

Just like a pizza with everything on it, you can go all the way with this frittata by adding more great toppings such as cooked shrimp, sausage, marinated artichoke hearts, mushrooms, bell peppers, and spinach!

HEALTHFUL HINTS

To reduce fat, use half the feta cheese and eliminate the Parmesan—you'll lose surprisingly little flavor! Eggbeaters or egg whites may be used in place of whole eggs to reduce cholesterol *and* fat.

Southwestern Breakfast Bites

My appreciation for Mexican food goes way back to one of my first jobs in the kitchen—when I was just fourteen—and it has continued ever since. The ingredients there had southwestern flair, and this is what I ate for breakfast, quite often in the form of scrambled eggs. These days, since I am always on the run and Rachel knows I am notorious for skipping breakfast, she will make these bites ahead and leave them in the refrigerator for me.

Yield:	**6 servings; 1 each**
Prep Time:	**10 minutes**
Cook Time:	**20 minutes**
Calories:	**210**
Total Fat:	**17 grams**
Saturated Fat:	**7 grams**
Carbohydrates:	**3 grams**
Net Carbohydrates:	**3 grams**
Fiber:	**0 gram**
Protein:	**14 grams**

4 ounces chorizo sausage, casings removed and crumbled (may use any breakfast sausage, the spicier the better)
2 tablespoons diced red onion
2 tablespoons diced red bell pepper
2 tablespoons diced green bell pepper
5 large eggs
¼ teaspoon kosher salt
⅛ teaspoon freshly ground black pepper
1 teaspoon chopped fresh cilantro
½ cup pepper shredded jack cheese
¼ cup diced tomatoes

SPECIAL EQUIPMENT: 6-cup muffin pan, lined with paper cups or sprayed with vegetable oil

1. Place the rack in the center position and preheat the oven to 350°F.

2. Add the chorizo, onion, and bell peppers to a sauté pan and cook over medium-high heat for 4 to 5 minutes until the sausage is fully cooked. (The oil from the sausage should be enough to cook in, but if needed, add a teaspoon or so of canola oil.) Remove from the heat and let cool.

3. Add the eggs, salt, pepper, and cilantro to a large bowl and mix well with a wooden spoon, then stir in the cooked sausage mixture.

4. Fill the muffin cups evenly with the finished mixture and sprinkle each with the pepper jack cheese and diced tomatoes. Bake for 15 to 20 minutes, until the eggs are firm, and serve warm.

MAKE IT MEMORABLE

Although great for breakfast, try using these tasty anytime treats with dinner in place of rice or potatoes or as a creative starter for a Mexican feast!

HEALTHFUL HINTS

Turkey sausage may be used to reduce fats considerably, but you'll most likely have to use 1 tablespoon canola oil to cook it. You can cut some corners and calories without losing flavor by using a couple of tablespoons of your favorite sugar-free salsa in place of the onion, pepper, and tomatoes in this recipe; just add the salsa to the eggs.

Sweets

Cinnamon Toast Pancakes

Like cinnamon toast? My grandmother used to make it for me as a kid and I remember that it was sooo easy to make. I soon found that I could make it for myself and why wouldn't I? It was like having "candy" for breakfast! We have re-created the flavors of cinnamon toast here using healthy alternatives such as almonds and milled flax seed. So curb that urge with this comforting, deliciously decadent, and—most of all—healthy alternative to all those useless whitestuffs we used to call food!

Yield:	**4 servings**
Prep Time:	**15 minutes**
Cook Time:	**6 minutes**
Calories:	**160**
Total Fat:	**11 grams**
Saturated Fat:	**1.5 grams**
Carbohydrates:	**8 grams**
Net Carbohydrates:	**4 grams**
Fiber:	**4 grams**
Protein:	**7 grams**

Nonstick vegetable cooking spray

BATTER

2 large eggs
¼ cup water
1 tablespoon vanilla extract, no sugar added
½ cup Almond Flour (page 85)
¼ cup milled flax seed
¼ cup sugar substitute (recommended: Splenda)
½ teaspoon baking powder
⅛ teaspoon salt
½ teaspoon baking soda

CINNAMON SPRINKLE

¼ teaspoon cinnamon
1 tablespoon sugar substitute (recommended: Splenda)
Butter, or fat-free margarine; fresh blueberries or strawberries, optional, for garnish

1. Grease a griddle or large skillet with nonstick cooking spray or butter and heat over medium heat.

2. Mix all the batter ingredients in a bowl with a wooden spoon until well blended.

3. Pour approximately 16 mini-cakes onto the hot griddle, and cook on the first side for 3 to 4 minutes until almost done, then flip and cook for just another minute or so to finish.

4. Mix together the cinnamon and sugar substitute and sprinkle over the hot cakes to serve. If desired, top with a pat of melted butter or fat-free margarine and garnish with fresh blueberries and strawberries.

MAKE IT MEMORABLE

Stack 4 pancakes on a plate, whip up some fresh heavy cream, and add a spoonful of cream and a few sliced strawberries stacked in between the layers!

HEALTHFUL HINTS

Eggbeaters or egg whites may be used in place of whole eggs. Milled flax seed has already been added for much needed healthy fiber, which isn't normally found in pancake recipes. Fresh berries may be added to the pancakes as they cook for another healthy breakfast entrée!

Strawberries and Mascarpone Cream Crêpes

These flourless crêpes are a quick and easy delight that will brighten up any breakfast and hit the spot when you are craving something decadent and delightful! They are sooo rich that they've kept me out of the local pancake house and away from those loaded waffles (loaded with sugar)!

Yield:	**4 servings**
Prep Time:	**10 minutes**
Cook Time:	**2 minutes each crêpe shell**
Calories:	**160**
Total Fat:	**13 grams**
Saturated Fat:	**7 grams**
Carbohydrates:	**4 grams**
Net Carbohydrates:	**3 grams**
Fiber:	**1 gram**
Protein:	**6 grams**

¼ cup whole milk ricotta cheese
2 large eggs
2 tablespoons sugar substitute (recommended: Splenda)
1½ teaspoons cinnamon
½ teaspoon vanilla extract, no sugar added
2 tablespoons butter or trans-fat-free margarine
½ cup chopped fresh strawberries
4 whole strawberries, optional, for garnish
¼ cup mascarpone cheese

1. Add all the ingredients, except the butter, berries, and mascarpone cheese, to a bowl and mix well with a whisk.

2. In a separate bowl, mix the mascarpone and sliced strawberries together with a fork until blended, and set aside.

3. Melt about a teaspoon of the butter in an 8-inch nonstick sauté pan over medium heat.

4. Drop 2 heaping tablespoons of the crêpe mix in the hot pan and immediately tilt the pan back and forth to help spread the mix thinly, to the size of the pan.

5. Cook for only a minute or two until set, and carefully flip the crêpe and cook for just another minute. (I tilt the pan slightly and let the crêpe slide a bit over the edge of the pan and gently grab the crêpe by the edges with two hands to flip, instead of using a spatula that can break the fragile crêpe.) Repeat this procedure until the mix is gone.

6. Fill each crêpe with 1 heaping tablespoon of the fresh strawberries and mascarpone mix and roll up loosely. Garnish with a strawberry fan, a dab of plain mascarpone cheese on top, and sprinkle the plate edges lightly with cinnamon.

NOTE: Crêpe shells may be wrapped with parchment or wax paper in between and then kept fresh refrigerated or frozen.

MAKE IT MEMORABLE

Strawberries are very low carb, but so are blueberries and raspberries. I love to mix all three, and then mix with the mascarpone cheese for a filling that explodes with color and flavor!

HEALTHFUL HINTS

If you aren't quite up to the decadence of the mascarpone cheese, replace it with fat-free cream cheese or just plain skip it! These crêpe shells are great simply stuffed with the fresh berries or even served by their lonesome, like pancakes.

Cranberry Pumpkin Muffins

You don't need to wait until Thanksgiving to make these hearty and healthy muffins. Flavorful and packed with tons of much needed fiber—eat them regular and keep regular! Here's a hint from Rachel. Since cranberries are seasonal, keep a bag in the freezer. If you can't find them, you can use equal amounts of walnuts or pecans in their place.

Yield:	6 servings
Prep Time:	15 minutes
Cook Time:	25 minutes
Calories:	200
Total Fat:	14 grams
Saturated Fat:	1.5 grams
Carbohydrates:	10 grams
Net Carbohydrates:	6 grams
Fiber:	4 grams
Protein:	8 grams

1½ cups Almond Flour (page 85)
¾ cup canned pumpkin (it must say 100% pure pumpkin on the label, not pie filling)
1 teaspoon baking powder
1 teaspoon baking soda
3 large eggs
¾ cup sugar substitute (recommended: Splenda)
1½ teaspoons pumpkin pie spice
1 teaspoon vanilla extract, no sugar added
⅛ teaspoon salt
½ cup chopped cranberries (fresh or frozen, no sugar added; may use chopped walnuts instead)

SPECIAL EQUIPMENT: 6-cup muffin pan with paper liners

1. Place the baking rack in the center of the oven and preheat the oven to 350°F.

2. Mix all the ingredients in a bowl with a wooden spoon until well blended. Fill the 6 paper-lined muffin cups about two-thirds full with the batter.

3. Bake for 20 to 25 minutes, until the muffin tops turn golden brown and a toothpick stuck in the center comes out clean.

4. Remove the muffins from the oven and let cool for 5 minutes. Serve warm or at room temperature, and refrigerate any leftovers in a sealed container.

MAKE IT MEMORABLE

Cut muffins in half, butter them, and place face down on a griddle or pan for 1 to 2 minutes, then serve with a pat of cream cheese. For dessert, cut in half and serve topped with pecans and fresh whipped cream.

HEALTHFUL HINTS

The sugar substitute may be cut to ½ cup and 4 egg whites may be used in place of the 3 whole eggs to lighten this recipe without altering the flavor much at all.

Coconut Macaroon Muffins

Christian clued us in to the fact that just because low carb allows fats in your diet, it's not a free-for-all. Trying to lessen excess fats when and wherever possible is just plain healthy! The fresh coconut and the natural oils in the almond flour keep these muffins moist and chewy without the heavy cream normally used in the recipe and without having to drench the muffins in butter or cream cheese to eat them. Try them straight up out of the tin!

Yield:	6 servings
Prep Time:	15 minutes
Cook Time:	20 minutes
Calories:	210
Total Fat:	17 grams
Saturated Fat:	4 grams
Carbohydrates:	7 grams
Net Carbohydrates:	4 grams
Fiber:	3 grams
Protein:	8 grams

1½ cups blanched Almond Flour (page 85) (blanched almond flour is made from raw almonds with the brown hulls removed; regular almond flour will turn the muffins brown)
½ tightly packed cup shredded unsweetened coconut (use fresh or unsweetened shredded, which can be found at health food stores)
1 teaspoon baking powder
2 large eggs
¾ cup sugar substitute (recommended: Splenda)
1½ teaspoons coconut extract, no sugar added
1 teaspoon vanilla extract, no sugar added
⅛ teaspoon salt
2 tablespoons unsalted butter, softened

SPECIAL EQUIPMENT: 6-cup muffin pan with paper liners

1. Place the baking rack in the center of the oven and preheat the oven to 350°F.

2. Mix all the ingredients in a bowl with a wooden spoon until well blended. Fill the 6 paper-lined muffin cups about two-thirds full with the batter.

3. Bake for 15 to 20 minutes, until the muffin tops turn golden brown and a toothpick stuck in the center comes out clean.

4. Remove the muffins from the oven and let cool for 5 minutes. Serve warm or at room temperature, no butter necessary. Refrigerate any leftovers in a sealed container.

MAKE IT MEMORABLE

Serve as a decadent dessert: cut in half, drizzle with rum, and top with fresh whipped cream.

HEALTHFUL HINT

If you are really watching fats, do like Anthony and Christian and use a trans-fat-free margarine.

Christian's Banana Bread Muffins

Christian invented this recipe when his girlfriend Elise swore off sugar. (I guess we have a way of doing that to people!) She needed only one bite before she had him making them every night. He kept going on and on about them, but five batches went by before Rachel and I could even get a taste! Finally, he woke us up one night and said, "Quick, quick . . . before they're gone again!"

2 cups Almond Flour (page 85)
1 teaspoon baking powder
3 egg whites
1 large egg
1 cup sugar substitute (recommended: Splenda)
1½ teaspoons banana extract
½ teaspoon vanilla extract, no sugar added
⅛ teaspoon salt
2 tablespoons unsalted butter, softened

Yield:	**6 servings**
Prep Time:	**15 minutes**
Cook Time:	**25 minutes**
Calories:	**250**
Total Fat:	**20 grams**
Saturated Fat:	**4 grams**
Carbohydrates:	**10 grams**
Net Carbohydrates:	**6 grams**
Fiber:	**4 grams**
Protein:	**9 grams**

SPECIAL EQUIPMENT: 6-cup muffin pan with paper liners

1. Place the baking rack in the center of the oven and preheat the oven to 350°F.

2. Mix all the ingredients in a bowl with a wooden spoon until well blended. Fill the 6 paper-lined muffin cups about two-thirds full with the batter.

3. Bake for 20 to 25 minutes, until the muffin tops turn golden brown and a toothpick stuck in the center comes out clean.

4. Remove the muffins from the oven and let cool for 5 minutes. Serve warm or at room temperature, no butter necessary. Refrigerate any leftovers in a sealed container.

MAKE IT MEMORABLE

Though the almond flour gives these muffins a nutty texture on their own, add ¼ cup chopped walnuts and you've got Banana *Nut* Bread Muffins.

HEALTHFUL HINT

Christian invented this recipe with a light trans-fat-free margarine in place of the butter, so you know you won't be sacrificing flavor!

April's Recipe for Success

I began my low-carb journey a little over one year ago and proudly refer to myself as "a skinny person in progress."

I'd struggled with my weight my whole life. When I gave birth to my first child at eighteen years old, I went up and over two hundred pounds. I figured I would just lose the extra weight, but that didn't happen, because within a few months I was pregnant again. With each passing year, I just got heavier and heavier. By the time my third child was born at age twenty-three, I was around 350 pounds. On a five-foot seven-inch frame, I was struggling each day to move around, let alone chase three beautiful kids under the age of five!

In 2002, my children's father lost his brave, three-year battle with cancer at the young age of thirty-four. *I* was in a tailspin healthwise. I was thirty-six years old at the time; I started having chest pains, was diagnosed with gout in my feet, and had diabetic tendencies. I managed to find a scale that went to 450 pounds and decided to find out exactly what I weighed. There was no way I could have been prepared for what I saw. I weighed 401 pounds! I was so devastated I cried all the way home. I was still very young, but I was falling apart, and would be facing an early grave if I didn't do something quickly!

I had to quit two jobs that year because I could barely walk across a room.

At my next job, I met a man who had lost a considerable amount of weight living a low-carb lifestyle called Atkins. Even in my denial, I couldn't help but be curious and asked him how he did it. Well, I had tried every other diet at this point, and I thought why not? I went online and researched like crazy and came across George and Rachel Stella's story. Here was a man who was in the same boat that I was, virtually a dead man if he didn't do something. What can I say? His story spoke right to me, and touched my heart. This family had lost over five hundred pounds by eating a fresh healthy low-carb lifestyle and if they could do it, so could I!

Today, after losing 175 pounds in fifteen months, I'm down to 225, only 50 pounds away from my goal. I am eternally grateful to the Stella family for their incredible inspiration, their wonderful cooking talent, and for sharing their lives, good and bad. It is because of them that I will now live to see my grandchildren and (God willing) great-grandchildren.

Satisfying Snacks

Snacking gets a bad rap. It *doesn't* have to be a bad thing! In fact, the more *smaller* meals you eat throughout the day, the better! They keep your body in a constant food-burning state, whereas waiting all day to eat results in your body *storing* food, unsure of when it will get more!

It isn't snacking that's so bad for you—it's what you snack *on.* Replacing your bad snack habits with new, healthy ones will leave you satisfied without the guilt! You don't necessarily have to eat a stalk of raw broccoli to get a *healthy* snack food crunch. But hey, if you're like me, you'd love to eat that broccoli dipped in some incredible **Herb Boursin Cheese Spread.** Or, you can just keep a tin of my ***Stella Style* Goldfish Crackers** or **Better Cheddar Cheese Crisps** on hand to curb the very worst of snack attacks!

The key to healthy snacking is to surround yourself with healthy—and *only* healthy—snack choices. I'm always cooking ahead, always cooking too much, so that my refrigerator is filled with bounties of great leftovers. I don't call my meals *Anytime Entrées* for nothing. They're truly great *anytime.* But if you're fresh out of leftovers and hours away from dinner, the recipes in this section should satisfy any snacker's appetite. So snack to it!

Curried Walnuts

Rachel and I are big believers in the health benefits of the omega-3 fatty acids found in salmon and, surprisingly, in walnuts. But it doesn't stop there; they are also rich in nutrients, fiber, and protein, yet low in saturated fats and cholesterol free! If that doesn't make you want to try them, how about the fact that they are just plain good by themselves or all spiced up like in this simple, delicious, and different recipe!

Yield:	**8 servings; ¼ cup each**
Prep Time:	**10 minutes**
Cook Time:	**20 minutes**
Calories:	**190**
Total Fat:	**18 grams**
Saturated Fat:	**3 grams**
Carbohydrates:	**4 grams**
Net Carbohydrates:	**2 grams**
Fiber:	**2 grams**
Protein:	**4 grams**

2 tablespoons butter
1 tablespoon curry powder
1 tablespoon sugar substitute (recommended: Splenda)
1 teaspoon kosher salt
⅛ teaspoon cayenne pepper
2 cups walnut halves

1. Preheat the oven to 350°F.

2. Melt the butter in a saucepan over medium heat and mix in the sugar substitute and the spices. Add the walnuts and toss to coat well.

3. Spread a single layer of the coated walnuts on a sheet pan and bake for 8 to 10 minutes. Remove, cool, and store on the counter in an airtight container for up to 1 week.

MAKE IT MEMORABLE

These walnuts make a great anytime snack, and are perfect served alongside fresh fruit and cheese for a party or holiday get together!

HEALTHFUL HINTS

Trans-fat-free margarine or canola oil may be used in place of the butter to lighten this recipe. The sodium may also be cut by using only ½ teaspoon salt without much difference in the flavor.

Boiled Spiced Edamame

We were filming the opening sequence of my show's first season in a natural foods store, and one of the producers asked if we wanted any edamame. We had no idea what he was talking about! He came back with these little green pods. We all loved soy, but had never actually eaten soybeans out of the pod! Now, it's one of our favorite snacks—with this recipe, they're just like boiled peanuts! The footage from that day was never used, but we were happy. We took away something great!

Yield:	**8 servings; 2 ounces each**
Prep Time:	**10 minutes**
Cook Time:	**10 minutes**
Calories:	**80**
Total Fat:	**2.5 grams**
Saturated Fat:	**0 gram**
Carbohydrates:	**6 grams**
Net Carbohydrates:	**3 grams**
Fiber:	**3 grams**
Protein:	**6 grams**

1 pound frozen edamame (green soybeans in the pods)
1 small fresh garlic clove, chopped
2 teaspoons salt (may use a no-sugar beef base in place of salt for a richer flavor)
1 teaspoon chili powder
¼ teaspoon onion powder
¼ teaspoon freshly ground black pepper
¼ teaspoon crushed red pepper flakes
⅛ teaspoon cayenne pepper

Add about 12 cups of water and all the ingredients to a large pot and boil the edamame for 10 minutes. Drain and season with a little more salt and chili powder, if desired, and serve warm or cold.

MAKE IT MEMORABLE

Edamame is perfect for late-night munchies, at lunch, or as an in-between snack, even on the go! You can also take them out of the husks, and blend them with just a bit of sour cream in a food processor. You'll have a quick and healthy bean dip that's great with Better Cheddar Cheese Crisps (page 64) or stuffed in celery!

HEALTHFUL HINT

To cut down on the sodium, boil the edamame without salt and then add a little bit of salt to taste after cooking. And of course, edamame is great without anything on it at all!

Fresh Raspberry Fruit Dip

I whipped this one up late at night when we had some fresh raspberries about to go bad. So into a blender they went, followed by some cream cheese, then it was only a matter of what to do with it? Too thick to drink, but lo and behold, it looked like a dip, tasted like a dip, so I dipped some cantaloupe in it and went to my room to show Rachel. All she said was "Book it Dan-O!" I hope that meant include it in the book; well, here it is. Enjoy!

Yield:	**16 servings; about 1 ounce each**
Prep Time:	**10 minutes**
Calories:	**60**
Total Fat:	**5 grams**
Saturated Fat:	**3 grams**
Carbohydrates:	**2 grams**
Net Carbohydrates:	**1 gram**
Fiber:	**1 gram**
Protein:	**1 gram**

8 ounces cream cheese, at room temperature
1 full pint fresh raspberries (they usually come in ½-pint containers, you will need 2)
1 teaspoon fresh lime juice
1 teaspoon fresh lemon juice (may use all lemon juice if lime juice is not available)
2 tablespoons sugar substitute (recommended: Splenda)
2 sprigs fresh mint, optional, for garnish

SPECIAL EQUIPMENT: blender or food processor

1. Keep a few raspberries aside and place all the remaining ingredients, except the mint, into the food processor or blender and pulse until somewhat smooth.

2. Remove, pour in a glass bowl or cantaloupe half and top with the reserved whole raspberries and sprigs of fresh mint for garnish, if desired. Serve as a dip right away or store in a covered nonreactive container and keep refrigerated for up to 3 days.

MAKE IT MEMORABLE

Kids love to dip and they love good food, too! Just cut up some cantaloupe and honeydew chunks, place them on skewers with whole strawberries, and let the dipping commence! (Stick the fruit-filled skewers right into the side of a cantaloupe half filled with the dip for a fun presentation!)

HEALTHFUL HINTS

Lighten up this cheese spread by choosing low-fat cream cheese or Neufchâtel cheese in place of regular. If the berries are good and sweet, the sugar substitute may be reduced or left out entirely with sweetness coming naturally from the berries.

Herb Boursin Cheese Spread

When Rachel and I cater parties, we frequently have a bunch of leftovers that I'm always trying to make something out of so that nothing goes to waste. Well, this recipe was a shot at using a bunch of leftover cream cheese while catering a big party. I threw this together at the last minute, and brought it with us as an extra that they didn't order. It stole the limelight. I might as well not have made anything else as it turned out to be the single most talked about food at the party! (Sometimes it's the little things . . .)

Yield:	12 servings; about 1 ounce each
Prep Time:	15 minutes
Chill Time:	2 hours
Calories:	90
Total Fat:	9 grams
Saturated Fat:	5 grams
Carbohydrates:	1 gram
Net Carbohydrates:	1 gram
Fiber:	0 gram
Protein:	2 grams

1 tablespoon fresh basil leaves
1 fresh garlic clove
2 tablespoons unsalted butter, softened
8 ounces cream cheese, softened
¼ cup sour cream, softened
¼ teaspoon kosher salt
⅛ teaspoon coarse freshly ground black pepper (freshly ground works best here)

SPECIAL EQUIPMENT: blender or food processor

1. Add basil leaves, garlic, and butter to the food processor or blender and pulse until minced.

2. Add the cream cheese, sour cream, salt, and pepper and pulse again until blended thoroughly, about 1 minute. Place in a covered nonreactive container and refrigerate at least 2 hours before serving. (Hint: If you spread it on a platter, it will chill much faster.)

MAKE IT MEMORABLE

This recipe is required to make our Ham, Asparagus, and Boursin Pinwheels (page 69). But there are many uses for this spread, as a dip for vegetables, stuffing celery, or my favorite, placing a scoop right on top of a hot cooked steak as it goes to the table. It will slowly melt; this makes it the best steak anyone has ever had!

HEALTHFUL HINTS

Lighten up this cheese spread by choosing low-fat sour cream and cream cheese or by using Neufchâtel cheese in place of regular. The butter may be replaced with trans-fat-free margarine.

Turkey Divan Roll-Ups

Turkey Divan crêpes were a French Continental favorite for me when I was a young chef in the seventies. This was at the Galt Ocean Mile area of Fort Lauderdale, Florida, just down the road from the infamous strip. Those were exciting days, and surrounding myself with such favorites ensures that I will never forget them! Food sure is some powerful *Mojo,* but that's another recipe!

Vegetable oil spray
8 slices, ½ ounce each, deli turkey breast (zero carb, check the label)
2 cups cooked broccoli, coarsely chopped (almost any leftover veggie works great here!)
2 ounces roasted red peppers, chopped
1 egg
½ cup shredded Swiss cheese
¼ cup grated Parmesan cheese
⅛ teaspoon kosher salt

⅛ teaspoon freshly ground black pepper
Wooden toothpicks, optional

Yield: 4 servings; 2 rolls each	
Prep Time:	15 minutes
Cook Time:	5 to 7 minutes
Calories:	140
Total Fat:	7 grams
Saturated Fat:	3.5 grams
Carbohydrates:	6 grams
Net Carbohydrates:	3 grams
Fiber:	3 grams
Protein:	14 grams

1. Preheat the oven to 350°F and spray a sheet pan with vegetable oil.

2. Add all the ingredients, except the turkey, to a bowl and mix well with a fork to make the filling.

3. Working over a sheet pan, fill each of the 8 slices of turkey breast with equal amounts of filling down the center, roll up and place open side down flat on the sheet pan, keeping all the rolls close together. (Wooden toothpicks may be used to hold the rolls closed if needed.)

4. Place the sheet pan in the oven and bake for 5 to 7 minutes, until bubbly hot. Serve immediately. (After cooking, the rolls may be refrigerated and then microwaved for on the go!)

MAKE IT MEMORABLE

These rolls make a great anytime snack or lunch, but I like to serve them as gourmet appetizers. Just slice and place on a skewer! You may also serve them atop any leftover salad mix you have and enjoy a chef's salad, *Stella Style*!

HEALTHFUL HINT

As always, low-fat cheeses may be used, and the amounts may be reduced by half without changing the flavor too much.

Devilish Deviled Eggs with Tuna

We always keep hard-boiled eggs on hand for a great anytime snack. The same goes for the cans of tuna that we use for quick lunches, so it was only a matter of time before they collided in our kitchen! The resulting creation are these deliciously different little devils of an egg that are a unique and filling way to serve up tuna fish, *Stella Style*!

Yield:	6 servings; 2 each
Prep Time:	15 minutes
Chill Time:	30 minutes
Calories:	240
Total Fat:	20 grams
Saturated Fat:	3.5 grams
Carbohydrates:	1 gram
Net Carbohydrates:	1 gram
Fiber:	0 gram
Protein:	12 grams

6 hard-boiled eggs, peeled
½ cup mayonnaise
1 (6-ounce) can white tuna in water, drained well
½ teaspoon white vinegar
2 tablespoons finely chopped celery
1 tablespoon finely chopped red onion
¼ teaspoon celery salt
⅛ teaspoon dry mustard
⅛ teaspoon freshly ground black pepper
¼ teaspoon paprika, optional, for garnish

1. Slice the hard-boiled eggs in half lengthwise. Remove the yolks and place them in a bowl with all the other ingredients, except the paprika, and mix until smooth.

2. Fill the egg white halves with heaping mounds of the tuna filling and then sprinkle paprika lightly over each. For best results, chill for at least 30 minutes before serving.

MAKE IT MEMORABLE

These eggs make a filling lunch by themselves, but are also perfect for parties, as a covered dish, at picnics, or alongside Jamaican BBQ Ribs (page 126) and Liz's Fast Fiesta Salad (page 104).

HEALTHFUL HINTS

You may lighten up this recipe by using a low-fat mayonnaise, or replace it altogether with plain low-fat yogurt.

Stella Style Goldfish Crackers

I don't mind being called cheesy, as long as you're talking about my favorite Goldfish crackers. For me, Goldfish crackers were always a comfort food growing up. I remember sitting around popping one after another into my mouth, and now I can once again, only without the guilt! These wholesome alternatives—32 "crackers" made from just 2 slices of cheese—prove that a little cheese goes a long way! Enjoy them as a snack, packed in lunches, or as a grab and go!

Yield:	**4 servings**
Prep Time:	**10 minutes**
Cook Time:	**7 minutes**
Calories:	**110**
Total Fat:	**9 grams**
Saturated Fat:	**5 grams**
Carbohydrates:	**.5 gram**
Net Carbohydrates:	**.5 gram**
Fiber:	**0 gram**
Protein:	**7 grams**

2 slices American cheese (not "processed cheese food")
½ teaspoon salt
⅛ teaspoon chili powder
⅛ teaspoon garlic powder

1. Preheat the oven to 400°F. Line a baking sheet with parchment paper.

2. Stack the slices of American cheese and cut them into 16 very small squares. Separate the pieces, and transfer them to a small bowl.

3. Add the salt, chili powder, and garlic powder and toss to combine.

4. Arrange the 32 cheese pieces in 4 rows of 8 on the parchment paper–lined baking sheet, leaving as much space in between each as possible. (A silicone baking mat works perfectly here and you can use it over and over.)

5. Bake until they puff up, are well browned (almost burnt), and crispy, 7 to 7½ minutes. If undercooked, they'll be soggy, so don't be afraid to check them and put them back in for more time, if needed.

6. Cool the crackers completely before serving; as they cool, they'll crisp up. Store on the counter in an airtight container for as long as a few days. Eat and enjoy!

MAKE IT MEMORABLE

Goldfish crackers come in many varieties, so why not have fun and use combinations of your favorite spices such as Cajun or curry to make something new? You can also place them in decorative, paper-lined tins to give as gifts or liven up a party!

HEALTHFUL HINT

No sugar added, low-fat cheese may be used to lighten up this recipe.

Better Cheddar Cheese Crisps

I really must stop naming my recipes like tongue twisters; that said, try saying Better Cheddar Cheese Crisps three times fast and then reward yourself with these Great Baked Super Duper Easy Shmeezy People Pleasers! These crisps can cool your cravings, too; just use them to take a dip!

Yield:	4 servings
Prep Time:	10 minutes
Cook Time:	7 minutes
Calories:	60
Total Fat:	4.5 grams
Saturated Fat:	3 grams
Carbohydrates:	0 gram
Net Carbohydrates:	0 gram
Fiber:	0 gram
Protein:	4 grams

2 ounces Cheddar cheese (any variety of Cheddar will work)
Cool Cucumber Chipotle Chutney, as needed (page 92) (optional; may use no sugar added fresh or store-bought salsa; we like Paul Newman's brand in a pinch!)

1. Preheat the oven to 400°F. Line a backing sheet with parchment paper.

2. Stack the Cheddar slices and cut them into about 24 small pieces. Arrange them on the parchment paper–lined baking sheet in 4 rows of 6, leaving as much space in between each as possible. (We find a silicone mat works perfectly in place of parchment paper and you can reuse it over and over!)

3. Bake until well browned and crispy, 7 to 7½ minutes. If undercooked, they'll be soggy, so don't be afraid to check them and put them back in for more time, if needed. (Hint: rotate the baking sheet halfway through for even cooking.)

4. Cool the crisps completely before serving; as they cool, they'll crisp up even more. Store on the counter in an airtight container for a few days, if they last! Eat them as a snack alone or they are great dipped into my Cool Cucumber Chipotle Chutney or salsa.

MAKE IT MEMORABLE

Use slightly crumbled crisps to top off any salad for a unique alternative to high-carb croutons!

HEALTHFUL HINT

Low-fat cheese can be used to lighten up this recipe; just make sure there are no added sugars in the ingredients.

Cheesy Pecan Cookies

The ultimate cheese. This cheese stands alone—the difference between this recipe and all the others in this book is that it is the king (the queen, too) of cheesy recipes. Really. In fact, this is the cheesiest of all the recipes, so I'll just stop here so you can see for yourself. Just smile and say . . . PECANS! (Ha!)

Yield:	**8 servings; 2 each**
Prep Time:	**15 minutes**
Chill Time:	**30 minutes**
Calories:	**130**
Total Fat:	**11 grams**
Saturated Fat:	**4.5 grams**
Carbohydrates:	**2 grams**
Net Carbohydrates:	**1 gram**
Fiber:	**1 gram**
Protein:	**6 grams**

1 cup shredded smoked Gouda cheese, at room temperature
¼ cup sour cream
1 tablespoon chopped fresh parsley
⅛ teaspoon kosher salt
36 pecan halves, the larger the better

SPECIAL EQUIPMENT: blender or food processor

1. Add everything, except the pecans, to the food processor or blender and run on medium until smooth and creamy.

2. Next, lay out 18 pecan halves on a tray or plate, place a good size dollop of the creamy cheese mixture on each, and then top with another pecan half to make 18 cheesy pecan "cookies"! Chill for 30 minutes and serve.

MAKE IT MEMORABLE

Try adding a couple of these to a salad in place of croutons! The same filling can be used to stuff celery ribs, or even made into mini-cheese balls that you can roll in Almond Flour (page 85). Both are favorites of kids! (and me)!

HEALTHFUL HINTS

Low-fat sour cream may be used. If you can't find low-fat Gouda, use your favorite low-fat cheese such as Swiss or Cheddar. Try using walnuts in place of pecans for a healthy change of pace!

Starters

Every good meal starts *somewhere.* Where to begin? Right here! The recipes in this section make delicious appetizers—strong proof that not all "finger foods" come from a box in your grocer's freezer section! I'd say that these are so easy to prepare that they're the only "convenience foods" you'll need!

Whether you're entertaining guests or treating yourself, few things are as deliciously decadent as a meal with more than one course. Of course!

Put out a platter of my **Jamaican Jerk Sea Scallop and Shrimp Brochettes** and my **Wood-Grilled Oysters with Dill Butter,** and make sure your guests save room for the main course! Especially if you're going to surprise them with my **Chicken Pesto Skewers** or **Melon and Prosciutto Bites.** Or if you'll help them indulge with my **Ham, Asparagus, and Boursin Pinwheels** or **Bacon-Wrapped Teriyaki Scallops**.

Sounds a lot like the last dinner party I held! As long as we don't forget the biggest hit of all, my **Bueno Jalapeños.**

Now that you're starting fresh, why not hold a party of your own to celebrate? We'll call it a *Stella Style Starters Shindig.* And now you've got the perfect menu!

Jamaican Jerk Sea Scallop and Shrimp Brochettes

Ham, Asparagus, and Boursin Pinwheels

Buffalo Shrimp Cocktail

Bueno Jalapeños

Wood-Grilled Oysters with Dill Butter

Chicken Pesto Skewers

Bacon-Wrapped Teriyaki Scallops

French-Style Mussels

Clams Parmesan

Melon and Prosciutto Bites

Jamaican Jerk Sea Scallop and Shrimp Brochettes

I grew up in South Florida, where there were little Ma and Pa stores on every corner. You could buy authentic Jamaican home-cooked meals, everything from curried goat, oxtail, and fried conch to my favorite back then, jerk chicken wings! I tried it all and learned a lot, and Caribbean flair foods became a big influence on my cooking. Jerk seasoning is so easy and fast to use that I think it's fair to say that I've pretty much tried it with everything—everything, except brochettes! So here I go!

Yield:	**12 servings; 2 brochettes per serving**
Prep Time:	**20 minutes**
Cook Time:	**5 minutes**
Calories:	**120**
Total Fat:	**5 grams**
Saturated Fat:	**0 gram**
Carbohydrates:	**0 gram**
Net Carbohydrates:	**0 gram**
Fiber:	**0 gram**
Protein:	**16 grams**

30 (8-inch) bamboo skewers
2 tablespoons Jamaican jerk seasoning (pick a brand with low carbs and sugars; I recommend Walkerswood brand)
¼ cup vegetable oil (recommended: canola)
1 pound (16 to 20) shrimp, peeled and deveined, tails on
1 pound fresh sea scallops, medium to large

1. Soak the bamboo skewers in water for 30 minutes to keep them from burning later. Preheat the grill to medium high or use an indoor grill top or grill pan over high heat.

2. Mix 2 tablespoons jerk seasoning with the vegetable oil in a bowl to thin and cut the hotness.

3. Lightly coat each piece of shrimp and scallop with the thinned jerk seasoning.

4. Thread 1 shrimp or scallop per stick to about 1 inch from the end.

5. Place the shrimp or scallop brochettes on the edges of the grill with the longest part of the stick hanging off the edge away from the fire. Stay close and turn the sticks by hand to keep from burning. Brochettes are done in just 3 to 4 minutes. Serve hot off the grill!

MAKE IT MEMORABLE

For a fun way to serve, stick the skewers straight out of the side of a cantaloupe half filled with Summer Squash Salsa (page 99) or some cantaloupe chunks!

HEALTHFUL HINTS

The oil is only to suspend the seasoning so it may be rubbed on the brochettes evenly and to keep them from sticking to the grill. Water will accomplish the same thing very effectively, and just before placing on the grill, you may swab your grill grate with vegetable oil on a cloth to prevent sticking.

Ham, Asparagus, and Boursin Pinwheels

I invented the Herb Boursin Cheese Spread that this recipe calls for from leftovers, but *then* I had some of the Boursin spread left over. Well, it was one of those hang onto the fridge nights when I took the leftover leftovers along with some, you guessed it, leftover cooked asparagus and made this wonderful *new* snack. It's so good, there were finally no leftovers!

Yield:	**8 servings; 4 pinwheels**
Prep Time:	**15 minutes**
Chill Time:	**30 minutes**
Calories:	**100**
Total Fat:	**8 grams**
Saturated Fat:	**5 grams**
Carbohydrates:	**3 grams**
Net Carbohydrates:	**2 grams**
Fiber:	**1 gram**
Protein:	**4 grams**

8 ounces Herb Boursin Cheese Spread (page 59)
8 slices, about ½ ounce each, deli lean ham (zero carb, check the label)
8 thick fresh asparagus spears, blanched for 2 minutes in boiling water (if asparagus is thin, blanch for only 1 minute and use 2 spears per roll)
32 cucumber slices
Whole fresh herbs or scallion, optional, for garnish

1. Spread a thin layer of the Boursin cheese mixture over each

slice of ham, place an asparagus spear in the center lengthwise, and roll the ham up around it.

2. Refrigerate for 30 minutes until firm, then cut each roll into four slices

3. Place each piece atop a cucumber round, and garnish the plate or tray with any whole fresh herbs or a simple whole scallion, if desired, and serve!

MAKE IT MEMORABLE

Use alternating fresh white asparagus with green; the white is hard to find fresh, but well worth the effort! And as always, placed atop any lettuces, this makes a wonderful gourmet salad!

HEALTHFUL HINTS

Follow the healthful hints on the Herb Boursin Cheese Spread to lighten it up. If you choose, you may use leaner turkey breast in place of the ham to reduce fat and sodium.

Buffalo Shrimp Cocktail

I love hot chicken wings—always have. They're easy, they're good, and they *used* to be inexpensive. Have you seen the price of chicken wings lately? You might as well buy shrimp! And besides that, people always expect me to make something fancy, even for impromptu card parties and the like. So here it is, all the flavor and texture of the wings, but made in a style fit for kings!

10 bacon slices
2 pounds peeled, deveined tail-on jumbo shrimp (called U-15 in chef-speak)
30 wooden toothpicks
½ cup Louisiana hot sauce (not Tabasco)

¾ cup blue cheese dressing, no sugar added
4 celery ribs, cut into sticks
1 lemon, cut into 6 wedges

Yield:	**6 servings; 5 pieces each**
Prep Time:	**20 minutes**
Cook Time:	**12 minutes**
Calories:	**320**
Total Fat:	**20 grams**
Saturated Fat:	**5 grams**
Carbohydrates:	**5 grams**
Net Carbohydrates:	**4 grams**
Fiber:	**1 gram**
Protein:	**30 grams**

1. Preheat the oven to 400°F.

2. Arrange the bacon slices on a baking sheet and bake until half-cooked, about 6 minutes. Let cool and cut each slice into thirds. Reserve the baking sheet; don't drain the fat.

3. Stretch one-third of a bacon slice tightly around the center of each shrimp, and secure with a toothpick.

4. Arrange the shrimp on the reserved baking sheet and bake until just cooked through and the bacon is crispy, about 6 minutes more.

5. Immediately transfer the shrimp to a bowl and gently toss with the hot sauce. To serve, pour the blue cheese dressing in a small serving bowl and place in the center of a serving platter, surrounded by the shrimp, celery sticks, and lemon wedges.

MAKE IT MEMORABLE

Try the same thing with sea scallops and serve them on the same platter together for a seafood medley that's sure to please everyone.

HEALTHFUL HINTS

Lighten this recipe by using turkey bacon in place of real bacon and try some Summer Squash Salsa (page 99) as a perfect alternative to the blue cheese dip.

Bueno Jalapeños

I was ten, and six of us were packed into a four-door '64 Ford Falcon moving south to Florida. I had never been more south than New York before and what do I remember most? The "South of the Border" billboard signs down I–95, of course! Years later I found myself pointing out those crazy signs to Anthony and Christian when traveling up the coast. I swear there was one that said, "We Have Bueno Jalapeños!" I don't know if South of the Border still has them, but *we* have Bueno Jalapeños—and now you do, too!

Yield:	**12 servings; 2 each**
Prep Time:	**15 minutes**
Cook Time:	**30 minutes**
Calories:	**150**
Total Fat:	**13 grams**
Saturated Fat:	**8 grams**
Carbohydrates:	**2 grams**
Net Carbohydrates:	**2 grams**
Fiber:	**0 gram**
Protein:	**6 grams**

Vegetable oil spray
1 cup shredded Monterey Jack cheese
1 cup shredded Colby cheese (may use Cheddar)
8 ounces cream cheese, softened
¼ cup cooked crumbled bacon, about 5 strips
½ teaspoon chili powder
¼ teaspoon kosher salt
¼ teaspoon garlic powder
⅛ teaspoon ground cumin
12 large fresh jalapeño peppers, about 1 pound, cut in half lengthwise and seeded (wear plastic gloves while seeding peppers and wash hands immediately afterward)
1 teaspoon paprika, for garnish

1. Preheat the oven to 300°F and spray a sheet pan with vegetable oil.

2. Add all the ingredients, except the peppers and paprika, to a bowl and mix well to combine.

3. Working over the sheet pan, spoon the cheese mixture into each of the 24 seeded jalapeño pepper halves, overfilling them slightly.

4. Sprinkle lightly on top with paprika and bake for about 30 minutes. Serve hot.

MAKE IT MEMORABLE

The perfect sauces to serve with these spicy devils are Cool Cucumber Chipotle Chutney (page 92), Summer Squash Salsa (page 99), or maybe just a simple cool ranch dressing.

HEALTHFUL HINTS

Lighten up this recipe two ways. First, use all low-fat versions of the cheeses, and second, simply make half as much filling and fill the peppers halfway! It's all bueno!

Wood-Grilled Oysters with Dill Butter

This is another classic recipe and true comfort food. I first made it at Café Max in Pompano Beach, Florida, back in the early eighties when Wolfgang's California cuisine was just taking off. It was a big hit then and a restaurant specialty that everyone was told they just *had* to order! Go ahead, make them, you'll see!

Yield:	4 servings
Prep Time:	20 minutes
Cook Time:	6 minutes
Calories:	100
Total Fat:	8 grams
Saturated Fat:	5 grams
Carbohydrates:	3 grams
Fiber:	0 gram
Protein:	2 grams

4 small pieces natural wood: mesquite, hickory, oak, recommended (if using chips, they must be soaked in water first to inhibit fast burning)
1 dozen raw oysters on the half-shell
Dill Butter (page 97)

1. Prepare white hot coals or preheat a gas grill to high.

2. Using a grill fork or similar heatproof tool, carefully lift the hot grate slightly and place only 3 or 4 small pieces of wood all around the edges of the grill, directly over the prepared coals or hot ceramic briquettes.

3. Before the wood catches fire, quickly place the opened oysters face up in the center of the grill, shut the lid, and let cook for 3 minutes at most. (Be careful not to put the oysters directly over any wood pieces or they will burn.)

4. Remove and top each grilled oyster with a small pat of dill butter and serve as it is melting and bubbly hot.

HELPFUL HINTS

You can easily open the oysters by placing them in a 400°F oven for a couple of minutes to loosen them up, and then the shells can simply be pried open with an ordinary pop bottle opener. (Do not overcook.)

Wood chips can be found in some grocery stores, but are almost always available at larger home improvement and building supply stores.

If your grill does not have a top, simply place the oysters all together and cover with a metal pie pan.

Chicken Pesto Skewers

This is a simple and easy appetizer that I frequently use for large parties because you can prep them ahead. Then just pop them in the oven a tray at a time as needed. This is a no-brainer that will surely come in handy if you ever have seventy-five hungry Italians around—like my last family reunion, where they were a big hit!

Vegetable oil spray
2 pounds boneless, skinless chicken breasts
¼ teaspoon kosher salt
¼ teaspoon freshly ground black pepper
16 (8-inch) bamboo skewers
8 tablespoons (½ cup) Basil Pesto (page 88)
Fresh basil tops, optional, for garnish
1 lemon, cut in wedges, optional, for garnish

1. Preheat the oven to 375°F and spray a sheet pan with vegetable oil.

2. Cut the chicken breasts into 16 equal strips about ½ inch wide and season with salt and pepper.

3. Thread 1 chicken strip per skewer until flat on the stick, and line up close together on the sheet pan.

4. Using a rubber spatula or spoon, spread a good layer of the pesto all over the tops of the chicken strips, keeping as much of the pesto as possible piled on top of the chicken.

Yield:	**8 servings; 2 skewers each**
Prep Time:	**20 minutes**
Cook Time:	**25 minutes**
Calories:	**210**
Total Fat:	**7 grams**
Saturated Fat:	**1.5 grams**
Carbohydrates:	**1 gram**
Net Carbohydrates:	**0 gram**
Fiber:	**0 gram**
Protein:	**35 grams**

5. Place in the oven and bake for about 25 minutes, or until fully cooked through. Serve hot garnished with fresh basil tops and lemon wedges, if desired.

MAKE IT MEMORABLE

These are perfect by themselves or served with a simple marinara sauce as a dip! Also try topping a whole boneless chicken breast and baking it for a great dinner entrée!

HEALTHFUL HINT

Use half as much pesto—cut fats, reduce calories, and still enjoy all the wonderful flavors of this starter!

Bacon-Wrapped Teriyaki Scallops

I could eat these all day long! The problem is that any appetizers like these teriyaki scallops are always *so* popular that by the time I turn around, *poof*—they're gone! I even tried to hide some in the kitchen once, but my black Labrador retriever, Baby, got to them first! I found the toothpicks, licked clean of the scallops and bacon, in a pile on the floor below the counter! I was going to remind you to remove the toothpicks before eating. But if Baby knew that, I guess I don't need to tell *you*!

Yield:	**8 servings; 2 pieces each**
Prep Time:	**20 minutes**
Chill Time:	**30 minutes to 2 hours**
Cook Time:	**16 minutes total**
Calories:	**120**
Total Fat:	**6 grams**
Saturated Fat:	**1.5 grams**
Carbohydrates:	**1 gram**
Net Carbohydrates:	**1 gram**
Fiber:	**0 gram**
Protein:	**14 grams**

TERIYAKI SAUCE

⅓ cup low-sodium soy sauce
2 tablespoons sesame oil
2 tablespoons rice wine vinegar, no sugar added (or may use dry sherry wine)
2 tablespoons apple cider vinegar
1½ tablespoons sugar substitute (recommended: Splenda)
1 tablespoon peeled and minced fresh ginger
1 tablespoon fresh lemon juice

1 pound large sea scallops, drained of any liquid (about 16 pieces)
8 bacon slices
16 wooden toothpicks

SPECIAL EQUIPMENT: large sealable plastic bag

1. Whisk all the teriyaki sauce ingredients together in a small saucepan and simmer over medium-high heat for 2 to 3 minutes, until the liquid reduces slightly. Remove from the heat and let cool for 10 minutes.

2. Add the drained scallops and cooled sauce to a bowl or large zip-lock bag and refrigerate for at least 30 minutes or up to 2 hours.

3. Preheat the oven to 400°F. Arrange the bacon on a baking sheet and bake until half-cooked, about 6 minutes. Let cool and cut each slice in half. Reserve the baking sheet; don't drain the fat.

4. Stretch one-half of a bacon slice around the outside of each marinated scallop, and secure with a toothpick.

5. Arrange the scallops on the reserved baking sheet and bake until just cooked through and the bacon is crispy, about 6 minutes more. Serve hot.

MAKE IT MEMORABLE

Try this perfect appetizer followed by a simple iceberg lettuce salad topped with Wasabe Ginger Vinaigrette (page 87), with Chili-Rubbed Baked Salmon (page 170) as the entrée.

HEALTHFUL HINTS

Lighten up this recipe by using turkey bacon in place of real bacon. A low-sodium soy sauce is always recommended.

French-Style Mussels

I find that many mussel dishes use too many ingredients, smothering the uniquely delicate and sweet liquor that is the secret of their subtle attraction! This recipe is classic in true French tradition. Its simplicity allows the natural flavors of the mussels to come through. (Make sure to enjoy the broth; it's the best part!)

Yield:	**6 servings**
Prep Time:	**15 minutes**
Cook Time:	**6 minutes**
Calories:	**170**
Total Fat:	**6 grams**
Saturated Fat:	**3 grams**
Carbohydrates:	**7 grams**
Net Carbohydrates:	**7 grams**
Fiber:	**0 gram**
Protein:	**17 grams**

2 tablespoons butter
1 cup chopped yellow or Spanish onion
2 tablespoons fresh thyme leaves, stemmed (may use 1 tablespoon dry thyme leaves)
½ teaspoon salt
2 pounds fresh mussels, washed and debearded
2 ounces dry white wine
Fresh whole thyme, optional, for garnish
1 lemon, cut into wedges, optional, for garnish

SPECIAL EQUIPMENT: large sauté or saucepan or small stockpot with fitting lid

1. Heat the butter in a large pan over medium-high heat. Add the onions, thyme, and salt and cook for just a minute.

2. Add the cleaned mussels to the pan and pour the wine over all.

3. Cover tightly and cook for only 4 to 5 minutes until the mussels begin to open. (Any mussels that do not open should be discarded.) Serve in large soup bowls or on a platter with the liquid and onions from the bottom of the pan poured over the mussels and garnish with fresh whole thyme and lemon wedges, if desired.

MAKE IT MEMORABLE

Make this into a hearty seafood stew by throwing in some peeled shrimp, sea scallops, and whole peeled tomatoes with the mussels. Voilà! A seafood feast in as little time as it takes to drive to a fancy French restaurant.

HEALTHFUL HINTS

To lighten up this recipe, trans fat-free margarine may be used to replace the butter. Or just leave out the butter and sauté the onions in the wine! Then finish the mussels exactly the same way.

Clams Parmesan

These stuffed clams have all the flavor of clams oreganata without all that breading that only fills you up before the main course. Instead, I add the same rich Italian flavors using fresh veggies and herbs and my favorite Parmesan cheese! The clams are a bit cheesier than what you may have had before, but then again, so am I!

Yield:	**8 servings; 3 clams each**
Prep Time:	**20 minutes**
Cook Time:	**5 minutes**
Calories:	**50**
Total Fat:	**1.5 grams**
Saturated Fat:	**.5 gram**
Carbohydrates:	**1.5 grams**
Net Carbohydrates:	**1.5 grams**
Fiber:	**0 gram**
Protein:	**7 grams**

Vegetable oil spray
2 dozen raw littleneck clams, opened on the half-shell
⅓ cup grated Parmesan cheese
1 tablespoon minced red onion
1 tablespoon chopped fresh flat-leaf parsley
1 teaspoon minced fresh garlic
½ teaspoon dry oregano
½ teaspoon dry basil
¼ teaspoon kosher salt
¼ teaspoon freshly ground black pepper
⅓ cup diced tomato
Juice of 1 lemon
Fresh parsley or basil tops, optional, for garnish

1. Place oven rack in the center position and set the oven to high broil. Spray a sheet pan with vegetable spray.

2. Place the unopened clams on the sheet pan and into the hot oven for just a minute or two, remove, and the clams will open easily by hand, or by carefully using a paring knife run along the inside of the shell cutting through the clams.

3. Add all the ingredients, except the diced tomato, lemon juice, and fresh parsley, to a bowl and mix well.

4. Working over the sheet pan, top each open clam on the half-shell with about 1 teaspoon of the mixture, sprinkle with the diced tomato, and squeeze the lemon juice over all.

5. Broil on the center rack for about 5 minutes, or until the clams start to bubble and brown slightly. Remove and serve hot, garnished with fresh parsley or basil, if desired.

MAKE IT MEMORABLE

These clams are definitely the start of something good, but why stop there? Try adding some fresh spinach and bacon to the mix for an entirely different stuffed clam that will leave you stuffed—I mean satisfied!

HEALTHFUL HINT

The Parmesan cheese may be replaced with trans-fat-free margarine or olive oil to lighten up the fats in this recipe.

Melon and Prosciutto Bites

Ever cut into a big honeydew melon or cantaloupe and wonder what you were going to do with it? Happens to me all the time! Well, try this new twist on presenting a classic gourmet appetizer that's perfect for any dinner party. These bites can be fancy by themselves or fun dipped in sauce for kids, but they are sure to please the most sophisticated palate with the simplest of ingredients and efforts.

Yield:	8 servings; 3 each
Prep Time:	15 minutes
Cook Time:	3 minutes
Calories:	30
Total Fat:	2 grams
Saturated Fat:	0 gram
Carbohydrates:	6 grams
Net Carbohydrates:	5 grams
Fiber:	1 gram
Protein:	2 grams

½ large cantaloupe, trimmed and seeded (about 2 cups)
¼ large honeydew melon, trimmed and seeded (about 1 cup)
4 ounces prosciutto, thinly sliced
24 pieces fancy plastic cocktail swords or long toothpicks
24 individual fresh basil leaves

1. Trim all the rind off the cantaloupe and honeydew halves and cut the trimmed melon into 2-inch squares about ½ inch thick. (Try to cut each melon piece as close to the same size as possible, about the size and thickness of a matchbook.)

2. Cut the prosciutto into 24 matching thin pieces as best you can. (If the prosciutto falls apart it can be pieced together, if needed.)

3. Thread on each cocktail stick alternating single pieces of cantaloupe, a basil leaf, honeydew, prosciutto, and end with another piece of cantaloupe all pushed tight together to form a 3-layer mini-sandwich.

MAKE IT MEMORABLE

Stick a strawberry on the end and serve these refreshing gourmet delights with some Fresh Raspberry Fruit Dip (page 58), poured into a cantaloupe half and served by sticking the bites right into the side of the filled melon for a treat the kids will truly love!

HEALTHFUL HINT

Get rid of the fat by simply leaving out the prosciutto for a great fruit treat for dipping!

Condiments, Spices, and Dressings

Almond Flour

DRESSINGS AND MARINADES

Basic Vinaigrette

Wasabe Ginger Vinaigrette

Basil Pesto

BBQ Rub

Herb Rub

SALSAS AND SAUCES

Cool Cucumber Chipotle Chutney

Easy Tzatziki Sauce

Foolproof Hollandaise Sauce

Low-Fat Hollandaise Sauce

Mornay Sauce

Dill Butter

Quick and Easy Ketchup

Summer Squash Salsa

Totally Tartar Sauce

Some would say that everything is in the details. If condiments really can make the meal, it's time to take more of the credit. Don't let some name brand ketchup get all the recognition! Make your own dressings and spices, so you can take all the glory while leaving all the *sugar* behind. (Along with the fillers and chemicals of store-bought condiments.)

Whether it's our **Quick and Easy Ketchup** or **Wasabe Ginger Vinaigrette,** even without added sugars, it isn't what's missing, it's what there: a taste beyond compare.

With just a few master recipes like these, you can change it up, adding amazing flavors for delicious combinations of all your favorite foods without an ounce of boredom. My **Herb Rub, Basil Pesto,** and **BBQ Rub** go well with just about any cut of meat, poultry, or seafood, whether you're baking, broiling, or grilling. They're that universal!

If you're ready to take it to the next level, go gourmet with my **Mornay Sauce** or **Foolproof Hollandaise Sauce**. You'd never find those in a jar—and you'll never cease to impress when serving them!

Success is taken in small steps, day by day, and meal by meal. So make the small things count! Make your condiments, spices, and dressings—*Stella Style*!

Almond Flour

Ground almonds have been used for centuries to make a sweet uncooked confection called marzipan. They're the perfect fresh alternative to white flour for baked goods. A strong antioxidant, loaded with vitamin E and fiber, their heart-healthy monounsaturated fats take the place of saturated or trans fats in recipes. (Trust me, I looked it up!) But all that goodness aside, almond flour adds a texture and flavor to muffins, cakes, and cookies that is unmatched by regular flours!

Yield:	**10 servings; ¼ cup each**
Prep Time:	**10 minutes**
Calories:	**140**
Total Fat:	**12 grams**
Saturated Fat:	**1 gram**
Carbohydrates:	**5 grams**
Net Carbohydrates:	**2 grams**
Fiber:	**3 grams**
Protein:	**5 grams**

10 ounces whole raw almonds (We buy a 10-ounce bag found in the produce department or baking aisle.) You may also use sliced raw almonds if you cannot find whole.

SPECIAL EQUIPMENT: food processor

1. Grind the almonds on high in a food processor for about 3 minutes until a grainy flour consistency.

2. Almond flour can be stored in an airtight container for up to 1 week on the counter or several months in the freezer.

MAKE IT MEMORABLE

Mix 1 serving of almond flour with half as much grated Parmesan cheese and use as an alternative to bread or cracker crumbs for lightly coating baked fish or chicken.

HEALTHFUL HINT

Always keep a bag of raw almonds in the house; they make good healthy snackin'!

Dressings and Marinades

Basic Vinaigrette

Cooking is easy and fun, at least it should be! That's always been my style and once you know how to make certain "basic" or "master" recipes like this vinaigrette, the sky's the limit for what you can do with just the simple switch of one ingredient here and there. Variety and goodness—both are key to eating *Stella Style*!

Yield:	**8 servings; 2 tablespoons each**
Prep Time:	**10 minutes**
Calories:	**200**
Total Fat:	**21 grams**
Saturated Fat:	**2.5 grams**
Carbohydrates:	**0 gram**
Fiber:	**0 gram**
Protein:	**0 gram**

1 teaspoon Dijon mustard
¼ cup red wine vinegar
⅛ cup white wine vinegar
1 small fresh garlic clove
1 teaspoon salt
½ teaspoon freshly ground black pepper
¼ teaspoon ground white pepper
⅓ cup extra virgin olive oil
½ cup canola oil
Salt

SPECIAL EQUIPMENT: blender

1. In a blender, combine the mustard, vinegars, garlic, and spices and mix on medium until completely blended.

2. With the blender still on, slowly pour in the olive oil in a continuous steady stream followed by the canola oil in the same fashion.

3. Remove the dressing from the blender and salt to taste, if necessary. The dressing will keep for 2 weeks refrigerated in a covered glass container.

MAKE IT MEMORABLE

Try this dressing on our Blackened Salmon Salad Niçoise (page 105) or use as a marinade for chicken and beef. Add different fresh herbs such as basil, tarragon, or cilantro to make a whole new and exciting flavor dressing, *Stella Style*!

Wasabe Ginger Vinaigrette

I went through a sushi and sashimi phase about ten years ago. I still love those simple ginger salads that came with the sushi, and the distinctive flavors of the hot wasabe, spicy ginger, and rice wine vinegar. And with this re-creation of the tasty salad dressing I remember so well, I can still enjoy the flavors I liked so much.

Yield:	**12 servings; 1 ounce each**
Prep Time:	**10 minutes**
Calories:	**130**
Total Fat:	**13 grams**
Saturated Fat:	**1 gram**
Carbohydrates:	**.5 gram**
Net Carbohydrates:	**.5 gram**
Fiber:	**0 gram**
Protein:	**0 gram**

1 tablespoon wasabe paste
1 teaspoon Dijon mustard
1 tablespoon fresh lemon juice
¼ cup rice wine vinegar
1 tablespoon peeled and minced fresh gingerroot
½ cup canola oil
¼ cup sesame oil
¼ teaspoon kosher salt
⅛ teaspoon freshly ground black pepper

SPECIAL EQUIPMENT: blender

1. In a blender on high speed, combine the wasabe paste, mustard, lemon juice, vinegar, and ginger for just a few seconds until smooth.

2. Turn the blender to a lower speed and slowly pour in first the canola then the sesame oil in a continuous stream until fully incorporated. Season with salt and pepper to taste and store refrigerated in a covered glass container for up to 1 month.

MAKE IT MEMORABLE

Place a head of shredded iceberg lettuce in a large bowl, add dressing, and toss. Serve individually in salad bowls sprinkled with parsley and garnish with lemon slices.

HEALTHFUL HINT

Use half as much oil and that much more rice wine vinegar. It will make a zestier dressing while lowering the fats.

Basil Pesto

From drizzling pesto over an antipasto platter filled with tomatoes, mozzarella, and peppers to stuffing a pork loin or topping a salad, the uses for a fresh basil pesto are limited only by the imagination! You can grill it on some big ol' shrimp or bake it on a chicken breast, but whatever the use, pesto adds gourmet flair and a flavor that's guaranteed to please!

Yield:	8 servings; 1 tablespoon each
Prep Time:	15 minutes
Calories:	120
Total Fat:	12 grams
Saturated Fat:	2 grams
Carbohydrates:	1 gram
Net Carbohydrates:	0 gram
Fiber:	1 gram
Protein:	2 grams

2 packed cups fresh basil leaves
⅓ cup extra virgin olive oil
3 tablespoons pine nuts (toast in a dry skillet over medium heat until lightly brown)
1 small fresh garlic clove (about ½ teaspoon chopped)
¼ teaspoon kosher salt
¼ teaspoon freshly ground black pepper
¼ cup grated Parmesan cheese

SPECIAL EQUIPMENT: food processor or blender

1. Place all the ingredients, except the Parmesan cheese, into a food processor or blender and pulse on high until almost a puree.

2. Pour into a glass bowl and stir in the Parmesan cheese to finish. Use immediately or may be refrigerated in a covered glass container for up to 1 week.

MAKE IT MEMORABLE

Pesto is perfect for topping chicken breast and the proof is in my simple Chicken Pesto Skewers (page 74). But there is *so* much more you can do with pesto, such as mix it with mayonnaise, spoonful for spoonful, to make an unbelievable salad dressing! What will you use it for?

HEALTHFUL HINTS

The olive oil may be reduced to ¼ cup, with the remaining amount of oil replaced with water, but when made this way, the pesto should be used right away and not stored.

BBQ Rub

Besides my blackening spice, this is another seasoning that I keep on hand for quick and easy cooking! It's simple to make, because it's made with ingredients everyone should already have in the kitchen. But it tastes like you drove all the way down South to get the recipe. Lucky for you, I did the traveling, and copied it here for you.

Yield:	**10 servings**
Prep Time:	**10 minutes**
Calories:	**60**
Total Fat:	**6 grams**
Saturated Fat:	**0 gram**
Carbohydrates:	**2 grams**
Net Carbohydrates:	**1 gram**
Fiber:	**1 gram**
Protein:	**0 gram**

¼ cup canola oil
2 tablespoons kosher salt
2 tablespoons paprika
1½ teaspoons freshly ground black pepper
2 teaspoons garlic powder
2 teaspoons onion powder

Place all the ingredients into a bowl and mix with a fork until a mudlike consistency. Store refrigerated for up to 3 weeks in a nonreactive, covered container.

MAKE IT MEMORABLE

This rub will instantly season pork, chicken, and beef for everything from roasting to grilling!

HEALTHFUL HINT

You may eliminate the oil and have a completely dry version that you can simply rub on when you are ready to use it.

Herb Rub

I love to use fresh herbs to garnish my plates; it's a signature for me. But I always have some left over that I just cannot use before it goes bad. Like fresh garlic, olive oil will help preserve fresh herbs in your refrigerator and still provide the same flavor weeks later. Once made, this herb rub will make your life a bit easier. All you need to do to cook with it is rub it on and bake, broil, grill, or sauté!

Yield:	**10 servings**
Prep Time:	**15 minutes**
Calories:	**110**
Total Fat:	**11 grams**
Saturated Fat:	**1 gram**
Carbohydrates:	**1 gram**
Net Carbohydrates:	**1 gram**
Fiber:	**0 gram**
Protein:	**0 gram**

½ cup fresh cilantro leaves, stemmed and washed
½ cup fresh basil leaves, stemmed and washed
½ cup fresh flat-leaf parsley, stemmed and washed
¼ cup extra virgin olive oil
¼ cup canola oil
2 tablespoons kosher salt
1 tablespoon paprika
1½ teaspoons freshly ground black pepper
2 teaspoons garlic powder
2 teaspoons onion powder

SPECIAL EQUIPMENT: food processor

Place all the ingredients into a food processor and blend on high for about 1 minute until a mudlike consistency. Remove and store refrigerated for up to 3 weeks in a covered nonreactive container.

MAKE IT MEMORABLE

Our favorite use for this rub is to make Herb-Roasted Chicken Breasts (page 153), but try it on meats, seafood, or vegetables. It's all good!

HEALTHFUL HINT

You may cut down on the oil by half and you'll have a thicker rub that you can simply thin with a little water when you are ready to use.

Salsas and Sauces

Cool Cucumber Chipotle Chutney

Say that three times fast! (See, I have fun cooking *and* naming recipes!) It was also fun inventing this healthy alternative to the traditionally sugar-laden chutneys or cocktail sauces. By the way, it's called "Cool" because when I was making it for the first time and let Rachel taste it, the first word out of her mouth was: "Cool!"

Yield:	12 servings; 2 tablespoons each
Prep Time:	10 minutes
Calories:	10
Total Fat:	0 gram
Saturated Fat:	0 gram
Carbohydrates:	1 gram
Net Carbohydrates:	1 gram
Fiber:	0 gram
Protein:	0 gram

1 medium seedless cucumber, diced small
1 Roma tomato, seeded and diced
¼ cup diced red bell pepper
¼ cup diced yellow bell pepper
2 tablespoons diced red onion
2 tablespoons chili sauce
1 teaspoon fresh lime juice
1 teaspoon Chipotle Tabasco Sauce
Salt and freshly ground black pepper to taste

Mix the ingredients together well in a glass bowl and chill before serving. Store refrigerated in a covered nonreactive container.

MAKE IT MEMORABLE

Enjoy atop Chili-Rubbed Baked Salmon (page 170), and wash it all down with a glass of White Wine Sangria (page 213)!

HEALTHFUL HINTS

This vegetable chutney makes a healthy and tasty alternative to salad dressing, and it is outstanding in place of cocktail sauce for oysters and shrimp!

Easy Tzatziki Sauce

Sounds Greek to me—and it is! But with no cooking involved, this classic cucumber and cream sauce is easier to make than it is to say! Although traditionally served with grilled marinated lamb and pork called souvlaki (page 124), I find it's also a refreshingly cool sauce that enhances almost any grilled fish, meat, or poultry.

1 cup sour cream
½ cup minced cucumber, peeled and seeded
½ teaspoon minced fresh garlic
½ teaspoon kosher salt

Add all the ingredients to a bowl and mix well. Store for up to 1 week refrigerated in a covered plastic or glass container.

Yield:	**6 servings; 2 tablespoons each**
Prep Time:	**10 minutes**
Calories:	**70**
Total Fat:	**7 grams**
Saturated Fat:	**4 grams**
Carbohydrates:	**1.5 grams**
Net Carbohydrates:	**1.5 grams**
Fiber:	**0 gram**
Protein:	**1 gram**

MAKE IT MEMORABLE

Serve traditionally with Pork Souvlaki (page 124), or as a sauce for grilled chicken, shrimp, or steak!

HEALTHFUL HINTS

You may lighten up this recipe by using low-fat sour cream or plain yogurt in place of the sour cream.

Foolproof Hollandaise Sauce

Making a hollandaise sauce can be a daunting task; maybe you've heard the horror stories when a chef messes up a batch before a Saturday night dinner rush. (I used to avoid using it just for that reason.)

At home, it's the same. Hollandaise is usually the last thing you make to top off a very special meal, a meal that counts on that sauce to make it all work! Follow this recipe carefully, and pay close attention to the cook's tips, and you will find that this hollandaise sauce will work every time. I promise that it really can be quite fast *and* easy!

Yield:	6 servings; 2 tablespoons each
Prep Time:	10 minutes
Cook Time:	5 minutes
Calories:	160
Total Fat:	17 grams
Saturated Fat:	11 grams
Carbohydrates:	0 gram
Net Carbohydrates:	0 gram
Fiber:	0 gram
Protein:	1 gram

2 egg yolks
2 tablespoons fresh lemon juice, about 1 lemon
Dash of cayenne pepper (less than ⅛ teaspoon)
¼ pound (1 stick) unsalted butter
Salt to taste (less than ⅛ teaspoon)

SPECIAL EQUIPMENT: blender or handheld wand blender with cup

1. In a blender cup, combine the egg yolks, lemon juice, and cayenne. Cover and blend on high for about 15 seconds, turn off, and let rest.

2. Meanwhile, melt the butter in a small saucepan over high heat until almost boiling and frothy; remove and immediately bring to the blender while keeping the butter as hot as possible.

3. With the egg mixture still in it, turn the blender on high and carefully pour in the hot butter, a little at a time, until it is all incorporated. If the sauce gets too thick, it only takes a couple drops of water to thin and you can continue.

4. Season lightly with salt to taste, if needed. Hollandaise must be used right away or store in a covered glass dish for up to 1 hour on the counter in a warm, not hot, environment; do not refrigerate or reheat.

NOTES: Cover the blender but remove the little center piece if your model has that feature when you are pouring the butter; otherwise, you will have to use a towel or your hand to keep splatters to a minimum.

Keep the butter as hot as possible and don't pour the butter in too fast or the sauce may break. And be careful, that butter is hot!

MAKE IT MEMORABLE

Hollandaise is the traditional finish to our *Stella Style* Baked Eggs Benedict (page 40), but also makes decadent delights of everything from vegetables to seafood or chicken to steaks!

HEALTHFUL HINT

If you are watching fats, try our Low-Fat Hollandaise Sauce (page 95).

Low-Fat Hollandaise Sauce

As a chef, it pained me at first to even *think* of making a lower fat version of such a deliciously decadent sauce as hollandaise. I was going to suggest skipping hollandaise altogether in recipes for those watching fats. Since *Stella Style* is about choices for *all* of us, I felt obliged to oblige, and thankfully so. This recipe fills the bill so nicely I use it myself now, all the time!

4 ounces fat-free cream cheese or Neuchâtel cheese, softened
3 tablespoons low-fat sour cream
1 tablespoon fresh lemon juice
1 teaspoon Dijon mustard
Dash of cayenne pepper (less than ⅛ teaspoon)
Salt to taste, if needed

Place all the ingredients in a small saucepan and whisk together over medium heat just until well blended and hot, but do not boil. Remove and serve warm. This may be refrigerated for up to 1 day and reheated, but this is not recommended.

MAKE IT MEMORABLE

Hollandaise is the traditional finish to our *Stella Style* Baked Eggs Benedict (page 40). This low-fat version holds up well to heat, making it a great sauce for everything from vegetables to seafood, chicken, and steaks!

HEALTHFUL HINT

Plain yogurt may be substituted for the sour cream to lower the fat even *more.*

Yield:	**6 servings; 2 tablespoons each**
Prep Time:	**10 minutes**
Cook Time:	**4 minutes**
Calories:	**30**
Total Fat:	**1 gram**
Saturated Fat:	**.5 gram**
Carbohydrates:	**1.5 grams**
Net Carbohydrates:	**1.5 grams**
Fiber:	**0 gram**
Protein:	**3 grams**

Mornay Sauce

Many sauces must be thickened with starches, but not this classic French white reduction sauce, making it perfect for low carb! I call it easy gourmet, because in a few short minutes you can turn a regular meal into something special, with hardly any extra effort!

2 tablespoons (¼ stick) unsalted butter
1 cup heavy cream
¼ cup dry white wine
1 small garlic clove, crushed
1 cup shredded Swiss cheese
½ cup freshly grated Parmesan cheese
¼ teaspoon kosher salt
⅛ teaspoon ground white pepper
Fresh Italian parsley optional, for garnish

Yield:	**8 servings; [illegible] ounces each**
Prep Time:	**10 minutes**
Cook Time:	**5 minutes**
Calories:	**190**
Total Fat:	**16 grams**
Saturated Fat:	**10 grams**
Carbohydrates:	**2 grams**
Net Carbohydrates:	**2 grams**
Fiber:	**0 gram**
Protein:	**8 grams**

1. Melt the butter in a medium saucepan over medium-high heat, add the cream, wine, and garlic, and let reduce for about [illegible] minutes.

2. Whisk in the Swiss and Parmesan cheeses, salt and white pepper; stir continuously for a couple of minutes more until the sauce becomes smooth and thick enough to put a heavy coat on the back of a spoon. Remove from the heat and serve immediately, garnished with fresh parsley, if desired.

MAKE IT MEMORABLE

Of course, this is the classic sauce to serve over Baked Stuffed Shrimp Mornay (page 181), but it can be a great topper for chicken breast, vegetables, and even as a fondue dip!

HEALTHFUL HINTS

Low-fat cheeses may be used and the cream can be replaced with unsweetened soy milk to reduce the fats considerably.

Dill Butter

I have used wonderful compound herb butters for more than twenty-five years and love their convenience! At any given time I have two or three different varieties in my freezer or refrigerator. Once you have all the ingredients in one place, you're only a few minutes away from an instant gourmet dinner!

¼ pound (1 stick) unsalted butter, softened
1 teaspoon minced garlic
2 tablespoons minced red onion
1 tablespoon chopped fresh parsley leaves
2 tablespoons chopped fresh dill, stems removed

⅛ teaspoon garlic powder
1 tablespoon kosher salt
¼ teaspoon freshly ground black pepper
Dash of white pepper
Dash of Worcestershire sauce
1 lemon, juiced

Yield:	**12 servings; 1 tablespoon each**
Prep time:	**15 minutes**
Calories:	**70**
Total Fat:	**7 grams**
Saturated Fat:	**5 grams**
Carbohydrates:	**0 gram**
Net Carbohydrates:	**0 gram**
Fiber:	**0 gram**
Protein:	**0 gram**

1. In a bowl with a wire whisk, mix together all the ingredients until well blended. It takes a bit of work, but it will mix together. (If you have trouble getting the liquid to combine, it may help to soften the butter just a bit more in the microwave for just a couple of seconds.)

2. Spoon the butter into a log shape about 2 inches around, place on a piece of saran wrap, and roll it up like a big cigar, twisting the ends shut. You may store the log in the refrigerator for 1 week or freeze for much longer.

MAKE IT MEMORABLE

Replace the dill with 2 tablespoons of any other fresh herb for a completely different butter. Try combinations of fresh grated ginger and teriyaki for tuna, or cilantro, basil, or mint for chicken, pork, and lamb. Gorgonzola and garlic go great with steak and veal. My favorite for swordfish is lemon and capers. Now, go have fun making your own combinations!

HEALTHFUL HINTS

To lighten things up, you can replace ¼ stick of butter with canola or olive oil for a healthier blend. If you're watching your saturated fats, all of the butter can be substituted with a trans-fat-free margarine.

Quick and Easy Ketchup

A quick and easy way to make our own ketchup was one of the first things we invented! Nothing fancy, but it sure does the trick without all those corn syrup solids you get with store bought. And did I say it was EASY? Believe me, when you want ketchup on that burger or dog, you're going to be grateful you don't have to start slaving over a stove just for ketchup! It's fresh, so remember to keep it refrigerated, and enjoy it in moderation, as it does still have natural tomato sugars!

8 ounces tomato sauce (make sure there is no sugar added in the ingredients list)
6 ounces tomato paste (make sure there is no sugar added in the ingredients list)
2 tablespoons white vinegar
¼ cup sugar substitute (recommended: Splenda)

Mix all the ingredients together in a small bowl. Refrigerate in a covered nonreactive container until needed for up to 2 weeks.

Yield:	24 servings; 1 tablespoon each
Prep Time:	5 minutes
Calories:	10
Total Fat:	0 gram
Saturated Fat:	0 gram
Carbohydrates:	2 grams
Net Carbohydrates:	2 grams
Fiber:	0 gram
Protein:	1 gram

Summer Squash Salsa

We always have plenty of our favorite vegetables, such as yellow squash and zucchini, in the refrigerator. When I needed to make a salsa one day and didn't have tomatoes, it was time to experiment! I was amazed at the way the flavors and colors worked so well to make this great alternative. The big difference turned out to be that instead of adding the hot and spicy touch to foods that regular salsa does, this version actually helps to cool down a hot and spicy dish!

2 tablespoons vegetable oil (recommended: canola)
1 cup small diced zucchini

Yield:	24 servings
Prep Time:	15 minutes
Cook Time:	5 minutes
Chill Time:	30 minutes
Calories:	15
Total Fat:	1 gram
Saturated Fat:	0 gram
Carbohydrates:	1 gram
Net Carbohydrates:	1 gram
Fiber:	0 gram
Protein:	0 gram

1 cup small diced yellow squash
½ cup small diced yellow bell pepper
¼ cup small diced red bell pepper
1 tablespoon sugar substitute (recommended: Splenda)
⅛ teaspoon kosher salt
⅛ teaspoon freshly ground black pepper
¼ cup small diced cantaloupe

1. Place the oil in a sauté pan and preheat over high heat.

2. Add all the ingredients, except the cantaloupe, and cook for only 2 minutes, just until tender.

3. Remove from the heat, drain, and spread out on a plate. Refrigerate quickly without a cover to stop the cooking.

4. When cooled, mix in the cantaloupe, cover, and refrigerate for at least 30 minutes before serving.

MAKE IT MEMORABLE

Serve as an accompaniment to spicy dishes such as Jamaican Jerk Sea Scallop and Shrimp Brochettes (page 68), or Jamaican BBQ Ribs (page 126). It's great with grilled chicken and fish, too!

HEALTHFUL HINTS

The vegetable oil can be replaced with water to lighten up this already healthy recipe, and the sugar substitute can be omitted altogether, changing only the sweetness, not the deliciousness!

Totally Tartar Sauce

Plain old sauces can be plain and boring, and boring just doesn't cut it with *Stella Style*! Something as simple as tartar sauce is no exception, because with a few gourmet touches that don't require extra work, the ordinary can easily become extraordinary! The proof is in this delightfully different and interesting condiment, everything you expect in a good tartar sauce and more—totally!

Yield:	24 servings; 1 tablespoon each
Prep Time:	10 minutes
Calories:	70
Total Fat:	7 grams
Saturated Fat:	1 gram
Carbohydrates:	1 gram
Net Carbohydrates:	1 gram
Fiber:	0 gram
Protein:	0 gram

1 cup mayonnaise
½ cup dill pickle relish
1 tablespoon minced red onion
1 tablespoon capers, chopped
1 tablespoon pitted black olives, chopped
1 tablespoon fresh lemon juice
¼ teaspoon kosher salt
⅛ teaspoon freshly ground black pepper
⅛ teaspoon garlic powder

Whisk all the ingredients together in a bowl. Refrigerate in a covered nonreactive container until needed for up to 1 week.

MAKE IT MEMORABLE

This sauce is especially designed to accompany Fried Ipswich Clams (page 177), or for any fish dish of your liking such as Monkfish Kebabs (page 175).

HEALTHFUL HINTS

Lighten up this recipe by using a low-fat or light mayo without sugars added, or try a low-fat plain yogurt as a total replacement for the mayo.

Jenny's Recipe for Success

Around four months ago, something in my mind clicked. I've been battling my weight for most of my life, but I noticed that when I exercised and ate fewer carbs, I was in top-notch shape. When I went back to eating "white" carbs, I ballooned up.

Last year, I had a beautiful baby boy—and one hundred extra pounds. When my son, Andrew, was born, I weighed 266! During the pregnancy, I ate everything and couldn't exercise due to complications. I lost thirty pounds after the birth, but then my weight stayed around 235 for months.

Then I watched George's show and bought his book. I knew that low carb was the answer, so earlier this year I started eating low carb and exercising. I haven't missed a single day's workout and I've done very well with food, eating lots of salad greens (no dressing), vegetables, and lean meats. I also kicked up my water intake, and that helped tremendously. In three and a half months of working very hard and watching what I eat, I've lost almost sixty pounds. When I feel stalled, I just reevaluate what I'm eating and how I've been exercising and make changes.

Besides the low-carb eating, the most important thing in my weight-loss journey has been the exercise. I put in at least sixty minutes per day. I get up at 4:45 so that I can get my hard exercise out of the way before the baby wakes up. Andrew and I like to take lots of walks throughout the day as well. When a workout gets too easy, I up the speed, incline, or intensity. I'm also going to start running with my husband, who is very supportive of my lifestyle change.

My primary motivation was to become healthy so that I can really enjoy my son. Before low carb, I was lucky to get dinner on the table before I collapsed into bed by 7:30 in the evening. Today, I can play with my son and and chase after him all day, exercise vigorously, make a gourmet dinner, *and* take care of my home. Low-carb eating helped me to regain my health and energy.

Low carb doesn't need to be boring, which was one of my problems with dieting in the past—becoming bored with the food. With chefs like George Stella out there, and with our own creative minds and determination, everyone can be in shape while eating great.

Salads and Soups

By now, you should know that I love my veggies. With so many fresh vegetables naturally low in carbohydrates, salads always make the perfect meal! If you're ever stuck in a restaurant and unsure of what to order, go with the salad. You can't lose!

Even when you're at home, I have a few salads of my own that are sure to give any restaurant a run for their money! From my **Grilled Portabella and Montrachet Salad** to my **Blackened Salmon Salad Niçoise,** they're sure to make anyone *green* with envy.

If you're looking for the perfect side dish for your next barbecue, **Liz's Fast Fiesta Salad** or my **Jicama Slaw** are always big hits. But if you're entertaining guests and *really* want to steal the show, why not kick things off with a mouth-watering bowl of **Mushroom Florentine Soup** or **Cream of Asparagus Soup?** They're so easy to prepare; it makes it even easier to *impress.*

Everything is in the details! So if your meals seem to be missing something, maybe it's a first course, such as a soup or salad. But don't rule out these recipes as merely primers for the main course, as they'll also make a great lunch or light dinner. So gather around the table—soup's on!

Liz's Fast Fiesta Salad

This recipe is courtesy of Elizabeth Levenson. I opened my local newspaper one morning and the headline read: Low Carb and Lovin' It! It wasn't about me; it was about Liz Levenson, an inspiring young woman who had successfully lost well over one hundred pounds living low carb! She really made an impression on me and lo and behold, a few months later, Liz and I met while shopping and I invited her to be on my show. Everyone loved the recipe she made on TV that day! "This dish is fast, simple, and tastes great for low-carbers and non-low-carbers alike," Liz told us as she cooked. "It's a great side to bring to a summer barbecue or picnic. It's full of flavor and a snap to prepare!"

Yield:	**8 servings**
Prep Time:	**10 minutes**
Cook Time:	**5 minutes**
Calories:	**250**
Total Fat:	**22 grams**
Saturated Fat:	**6 grams**
Carbohydrates:	**7 grams**
Net Carbohydrates:	**4 grams**
Fiber:	**3 grams**
Protein:	**7 grams**

1 (16-ounce) bag frozen broccoli florets
1 (16-ounce) bag frozen cauliflower florets
1 cup ranch dressing (most brands have 1 gram carbohydrate or less)
1 cup shredded Cheddar cheese
5 slices bacon, cooked and crumbled
3 scallions

1. Defrost the frozen broccoli and cauliflower in the microwave for approximately 5 minutes. They should come out still cold, but not icy.

2. Toss the broccoli and cauliflower with the ranch dressing and make sure that all the pieces are evenly coated.

3. Add the shredded Cheddar and bacon and mix well. Cover and refrigerate for 1 hour or as long as overnight. Thinly slice the scallions on an angle and sprinkle on top of the salad for garnish when ready to serve.

MAKE IT MEMORABLE

I agree with Liz. Take this salad to a picnic or barbecue, and enjoy it with some Jamaican BBQ Ribs (page 126) and BBQ Baked Soybeans (page 202)!

HEALTHFUL HINT

You may use low-fat Cheddar cheese and ranch dressing or cooked turkey bacon to lighten up this recipe.

Blackened Salmon Salad Niçoise

This wonderful and classic gourmet salad is a great way to use leftovers! Sure, you can make it from scratch very easily, but it's a perfect way to make a completely different meal the day after when you have that leftover salmon, blackened or otherwise. This salad is *so* chockful of goodness, you won't even notice that it's missing the white potatoes it normally calls for!

Yield:	2 servings
Prep Time:	30 minutes
Cook Time:	12 minutes
Calories:	540
Total Fat:	26 grams
Saturated Fat:	4 grams
Carbohydrates:	17 grams
Net Carbohydrates:	13 grams
Fiber:	4 grams
Protein:	48 grams

¼ pound fresh green beans, ends trimmed
4 ounces Basic Vinaigrette (page 86)
4 cups field greens (any lettuce mix will do)
1 Roma tomato, cut into 6 wedges
4 ounces marinated artichoke hearts
2 hard-boiled eggs, halved
¼ cup pimiento stuffed green olives (may use any variety olives)
Two 6-ounce Blackened Salmon fillets (page 168)
1 tablespoon minced red bell pepper
1 tablespoon minced green bell pepper

1. Place a small pot of water over high heat to boil. Drop the trimmed green beans in boiling water and cook for about 5 minutes or until tender but still crispy.

2. While the green beans are cooking, make the vinaigrette.

3. When the green beans are done, place them in an ice bath to cool; strain and reserve.

4. Pile the lettuce mix high in the center of 2 plates. Place 3 wedges of tomato around each of the 2 plates in a starburst fashion with an artichoke heart in between. Then add an egg half on either side of each salad and scatter evenly with the green beans and olives.

5. Make and top the salad with the blackened salmon fillets. Drizzle with the vinaigrette and sprinkle the bell peppers around the edges of the plate for garnish. Serve immediately.

MAKE IT MEMORABLE

Save time at lunch or dinner by preparing the entire salad and dressing ahead; just keep them separate in the refrigerator. Cook or reheat the salmon just before you're ready to serve the meal, and remember too that salmon cooks very quickly!

HEALTHFUL HINTS

Boneless and skinless chicken breast may be used in place of the salmon for a lower fat version, or enjoy the salad by itself without the protein. It's all good!

Grilled Portabella and Montrachet Salad

I first tried grilling goat cheese wrapped in lettuce leaves back in the early eighties, when Wolfgang Puck's California cuisine was just taking off. We chefs were definitely paying attention! Who knew you could grill so many foods? And believe me, we tried them all—from oysters to ducks to peaches and strawberries, it all hit the grill then. The funny thing is, most of it worked! But don't take my word for it—fire up the grill! I know you'll love the creaminess of the rich, warmed Montrachet as it melts slightly, perfectly complementing the grilled portabellas and walnuts.

Yield:	**4 servings**
Prep Time:	**15 minutes**
Cook Time:	**8 minutes**
Calories:	**240**
Total Fat:	**20 grams**
Saturated Fat:	**7 grams**
Carbohydrates:	**6 grams**
Net Carbohydrates:	**4 grams**
Fiber:	**2 grams**
Protein:	**9 grams**

4 ounces Montrachet goat cheese, cut into 4 equal rounds
4 large outer leaves radicchio lettuce
3 medium portabella mushroom caps, stems removed
2 tablespoons extra virgin olive oil, plus more for the cheese
½ teaspoon kosher salt
⅛ teaspoon freshly ground black pepper
2 tablespoons fresh lemon juice
2 tablespoons sherry vinegar or red wine vinegar
7 ounces (about 3 cups) mesclun lettuce mix
¼ cup roasted red pepper strips
¼ cup shelled walnut halves
1 lemon, cut into wedges

SPECIAL EQUIPMENT: grill or grill pan

1. Preheat an outdoor grill or cast-iron grill pan to medium-high.

2. Working on a baking sheet, wrap each round of cheese in a radicchio leaf like an egg roll, and pinch them a little to help them keep their shape. Arrange them on one side of the baking sheet.

3. Place the mushroom caps on the other side of the baking sheet; drizzle with the olive oil and season with salt and pepper.

4. Grill the mushrooms until tender and juicy, turning once, about 6 minutes.

5. Lightly drizzle the wrapped goat cheese with oil and grill until slightly charred and warm, turning occasionally, about 1 minute. Immediately remove and slice in half on the diagonal.

6. Slice the grilled mushroom caps into strips and add them to a bowl with the lemon juice and sherry wine vinegar. Toss to combine.

7. In a bowl, toss the lettuce mix with the mushrooms and juices and arrange in 4 salad bowls.

8. Arrange 2 goat cheese halves in the center of each bowl, and distribute the sliced mushrooms over the top.

9. Sprinkle each salad with red pepper strips and walnuts, and serve garnished with lemon wedges.

MAKE IT MEMORABLE

This salad is a meal in itself, or it makes a great start to a gourmet dinner of Tilapia and Prawn Mousse Roulades (page 183), with Chocolate Pecan Truffles (page 220) for dessert.

HEALTHFUL HINT

This recipe can be lightened up by replacing the goat cheese with lower fat Neufchâtel cheese.

Grilled Rosemary-Ginger Pork Tenderloin and Peach Salad

I'm tempted to tell you that this recipe takes less time to make than it does to say the title, but I can't say that. I *can* guarantee that you won't forget the name after you've tasted it! This gourmet, high in protein salad highlights pork tenderloins, the "filet mignon" of pork, and is a full meal in itself! Being the leanest and most tender cut, the pork tenderloin doesn't usually get the attention and respect it deserves. So, if you're looking to truly "WOW" someone with something decidedly different and outrageous, this is definitely the meal to make!

Yield:	**4 servings**
Prep Time:	**15 minutes**
Inactive Prep Time:	**3 hours**
Cook Time:	**10 minutes**
Calories:	**320**
Total Fat:	**14 grams**
Saturated Fat:	**4 grams**
Carbohydrates:	**10 grams**
Net Carbohydrates:	**6.5 grams**
Fiber:	**3.5 grams**
Protein:	**38 grams**

⅓ cup extra virgin olive oil
⅓ cup sherry vinegar
1½ tablespoons peeled, grated fresh ginger
1 tablespoon coarsely chopped fresh rosemary plus 4 whole sprigs, for garnish
½ teaspoon kosher salt
¼ teaspoon freshly ground black pepper
¼ teaspoon crushed red pepper flakes
2 (12-ounce) pork tenderloins, trimmed
2 firm ripe peaches, pitted and halved
4 small yellow tomatoes, cored and halved
12 large radicchio leaves
6 cups cut romaine lettuce (about 1 large head)
¼ cup crumbled Gorgonzola cheese

SPECIAL EQUIPMENT: gallon-sized sealable plastic bag

1. Whisk together the oil, vinegar, ginger, rosemary, salt, pepper, and red pepper flakes in a bowl.

2. Transfer half of the marinade to the gallon-sized sealable plastic bag with the pork. Marinate the pork in the refrigerator for at least 2 hours and up to overnight. Refrigerate the remaining marinade and reserve for the peaches and tomatoes.

3. When ready to cook, build a charcoal fire or preheat a gas grill. Remove the pork from the bag and discard the used marinade.

4. Place the tenderloins on the grill and cook, turning once, until cooked medium rare, or when an instant-read thermometer stuck in the thickest part reads 145°F, about 10 minutes. Transfer the pork to a cutting board, cover loosely with foil, and let rest for 5 minutes before cutting the tenderloins on the diagonal into 8 slices each.

5. Meanwhile, toss the peach and tomato halves in a bowl with the reserved marinade. Place them cut side down on the grill, and cook until lightly browned but still firm, about 4 minutes. Transfer to the cutting board and cut each peach half into thirds.

6. To serve, fan 3 radicchio lettuce leaves on each of 4 plates and place one-quarter of the romaine (1½ cups) in the center of each.

7. On one side of each plate, place 4 slices of pork and on the other side, place 3 peach wedges and 2 tomato halves.

8. Sprinkle each plate with the cheese and drizzle with 2 tablespoons of the reserved marinade. Garnish each plate with a rosemary sprig and serve.

MAKE IT MEMORABLE

This salad covers all the bases as a meal, but doesn't leave you stuffed. That means there might be room for a tempting dessert such as a slice of Lemon Meringue Pie (page 235) or even some refreshing Frozen Custard Ice Cream (page 242).

HEALTHFUL HINTS

Cutting the fats and calories here can easily be accomplished by replacing the Gorgonzola cheese with healthier alternatives such as roasted red peppers, marinated artichoke hearts, or olives. And since there is plenty of pork tenderloin to go around, you can cook both but use only one, freezing the other.

Iceberg Prairie Salad with Smoky Green Chile Ranch Dressing

I promise this is the longest name I will ever use for a recipe! Making food exciting is an important part of enjoying your meals, and enjoying your meals is a key factor in successfully changing your eating habits for the long term. Iceberg is my favorite lettuce and I am always throwing whatever is in the refrigerator on top of it, such as the olives and peppers in this recipe. The dressing is a result of experimentation: I wanted to include one of my new favorite ingredients, chipotle pepper hot sauce. Once you've tried it, you'll definitely understand the name of this recipe, especially when you are guzzling that water! (The water is great for you, too!)

Yield:	4 servings
Prep Time:	10 minutes
Calories:	115
Total Fat:	10 grams
Saturated Fat:	1.5 grams
Carbohydrates:	5 grams
Net Carbohydrates:	3 grams
Fiber:	2 grams
Protein:	1 gram

4 cups shredded iceberg lettuce
3 small yellow tomatoes, quartered (may use 4 cherry tomatoes, cut in half)
20 oil-cured black olives, pitted
4 large radishes, sliced
Smoky Green Chile Ranch Dressing (recipe follows)
2 scallions, thinly sliced

1. Pile equal amounts of lettuce in the center of 4 bowls.

2. Top each salad with the tomatoes, olives, and radishes, drizzle 2 tablespoons of the dressing over each, and sprinkle with the scallions. Serve.

MAKE IT MEMORABLE

Top this salad with any leftover protein such as cooked chicken or turkey breast or our favorite, Chili-Rubbed Baked Salmon (page 170), for a complete lunch or dinner, leaving you with enough room for some Breadless Bread Pudding (page 230).

HEALTHFUL HINTS

This is a healthy salad already, but you can still reduce the fats and calories by using fewer olives and only a small amount of dressing, or replace the dressing altogether with a drizzle of fresh lemon juice and olive oil.

Smoky Green Chile Ranch Dressing

Yield:	about 12 servings
Calories:	90
Total Fat:	9 grams
Saturated Fat:	1.5 grams
Carbohydrates:	1 gram
Net Carbohydrates:	1 gram
Fiber:	0 gram
Protein:	0 gram

1 cup low-carb ranch dressing (recommended: no more than 1 carb per 2 tablespoons)
1 (4-ounce) can diced green chiles, drained
2 teaspoons chipotle pepper sauce (recommended: Tabasco)
1 teaspoon finely chopped cilantro leaves
1 garlic clove, minced

Whisk all the ingredients together in a bowl. Refrigerate until needed.

Riviera Omelet (p. 32); Cinnamon Toast Pancakes (p.46)

Pork Souvlaki with Easy Tzatziki Sauce (p. 124); Grilled Portabellas, Peppers, and Squash (p. 190)

Blackened Salmon Salad Niçoise (p. 105); Basic Vinaigrette (p. 86); Cream of Asparagus Soup (p. 119); Better Cheddar Cheese Crisps (p.64)

Jamaican BBQ Ribs *(p. 126)**;*
BBQ Baked Soybeans *(p. 202)*

Herb-Roasted Chicken Breasts (fresh Herb Rub [p. 90] for chicken) (p. 153)

Family-Style Chicken (p. 152); Roasted Vegetables (p. 191); Cauliflower "Mac" and Cheese Casserole (p. 203)

Rachel's Marvelous Macaroons (p. 222); Pumpkin Pound Cake (p. 229); (Almond Flour [p. 85] for macaroons and cake); Balsamic-Grilled Strawberries and Cream (p. 238)

Stella Style *Goldfish Crackers (p. 63); Chocolate Pecan Truffles (p. 220)*

Stella Style Chef's Salad

I'm sitting in an airplane on the way to my high school band reunion in Florida. (Yes, I was a band geek ever since I played the snare drum at my kindergarten graduation.) What does this have to do with a chef's salad? Well, I'm sitting here starving once again on an airplane, and as usual everything offered has sugars or starches or something that I prefer to avoid. Why can't they just put a chef's salad like this one—without fried noodles, croutons, or sugary dressings—on the menu? It *would* be nice, but for now, better bring your own!

Yield:	**2 servings**
Prep Time:	**15 minutes**
Cook Time:	**5 minutes**
Calories:	**220**
Total Fat:	**15 grams**
Saturated Fat:	**4.5 grams**
Carbohydrates:	**8 grams**
Net Carbohydrates:	**5 grams**
Fiber:	**3 grams**
Protein:	**16 grams**

SALAD

4 cups mesclun salad mix
¼ cup quartered marinated artichoke hearts
¼ cup roasted red pepper strips
¼ cup grape tomatoes
2 tablespoons red wine vinegar
1 tablespoon extra virgin olive oil
⅛ teaspoon freshly ground black pepper
⅛ teaspoon kosher salt
6 oil-cured black olives, such as kalamata or Gaeta, pitted
2 pepperoncini

PINWHEELS

2 ounces deli-sliced mozzarella cheese, at room temperature (1 long rectanglar slice or 2 square slices)
2 ounces prosciutto, thinly sliced (may use boiled ham)

SPECIAL EQUIPMENT: 2 heavy-duty, gallon-sized resealable plastic bags

1. Prepare the salad: Place the salad mix in one of the plastic bags and keep refrigerated.

2. Combine the remaining ingredients in the second plastic bag and shake to mix.

3. Make the pinwheels: Layer each slice of mozzarella with prosciutto; roll it up and tightly squeeze to keep its shape.

4. Slice each roll into 4 equal pinwheels and place them in the bottom of the bag with the vegetables and refrigerate.

5. To serve, arrange the salad mix in 2 bowls and divide the vegetables and pinwheels evenly over each.

MAKE IT MEMORABLE

This salad makes a great covered dish to bring to a family gathering, especially if you are not sure what other foods may be there. Just make extra and arrange it in a large family-style bowl when you get to the gathering; it's always a crowd pleaser.

HEALTHFUL HINTS

It's easy to lighten the fats in this recipe; simply use any type of low-fat cheese you prefer and trade the prosciutto for sliced roast turkey breast.

Chicken Fajita Salad

Whenever you're in a restaurant and you see those sizzling fajita platters marched through the dining room, you know you're regretting whatever it is *you* just ordered! Well, ordinarily, everything on a fajita plate is fresh and naturally low carb, that is, until they hand you the tortillas. But who needs a tortilla, when all the flavor is inside? I created this delicious dinner salad to curb my sizzling fajita platter envy! Let's see who's jealous now!

2 tablespoons canola oil
1 cup sliced red and green bell peppers, fresh or frozen
12 ounces leftover cooked chicken, shredded
1 teaspoon chopped fresh cilantro leaves
¼ teaspoon minced fresh garlic
¼ teaspoon kosher salt
¼ teaspoon freshly ground black pepper

Yield:	**4 servings**
Prep Time:	**10 minutes**
Cook Time:	**8 minutes**
Calories:	**260**
Total Fat:	**11 grams**
Saturated Fat:	**3 grams**
Carbohydrates:	**4 grams**
Net Carbohydrates:	**2 grams**
Fiber:	**2 grams**
Protein:	**31 grams**

½ tablespoon ground cumin
½ teaspoon chili powder
½ cup shredded mozzarella cheese
10 ounces salad mix
4 sprigs whole cilantro, optional, for garnish
1 lime, cut into 8 wedges, optional, for garnish

1. Heat the oil in a large skillet over medium-high heat. Add the peppers, cooked chicken, and seasonings and cook for about 4 minutes, or until the peppers are tender.

2. Turn off the heat and top the hot chicken and peppers with the cheese and let melt.

3. Meanwhile, divide the salad mix evenly among 4 bowls and top each with equal amounts of the hot chicken fajita mix and garnish with cilantro sprigs and lime wedges, if desired. Serve hot.

MAKE IT MEMORABLE

Top off this south-of-the-border trip with a refreshing White Wine Sangria (page 213).

HEALTHFUL HINTS

The chicken can be cooked with less oil, adding all natural chicken broth in small amounts if the pan gets too dry. The cheese can be replaced with low-fat or even soy mozzarella to make it even lighter.

Shaved Zucchini Parmesan Salad

A classic salad for a classic vegetable! I was making this salad way before low carb was popular. It's a traditional Italian dish that can be whipped together in minutes using a vegetable that we always have on hand—zucchini! From baking to grilling, zucchini is a versatile vegetable that loves to perform. So let your dining-room table be the stage!

Yield:	**4 servings**
Prep Time:	**20 minutes**
Calories:	**180**
Total Fat:	**16 grams**
Saturated Fat:	**3 grams**
Carbohydrates:	**6 grams**
Net Carbohydrates:	**3 grams**
Fiber:	**3 grams**
Protein:	**4 grams**

4 tablespoons extra virgin olive oil
1 tablespoon red wine vinegar
1 tablespoon fresh lemon juice
1 tablespoon capers, chopped
1 tablespoon fresh basil leaves, finely sliced, plus 4 whole sprigs, for garnish
1 small fresh garlic clove, chopped
½ teaspoon kosher salt
¼ teaspoon freshly ground black pepper
½ cup thinly sliced red onion
2 cups sliced fresh zucchini, or 1 large zucchini cut into very thin sticks about 2 inches in length
8 radicchio leaves
4 cups cut romaine lettuce (about ½ head)
¼ cup shaved Parmesan cheese
½ lemon, cut into 4 wedges, optional, for garnish

1. In a bowl, whisk together the oil, vinegar, lemon juice, capers, basil, garlic, salt, and pepper.

2. Add the onion and sliced zucchini and toss with the marinade to coat.

3. Fan 2 radicchio lettuce leaves on each of 4 plates, place one-quarter of the romaine in the center and top with equal amounts of the marinated zucchini.

4. Drizzle all the remaining marinade on top of each salad and sprinkle with shavings of Parmesan. Garnish the plates with sprigs of fresh basil and lemon wedges, if desired and serve immediately.

MAKE IT MEMORABLE

This salad is a rich start to a perfect Italian meal of Chicken Saltimbocca (page 162). And if you have room, there is always some Tiramisù for You (page 232)!

HEALTHFUL HINTS

This recipe can be lightened up by cutting the olive oil to 2 tablespoons and adding 1 tablespoon more of both red wine vinegar and lemon juice as a replacement. The capers may be eliminated or replaced with diced red bell peppers to cut down on the sodium.

Jicama Slaw

Jicama reminds me of green apple in flavor and resembles a rutabaga, another root vegetable, the family from which this unusual *vege-fruit* derives! I enjoy trying to find uses for it, which can be quite a challenge. For instance, you must always cut jicama very thin, otherwise, it can be tough to eat or cook. With care and proper use, jicama provides a unique texture and flavor that is unmatched by other vegetables and fruits.

Yield:	**6 servings**
Prep Time:	**15 minutes**
Inactive Prep Time:	**2 hours**
Calories:	**70**
Total Fat:	**3 grams**
Saturated Fat:	**0 gram**
Carbohydrates:	**10 grams**
Net Carbohydrates:	**6 grams**
Fiber:	**4 grams**
Protein:	**3 grams**

1 tablespoon red wine vinegar
1 tablespoon apple cider vinegar
2 packets sugar substitute, more or less, depending on your taste (recommended: Splenda)
2 cups jicama root, peeled and shredded with a mandoline or cheese grater
4 ounces red cabbage, shredded
4 ounces bean sprouts
1 teaspoon celery seeds
½ teaspoon kosher salt
⅛ teaspoon freshly ground black pepper
¼ cup walnuts, coarsely chopped

In a large bowl, mix all the ingredients, tossing to combine. Chill for 2 hours before serving.

MAKE IT MEMORABLE

This is the start of a great picnic served up with some Jamaican BBQ Ribs (page 126) and a side of BBQ Baked Soybeans (page 202).

HEALTHFUL HINT

You may leave out the sugar substitute for a more tart and refreshing healthy recipe.

Cream of Asparagus Soup

When asparagus goes on sale, you just know it's time to celebrate spring with a recipe like this one. Asparagus is perfect for grilling, stir-fry, salads, and soups, and with cream of asparagus soup, there's no slaving over a hot stove all day. By using reduced chicken stock, much less cream is needed to make it rich and creamy! So spring into the kitchen and get cookin'!

Yield:	2 servings
Prep Time:	10 minutes
Cook Time:	10 minutes
Calories:	270
Total Fat:	24 grams
Saturated Fat:	16 grams
Carbohydrates:	8 grams
Net Carbohydrates:	6 grams
Fiber:	2 grams
Protein:	9 grams

1 tablespoon unsalted butter (may use trans-fat-free margarine)
8 ounces fresh asparagus, ends trimmed and cut into 1-inch lengths
1 tablespoon minced red onion
1 garlic clove, minced
½ teaspoon kosher salt
¼ teaspoon freshly ground black pepper
2½ cups no-sugar, low-sodium chicken broth (may use vegetable broth for vegetarian)
½ cup heavy cream, at room temperature
1 teaspoon sour cream, optional

SPECIAL EQUIPMENT: immersion blender

1. Heat the butter in a large pan over medium-high heat. Add the cut asparagus, red onion, garlic, salt, and pepper and cook while stirring for about 5 minutes.

2. Add the broth, raise the heat to high, and continue cooking until reduced by half, about 4 more minutes.

3. Remove from the heat, pour the soup into a tall plastic container and puree using an immersion blender. Return the puree to the pan and heat over high heat, while stirring in the cream. Divide the soup between 2 bowls and serve garnished with ½ teaspoon dollop of sour cream in each, if desired.

MAKE IT MEMORABLE

Make this soup into a simple but glorious meal by adding a few Better Cheddar Cheese Crisps (page 64) and a wedge of iceberg lettuce with Basic Vinaigrette (page 86).

HEALTHFUL HINTS

To lighten up this recipe, Christian uses unsweetened soy milk (we use Silk brand) as a low-fat alternative to the heavy cream because it has a similar rich and thick body. Also, for garnish, there are no-sugar-added low-fat sour creams available these days as well!

Mushroom Florentine Soup

No need for cornstarch or a white flour roux to thicken a soup when a simple French reduction will work! When I started putting on all the weight, I was cooking French Continental cuisine and serving it to others, but not eating it myself. If I had only remembered to enjoy my own cooking all those years, things might have been very different. This soup is a reminder that making better choices (such as using this method to thicken a soup instead of using refined flours) can make all the difference in the world!

Yield:	**2 servings**
Prep Time:	**10 minutes**
Cook Time:	**10 minutes**
Calories:	**320**
Total Fat:	**28 grams**
Saturated Fat:	**17 grams**
Carbohydrates:	**7 grams**
Net Carbohydrates:	**5 grams**
Fiber:	**2 grams**
Protein:	**10 grams**

1 tablespoon unsalted butter
6 ounces button mushrooms, cleaned and sliced
1 tablespoon minced red onion
1 garlic clove, minced
½ teaspoon kosher salt
¼ teaspoon freshly ground black pepper
2½ cups beef broth, no sugar, low sodium
2 tablespoons white wine
1 cup spinach leaves, washed and stems trimmed
½ cup heavy cream, at room temperature
12 enoki mushroom stems, bottoms removed, optional, for garnish

SPECIAL EQUIPMENT: **immersion blender or blender**

1. Heat the butter in a large pan over medium-high heat. Add the mushrooms, red onion, garlic, salt, and pepper and cook, stirring, until lightly browned, about 5 minutes.

2. Add the broth and wine, raise the heat to high, and continue cooking until reduced by half, about 4 more minutes.

3. Remove from the heat, pour half the soup into a tall plastic container cup, and puree using an immersion blender (may use a drink blender).

4. Return the puree to the pan and heat over high heat, while stirring in the spinach and cream in batches.

5. Divide the soup between 2 bowls and serve garnished with 6 enoki stems apiece, if desired.

MAKE IT MEMORABLE

This soup makes a great lunch or a quick start to a gourmet dinner of Grilled Herb Lamb Chops (page 144), accompanied by Cauliflower Rice Pilaf (page 199) and Roasted Vegetables (page 191).

HEALTHFUL HINTS

This recipe is easily lightened up by replacing the butter with trans-fat-free margarine and the heavy cream with unsweetened soy milk.

Meats

I keep hearing more and more about the health benefits of protein. Protein is an important component of every cell in our bodies, but we keep no protein reserves, so it's important to eat protein on a daily basis.

Beef is the number one food source of protein, and it *isn't always* loaded with saturated fats. Leaner cuts can be identified by the appearance of words such as "loin" or "round" in their names, such as *top sirloin* or an *eye-round roast.* And just because they're lean doesn't mean you *have* to overindulge! One 8-ounce steak is packed with your entire daily requirement of protein.

Pork is a favorite in my house, so I like to buy the whole tenderloin on sale and freeze it in sections; I get several meals out of one tenderloin. A well-trimmed pork tenderloin is nearly as low in fat as skinless chicken breasts and is high in vitamin B_{12}, which helps your body metabolize carbohydrates and fat. In fact, through changes in feeding, pork has an average of 31 percent less fat than it did just twenty years ago!

That's no bologna. And neither is my take on the Greek classic **Pork Souvlaki with Easy Tzatziki Sauce** or my mouthwatering **Mojo Pork Roast.**

If it's a steak you're after, don't dare miss out on the **Herbed Filet Mignon with Red Wine Mushrooms.** Chockful of flavor, but not fat!

And remember, just because these recipes *sound* like entrées doesn't mean you can eat them only at the dinner table! Why not make a lunch of **Cuban Lettuce Wraps** or one of my **Boredom-Bashing Burger Ideas**? Why not have some leftover **Herb-Roasted New York Strip Sirloin** and eggs for breakfast? *Stella Style* is all about being creative, so there's no need to stick to the average breakfast, lunch, and dinner paradigm if you don't want to!

No matter what time of day, the following protein-packed recipes are guaranteed to please!

Pork Souvlaki with Easy Tzatziki Sauce

I have been making this recipe forever, and it always brings back memories of my good friend, Paul Manolakos. Paul came from a Greek family, and his mother always seemed to be cooking and baking when I was over, which was practically every day when I was a teenager. Much like with my own Italian family, you could never leave his house without eating something (which wasn't hard to do because his mother made some of the best food I have ever tasted in my life). Souvlaki was one of my favorite things. Paul's mother made it with lamb, but I prefer pork; either way, it's a recipe everyone always loves!

Yield:	**4 servings; 2 skewers each**
Prep Time:	**15 minutes**
Cook Time:	**10 minutes**
Calories:	**440/370 w/o sauce**
Total Fat:	**24 grams/17 grams**
Saturated Fat:	**9 grams/ 4.5 grams**
Carbohydrates:	**3 grams/ 2 grams**
Net Carbohydrates:	**3 grams/ 2 grams**
Fiber:	**0 gram/0 gram**
Protein:	**50 grams/49 grams**

Eight 8-inch bamboo skewers
2 tablespoons extra virgin olive oil
2 tablespoons chopped fresh oregano leaves, plus 4 sprigs, for garnish (may use 1½ tablespoons dry oregano)
2 tablespoons finely chopped red onion
1½ teaspoons kosher salt
1 teaspoon freshly ground black pepper
2 garlic cloves, chopped
2½ pounds boneless pork loin, trimmed of all fat and cut into 1½-inch cubes
1 lemon, cut into wedges, optional, for garnish
8 tablespoons Easy Tzatziki Sauce (page 93)

SPECIAL EQUIPMENT: gallon-sized sealable plastic bag; grill or grill pan

1. Soak 8 bamboo skewers in water for 30 minutes to 1 hour. (This will keep them from burning later.)

2. Whisk together the oil, oregano, onion, salt, pepper, and garlic in a bowl.

3. Transfer the marinade to the plastic bag with the pork cubes and shake to coat well. Refrigerate for at least 30 minutes or up to 12 hours.

4. Preheat a grill or grill pan to high.

5. Remove the pork from the marinade and the skewers from the water, and thread 4 to 5 pieces of pork onto each skewer.

6. Place the skewers on the edges of the grill with the longest part of the stick hanging off the edge away from the fire. Stay close by and turn the sticks by hand to keep from burning. Skewers are done in just 4 to 5 minutes on each side. Serve skewers accompanied by 1 tablespoon each of Easy Tzatziki Sauce and garnish with sprigs of fresh oregano and lemon wedges, if desired.

MAKE IT MEMORABLE

Throw some Grilled Portabellas, Peppers, and Squash (page 190) on the fire along with the souvlaki for a healthy side or serve atop a salad of shredded iceberg and sliced tomatoes. Or for a party, put less meat per stick and serve skewers straight out of the side of half a cantaloupe filled with melon balls as an appetizer!

HEALTHFUL HINT

If you've added whole wheat and whole grains to your diet, try serving the souvlaki traditionally, on top of whole wheat pita bread mounded with shredded iceberg lettuce and topped with tzatziki sauce.

Jamaican BBQ Ribs

I just can't seem to get away from that Caribbean, or should I say "Floribean," influence; it's been built into my cooking style ever since my days as a young chef in south Florida. We all need a little spice in our lives, and these jerk-style ribs really get things heated up! Since I've always thought that grilling should be easy, these prebaked ribs can be made days ahead of time, so they're ready when you are. No problem!

Yield:	**8 servings**
Prep Time:	**20 minutes**
Inactive Prep Time:	**1 hour**
Cook Time:	**2 hours 10 minutes**
Calories:	**340**
Total Fat:	**28 grams**
Saturated Fat:	**10 grams**
Carbohydrates:	**1 gram**
Net Carbohydrates:	**1 gram**
Fiber:	**0 gram**
Protein:	**18 grams**

Vegetable oil spray
1 tablespoon dried thyme leaves
2 teaspoons kosher salt
1 teaspoon onion powder
1 teaspoon cayenne pepper
1 teaspoon freshly ground black pepper
¼ teaspoon garlic powder
¼ teaspoon ground nutmeg
¼ teaspoon ground cloves
½ cup water
2 tablespoons extra virgin olive oil
3 pounds pork spareribs (racks cut in half to fit into a gallon zip-lock plastic bag)

1. Whisk together all the marinade ingredients in a bowl and place in the plastic bag with the ribs. Chill for at least 1 hour, turning the bag occasionally to marinate evenly.

2. Place the rack in the center position and preheat the oven to 290°F. Spray a sheet pan with vegetable oil.

3. Remove the ribs from the bag, discard the marinade, and lay the ribs meaty side up on the prepared sheet pan.

4. Cover tightly with aluminum foil and bake for about 2 hours, or until the meat is almost falling off the bone.

5. Remove from the oven and drain any liquid immediately. Place the ribs meaty side down on the grill and grill for just about 5 minutes on each side until well marked and heated through. Cut into individual pieces to serve. (If not grilling right away, cool and refrigerate baked ribs, covered, for up to 3 days or until ready to grill.)

MAKE IT MEMORABLE

Serve these ribs with some of Rachel's BBQ Baked Soybeans (page 202), and round it out with some of my Jicama Slaw (page 118).

HEALTHFUL HINTS

Try using the same marinade for leaner cuts of meats such as boneless, skinless chicken breast, pork tenderloin, or shrimp, and bake, broil, sauté, or grill!

Mojo Pork Roast

Mojo Criollo is a marinade very much like Italian dressing that is infused with wonderful Caribbean flavors. It's as common in the Miami area as the shining sun. Used to marinate and cook pork, it adds a tangy flavor, resulting in a tender roast that falls apart when pulled with a fork. When I was younger, you could get Mojo pork roast on almost any street corner in Miami. All the little shops had it, and that tradition continues today because Mojo is a true Cuban comfort food! So why not take this recipe and get your Mojo on!

Yield:	**12 servings; 6 ounces each**
Prep Time:	**15 minutes**
Cook Time:	**2 to 2½ hours**
Calories:	**390**
Total Fat:	**28 grams**
Saturated Fat:	**9 grams**
Carbohydrates:	**0 gram**
Net Carbohydrates:	**0 gram**
Fiber:	**0 gram**
Protein:	**23 grams**

1 (5-pound) bone-in fresh pork shoulder half (preferably arm picnic)
1 (16-ounce) bottle no-sugar-added Italian dressing (recommended: Paul Newman's Olive Oil and Vinegar)
Juice from 2 limes
2 tablespoons chopped fresh cilantro
1 tablespoon kosher salt
¼ teaspoon freshly ground black pepper
3 bay leaves

SPECIAL EQUIPMENT: roasting pan with rack

1. Preheat the oven to 325°F.

2. Score the fat and skin on the pork shoulder in a hatch-mark fashion.

3. Place the shoulder in a roasting pan lined with a rack, and pour the dressing over it.

4. Rub the shoulder with the remaining ingredients and roast uncovered for 1 hour.

5. After the first hour, tent the shoulder loosely with aluminum foil and continue roasting while basting occasionally, until the meat starts to easily pull apart from the bone, about 1½ hours more. Transfer the shoulder to a cutting board and let rest for 15 minutes. Trim off any excess fat and cut into thin slices.

MAKE IT MEMORABLE

Serve this wonderful Cuban comfort food with Spinach, Roasted Peppers, and Artichoke Sauté (page 192), and wash it down with a Frozen Margarita (page 214). The leftovers are perfect for making Cuban Lettuce Wraps (page 131). Olé!

HEALTHFUL HINTS

Although most of the fat renders out of the pork roast during the slow cooking, you can lighten this recipe by using half as much of the marinade and choosing a leaner cut of pork, such as pork loin or tenderloin.

Uncle Al's Sausage and Peppers Casserole

When I was very young, every time we visited my Uncle Al's house he would be making his famous hot sausage and peppers dish. It was *so* spicy and hot that I remember thinking that it made me a man to be able to eat it. It really was way too hot for me back then, but I wasn't about to admit it! Today, it's a comfort food that reminds me of those carefree times growing up in Monroe, Connecticut—and of my late Uncle Al. His tradition lives on in my family, and maybe now also in yours. *Mangia!*

Yield:	8 servings
Prep Time:	30 minutes
Cook Time:	46 minutes
Calories:	340
Total Fat:	19 grams
Saturated Fat:	4 grams
Carbohydrates:	11 grams
Net Carbohydrates:	7 grams
Fiber:	4 grams
Protein:	30 grams

¼ cup extra virgin olive oil
2 pounds (about 8 links) fresh turkey sausage, cut in half
1 medium red onion, quartered and separated into rings
1 red bell pepper, cored, seeded, and cut into 1-inch-wide strips
1 green bell pepper, cored, seeded, and cut into 1-inch-wide strips
1 yellow bell pepper, cored, seeded, and cut into 1-inch-wide strips
1 pound green beans, ends trimmed and halved
1 (14-ounce) can no-sugar-added diced tomatoes
3 garlic cloves, chopped
2 tablespoons chopped fresh basil, plus some leaves, for garnish
1 teaspoon dried oregano
¼ teaspoon crushed red pepper flakes
¼ teaspoon freshly ground black pepper
8 ounces button mushrooms
4 marinated hot cherry peppers, optional
Shaved Parmesan cheese, optional, for garnish

SPECIAL EQUIPMENT: oval gratin dish

1. Preheat the oven to 375°F.

2. Heat 2 tablespoons of the oil in a large skillet over medium heat. Add the sausage and cook, stirring occasionally, until browned, about 6 minutes. (Don't fully cook the sausage, as it will be finished in the oven.) Drain the fat from the skillet.

3. Meanwhile, heat the remaining 2 tablespoons oil in another large skillet over medium-high heat. Add the onion and peppers and cook, stirring, until tender, about 2 minutes.

4. To the second skillet, add the remaining ingredients except for the mushrooms, cherry peppers, and Parmesan and cook, stirring occasionally, for another 3 minutes.

5. Combine the sausage, vegetable mixture, mushrooms, and cherry peppers in the gratin dish. Bake, uncovered, until well browned, about 40 minutes. Serve garnished with basil leaves, cherry peppers, and Parmesan cheese, if desired.

MAKE IT MEMORABLE

This casserole is always at the center of our family gatherings, accompanied by favorite appetizers of ours, such as Chicken Pesto Skewers (page 74) or Clams Parmesan (page 79). And if you want to end it all in ecstasy, try our most decadent dessert to date, Tiramisù for You (page 232)!

HEALTHFUL HINTS

Although turkey sausage has less fat than pork sausage, check the ingredients to make sure the brand you are using does not have sugar added, and boneless, skinless chicken breast may be used as a lean alternative to any sausage.

Cuban Lettuce Wraps

When driving through rural Miami, you will see lunch counters and trucks on practically every street that serve-up some of the best traditional Cuban comfort foods. You could get my favorite sandwich at every street corner, and you still can today. The Cubano is a giant sandwich made with two kinds of pork, cheese, pickles, and just the right amount of mustard, grilled hot on a white sub roll.

I still enjoy those wonderful combinations of flavors today as a satisfyingly different lettuce wrap—without all that white bread filler! *Muy Bueno!*

Yield:	**4 servings**
Prep Time:	**8 minutes**
Cook Time:	**2 minutes**
Calories:	**360**
Total Fat:	**24 grams**
Saturated Fat:	**8 grams**
Carbohydrates:	**3 grams**
Net Carbohydrates:	**2 grams**
Fiber:	**1 gram**
Protein:	**28 grams**

8 slices (about ¼ pound) boiled no-sugar-added ham
8 slices (about ¼ pound) Swiss cheese
8 slices Mojo Pork Roast (page 127)
1 kosher dill pickle, thinly sliced lengthwise
2 teaspoons yellow mustard
4 outer leaves iceberg lettuce
16 wooden toothpicks

1. On a microwave-proof plate, layer 2 slices ham, 1 slice cheese, 2 slices pork roast, 1 slice pickle, and 1 more slice of cheese.

2. Heat in the microwave for about 30 seconds, just long enough to melt the cheese.

3. Spread ½ teaspoon mustard on the inside of a lettuce leaf, top with the heated layered meat and cheese, and roll it up. Secure with toothpicks. Repeat to make 4 wraps.

MAKE IT MEMORABLE

Try using these rolls to top the *Stella Style* Chef's Salad (page 113), in place of the Italian meats, for an entirely different salad! Or take them to school or work along with a zip-lock bag of some Curried Walnuts (page 56), a few berries, and a frozen bottle of water that will keep it all cold until lunch.

HEALTHFUL HINTS

Low-fat Swiss cheese and ham may be used to lighten up this recipe. The Mojo Pork Roast may be replaced with deli sliced pork roll, or simply follow the Healthful Hints in the Mojo Pork Roast recipe and use a leaner cut of pork such as boneless pork loin or tenderloin.

Crazy Egg Meatloaf

I had just invented the recipe and cut the first slice when Christian exclaimed, "That's a crazy-looking meatloaf!" That was all I needed to hear, and the recipe had a name! It's a fitting name, too, because of the crazy way this dish was invented; after Easter, we had tons of leftover colored hard-boiled eggs, and I decided to just stuff a meatloaf with them. The result was a very unique dish that demands conversation. It's easy and quick to make—just make sure to follow the recipe . . . eggs-actly!

Yield:	**8 servings**
Prep Time:	**30 minutes**
Cook Time:	**1 hour and 15 minutes**
Calories:	**230**
Total Fat:	**10 grams**
Saturated Fat:	**4 grams**
Carbohydrates:	**4 grams**
Net Carbohydrates:	**3 grams**
Fiber:	**1 gram**
Protein:	**30 grams**

2 pounds ground chuck (may use meat loaf mix with ground pork)
2 large eggs
½ cup grated Parmesan cheese
¼ cup small diced red onion
¼ cup diced roasted or raw red bell pepper
2 tablespoons chopped fresh parsley leaves
2 garlic cloves, minced
½ teaspoon dried oregano
½ teaspoon dried basil
1 teaspoon kosher salt
½ teaspoon freshly ground black pepper
5 hard-boiled eggs, peeled
4 tablespoons Quick and Easy Ketchup (page 99), optional

1. Preheat the oven to 350°F.

2. In a large bowl, mix together the beef, eggs, Parmesan, vegetables, herbs, and seasonings.

3. Place half of the mixture into a 9-by-5-inch loaf pan.

4. Line the hard-boiled eggs end to end down the center and cover with the remaining beef mixture and press down lightly.

5. Spread the no-sugar ketchup, if desired, over the top of the meatloaf and bake for about 1 hour and 15 minutes, or until the temperature on an instant-read thermometer registers 165°F. Drain the fat and let rest at least 10 minutes before cutting into 8 equal slices.

MAKE IT MEMORABLE

Serve this family comfort meal with Liz's Fast Fiesta Salad (page 104) and simple Baked Zucchini Fries (page 198).

HEALTHFUL HINTS

The vegetables in this recipe will help keep this dish moist, so a very lean ground beef such as ground sirloin can be used to limit fats. Leave off the sugar-free ketchup and use low-fat cheese to lighten it up even more.

Ernie's Greco-Roman Rib Eyes

Rachel's dad, Ernie, does a lot of the cooking in her family, and my mother-in law, Claire, always helps (very much the way Rachel and I cook together)! We all love Greek food, especially Rachel, so her father sends us recipes to try all the time. This one turned out to be a surefire winner and a new favorite around here! Anyone can make this simple steak, overflowing with traditional Greek flavors that turn an everyday meal into a Mediterranean adventure. Is *your* passport up to date?

Yield:	**4 servings; 10 ounces each**
Prep Time:	**10 minutes**
Cook Time:	**12 minutes**
Calories:	**475**
Total Fat:	**30 grams**
Saturated Fat:	**11 grams**
Carbohydrates:	**3.5 grams**
Net Carbohydrates:	**3.5 grams**
Fiber:	**0 gram**
Protein:	**43 grams**

2 tablespoons extra virgin olive oil
1 tablespoon chopped fresh oregano (may use 1 teaspoon dried oregano)
1 small garlic clove, minced
1 teaspoon kosher salt
½ teaspoon freshly ground black pepper
4 (8-ounce) boneless rib-eye steaks
½ cup feta cheese, crumbled
¼ cup kalamata olives, pitted and chopped
¼ cup diced roasted red peppers
2 tablespoons fresh lemon juice
4 sprigs fresh oregano, optional, for garnish
1 lemon, cut into 8 wedges, optional, for garnish

SPECIAL EQUIPMENT: grill or grill pan

1. Preheat a grill to high or an indoor cast-iron grill pan over medium-high heat.

2. Combine the olive oil, chopped oregano, garlic, salt, and pepper in a bowl.

3. Place the steaks on a sheet pan and rub each generously on all sides with the herb rub.

4. Grill the steaks over high heat 2 to 3 minutes on each side, flipping the steaks twice. Rotate the steaks on the grill grate 45 degrees to create an attractive crisscross pattern and cook them more or less to desired doneness.

5. Remove the steaks from the grill and immediately top each with equal amounts of feta cheese, olives, and peppers and sprinkle the lemon juice over all. Serve steak on 4 plates garnished with a sprig of fresh oregano and 2 lemon wedges, if desired.

MAKE IT MEMORABLE

Start your Mediterranean adventure with some Chicken Pesto Skewers (page 74), and then finish your journey with Fresh Berries and Sabayon (page 240).

HEALTHFUL HINTS

You may use a leaner cut of beef such as filet mignon or cut the feta cheese amount by half to reduce the fat in this recipe. Or try this method with a leaner protein such as chicken breast or even a fish fillet.

Boredom-Bashing Burger Ideas

You got me; this really isn't a recipe at all! But it is a great list of interesting ways to top the good ol' hamburger, turning our favorite eat into a gastronomical feat! Whether you've gone bun-free or use whole wheat, these ideas will satisfy and keep your interest high. But you better get to trying them soon, because even if you start right now, you won't run out of ideas until about the year 2020!

Top your grilled, broiled, or pan-fried hamburger with any of these tantalizing combinations and then serve them up properly with lettuce, tomato, and dill pickle wedges.

1. **Greek Burger: Crumbled feta cheese, chopped kalamata olives, and Easy Tzatziki Sauce (page 93).**
2. **Brie Burger: Brie cheese, Canadian bacon, and sautéed onions**
3. **Pizza Burger: pizza sauce, mozzarella cheese, and pepperoni**
4. **Blue Burger: Gorgonzola cheese, sautéed crimini mushrooms, and pine nuts**

5. **Stuffed Burger: Swiss cheese, bacon, and mushrooms**
6. **California Burger: Monterey Jack cheese, avocado, and bean sprouts with ranch dressing**
7. **Corned Beef Burger: Swiss cheese, sliced deli corned beef, and stone-ground mustard**
8. **Pesto Burger: roasted red bell pepper, Basil Pesto (page 88), and mayonnaise**
9. **Southern Pecan Burger: Gruyère cheese, pecans, stone-ground mustard, and mayonnaise**
10. **Chicago Dog Burger: dill pickle relish, chopped green bell pepper, sliced banana peppers, chopped black olives, with Quick and Easy Ketchup (page 99), Dijon mustard, and mayonnaise.**

MAKE IT MEMORABLE

Mix up the toppings to come up with many more types. And if you really want to mix things up, try *stuffing* the burgers with the toppings for an even more interesting way to enjoy a burger!

HEALTHFUL HINTS

If you're watching your fats, use ground turkey meat to make the burgers and choose low-fat cheeses.

Grilled Marinated Flank Steak

Flank steak certainly has risen in popularity over the years, and like anything good, so has the price. I remember when it was just about the least expensive cut of meat in the kitchen. This deliciously different, succulent cut of beef truly was a chef's secret, because when cooked medium rare and sliced thin, it melts in your mouth like a filet mignon!

Yield:	**6 servings; approximately 7 ounces each**
Prep Time:	**15 minutes**
Inactive Prep Time:	**1 hour or overnight**
Cook Time:	**15 minutes**
Calories:	**360**
Total Fat:	**21 grams**
Saturated Fat:	**6 grams**
Carbohydrates:	**1 gram**
Net Carbohydrates:	**1 gram**
Fiber:	**0 gram**
Protein:	**38 grams**

¼ cup extra virgin olive oil
¼ cup dry red wine
2 tablespoons fresh lime juice
½ cup chopped fresh cilantro, plus 6 whole sprigs, for garnish
2 small garlic cloves, crushed
1 tablespoon chopped red onion
½ teaspoon kosher salt
¼ teaspoon freshly ground black pepper
¼ teaspoon crushed red pepper flakes
2½ pounds flank steak
1 lime, cut into 8 wedges, optional, for garnish

SPECIAL EQUIPMENT: gallon-sized sealable plastic bag; grill or grill pan

1. Whisk the oil and all the other ingredients, except the steak and lime, together in a bowl and transfer the marinade to the plastic bag with the flank steak.

2. Marinate the steak in the refrigerator for at least 1 hour and up to overnight. (Place the bag on a tray or plate as the bag could leak.)

3. When ready to cook, preheat a gas grill to high or place an indoor cast-iron grill pan over medium-high heat.

4. Remove the steak from the bag and discard the used marinade.

5. Place the flank steak on the grill and cook for about 7 minutes on each side, turning once, until cooked medium rare, or when an instant-read thermometer stuck in the thickest part reads 145°F. Transfer the steak to a cutting board, cover loosely with foil, and let rest for 5 minutes before cutting across the grain of the meat. Serve garnished with fresh cilantro sprigs and sliced fresh lime wedges, if desired.

MAKE IT MEMORABLE

Start this south-of-the-border entrée off right with an Iceberg Prairie Salad with Smoky Green Chile Ranch Dressing (page 111), team it up with a posse of Grilled Portabellas, Peppers, and Squash (page 190), and head your thirst off at the pass with a refreshing White Wine Sangria (page 214).

HEALTHFUL HINTS

Try these same marinade ingredients with leaner cuts of meats such as boneless, skinless chicken breast to save on fat.

Ground Beef Stroganoff

My mother made stroganoff quite a bit when I was growing up; as I continue many of my mom's traditions today, I like to make it for my own family. This was a favorite of hers and now, I know why—it's a great way to quickly, easily, *and* inexpensively feed the entire family! These days, Rachel makes it for us and we all love it! So go ahead and beef up your Sunday family meal. I know your family will love it, too!

2 tablespoons canola oil
2 cups chopped celery
⅓ cup chopped red onion
2½ pounds lean ground beef
1 teaspoon beef base, lowest sugar possible
10 ounces button mushrooms, cleaned and sliced
¼ teaspoon minced fresh garlic
½ teaspoon kosher salt
¼ teaspoon freshly ground black pepper
1 tablespoon chopped fresh dill
8 ounces sour cream
1 tablespoon dill pickle relish (not sweet)
Few sprigs fresh dill, optional, for garnish

Yield:	**8 servings**
Prep Time:	**10 minutes**
Cook Time:	**20 minutes**
Calories:	**280**
Total Fat:	**14 grams**
Saturated Fat:	**6 grams**
Carbohydrates:	**6 grams**
Net Carbohydrates:	**5 grams**
Fiber:	**1 gram**
Protein:	**30 grams**

1. Heat the oil in a large skillet over medium-high heat. Add the celery and onion and cook, stirring often, until slightly tender.

2. Add the ground beef and cook, stirring often, until browned. Skim off the excess grease.

3. Add the beef base, mushrooms, garlic, pickle relish, and spices and simmer for 4 to 5 minutes more, while stirring.

4. Remove from the heat, stir in the sour cream, and serve garnished with sprigs of fresh dill, if desired.

MAKE IT MEMORABLE

Normally stroganoff is served alongside egg noodles, but it's delicious over a mound of Cauliflower Rice Pilaf (page 199). And you can go gourmet by using any combination of wild mushrooms in place of the simpler button variety, such as two of my favorites, portabella and shiitake.

HEALTHFUL HINTS

You may use low-fat sour cream to lessen the fats. In a separate pan, over high heat, you may reduce 1 cup of no-sugar beef consommé to ¼ cup liquid for a healthier alternative to the beef base.

Herbed Filet Mignon with Red Wine Mushrooms

Who doesn't enjoy the occasional treat of a tender and juicy rare filet mignon? It doesn't get much better than when it comes smothered with mushrooms and red wine. The simplicity of this recipe more than makes up for the extra cost. It's a real treat to enjoy a gourmet meal—in minutes—after that long hard day! Luckily, these days, filet mignon seems to go on sale quite often. As low as $7.99 a pound, it's a real bargain, and Rachel has taught me to be all about the sales!

Yield:	2 servings
Prep Time:	10 minutes
Cook Time:	10 minutes
Calories:	280
Total Fat:	13 grams
Saturated Fat:	3.5 grams
Carbohydrates:	3 grams
Net Carbohydrates:	2 grams
Fiber:	1 gram
Protein:	34 grams

1 tablespoon extra virgin olive oil
12 ounces beef tenderloin, cut into six 2-ounce medallions
¼ teaspoon kosher salt
¼ teaspoon freshly ground black pepper
1 tablespoon chopped red onion
¼ teaspoon chopped garlic
1 cup sliced button mushrooms
½ cup red wine
½ teaspoon chopped fresh rosemary, plus sprigs, optional, for garnish
2 tablespoons roasted red pepper strips, optional, for garnish

1. Place the oil in a large sauté pan over high heat until almost smoking hot.

2. Season both sides of the tenderloin medallions with salt and pepper and add to the hot pan.

3. Add the onion, garlic, and mushrooms and continue to sear the beef for about 2 minutes.

4. Turn the medallions over, add the wine and rosemary, and cook just until the liquid is reduced, about 2 minutes more, and remove from the heat. Serve on 2 plates, garnished with roasted red pepper strips and fresh rosemary sprigs, if desired.

MAKE IT MEMORABLE

Before you start cooking this delish dish on top of the stove, make Green Beans Casserole (page 188), get it in the oven, and it will be done at about the same time as you finish the filet mignon! Likewise, if you have Baked Meringue Cookies (page 226) ready to go in the oven when the green beans come out, dessert will be ready when you are done eating! Planning ahead will make things *so* easy!

HEALTHFUL HINT

Boneless, skinless chicken breast fillet cut thin can be used in place of the beef. It lowers the fats and makes a whole new dish that is very similar to chicken marsala.

Steph's Chuck Pot Roast

My mother was a big influence on my cooking. I remember her always being in the kitchen, turning the grapes in our backyard into grape jelly, and preparing regular family meals like this pot roast! Looking back, I realize how much my sister, Stephanie, who still cooks exactly like my mom, influenced me, too. Much of what I attribute to my mom just may be from my big sister! Like this one, which is my mom's, by way of Steph. Thanks, sis!

Yield:	6 servings
Prep Time:	20 minutes
Cook Time:	2 hours
Calories:	390
Total Fat:	15 grams
Saturated Fat:	4 grams
Carbohydrates:	1 gram
Net Carbohydrates:	1 gram
Fiber:	0 gram
Protein:	65 grams

2 tablespoons canola oil
4 pounds boneless chuck roast
½ teaspoon kosher salt
½ teaspoon freshly ground black pepper
¼ teaspoon garlic powder
½ teaspoon dry oregano
½ teaspoon dry basil
¼ teaspoon dry marjoram
2 large bay leaves
4 cups beef consommé, low sodium and no sugar
2 tablespoons tomato paste

1. Preheat the oven to 325°F.

2. Add the oil to a large skillet or Dutch oven pot and place over medium-high heat until almost smoking hot.

3. Season the roast with the salt, pepper, and garlic powder and place in the hot skillet.

4. Sear on each side for 4 to 5 minutes until browned and then add the remaining ingredients, cover, and bake for about 2 hours, until very tender and almost falling apart. (Keep an eye on the roast to make sure the liquid does not all evaporate. If it does, add a bit of water and lower the heat a tad, as it may be too high.)

MAKE IT MEMORABLE

Follow the recipe for Roasted Vegetables (page 191), but instead of baking the veggies, as the recipe directs, simply put them right in with this pot roast during the last ½ hour of cooking for an amazing family meal!

HEALTHFUL HINT

The longer and slower you cook a pot roast, the more fat is rendered out of it. The fat can be skimmed off the broth and discarded before serving.

Herb-Grilled Lamb Chops

Rachel was the one who pointed out that there wasn't a single recipe for lamb in my first book, and at first I didn't believe her! While we don't eat it every day, I'm always preparing it for parties. I recently catered my own family reunion, and this is exactly how I prepared the lamb chops. Everyone was very impressed. Now I bestow that same power to impress your guests—to you!

Yield:	4 servings; 8 ounces each
Prep Time:	15 minutes
Cook Time:	8 minutes
Calories:	520
Total Fat:	28 grams
Saturated Fat:	8 grams
Carbohydrates:	1 gram
Net Carbohydrates:	1 gram
Fiber:	0 gram
Protein:	67 grams

3 tablespoons extra virgin olive oil
1 tablespoon chopped fresh rosemary leaves
1 tablespoon chopped fresh thyme leaves
1 tablespoon chopped fresh mint, plus 4 sprigs, for garnish
¼ teaspoon chopped fresh garlic (about 1 small clove)
1 teaspoon kosher salt
½ teaspoon freshly ground black pepper
8 lamb loin chops, about 4 ounces each
1 fresh lemon, for juice
1 fresh lemon, sliced, and fresh mint sprig, optional, for garnish

SPECIAL EQUIPMENT: grill or grill pan

1. Preheat a grill to high or an indoor cast-iron grill pan over medium-high heat.

2. Combine all the ingredients, except the lamb and lemon, in a small bowl and mix well.

3. Rub the lamb chops generously on all sides with the herb mixture.

4. Place the chops on the grill and cook for about 4 minutes on each side, turning once, until cooked medium rare to rare, or when an instant-read thermometer stuck in the thickest part reads 145°F.

5. Remove the chops from the grill and squeeze the juice of 1 lemon over all. Serve 2 chops to a plate, garnished with a sprig of fresh mint and a slice of lemon, if desired.

MAKE IT MEMORABLE

Since you have the grill fired up, I suggest serving Grilled Portabella and Montrachet Salad (page 107), the perfect starter for this meal! To mix it up, go European and serve the salad after the meal, for a refreshing finish.

HEALTHFUL HINT

You may use 1 tablespoon Dijon mustard thinned with 2 tablespoons water in place of the olive oil to lighten the fats in this recipe and add flavor at the same time!

Ginger Pan-Fried Pork Chops

I bought a full pork loin on sale, and that meant we were having pork for dinner four days in a row! Needless to say, on the fourth day we wanted something new. We needed to get inventive! When I found the gingerroot in my crisper drawer, I knew it was time for my own take on Thai food. Not only were these pork chops different, they were awesome! We could have kicked ourselves for not coming up with it earlier but, instead, we concentrated on eating. Then all we could do was wait for the grocery store to put that pork loin on sale again!

Yield:	**2 servings; 6 ounces each**
Prep Time:	**10 minutes**
Cook Time:	**10 minutes**
Calories:	**280**
Total Fat:	**11 grams**
Saturated Fat:	**3 grams**
Carbohydrates:	**1 gram**
Net Carbohydrates:	**1 gram**
Fiber:	**0 gram**
Protein:	**37 grams**

1 tablespoon extra virgin olive oil
Four 3-ounce boneless center cut loin pork chops (may use any cut)
¼ teaspoon kosher salt
¼ teaspoon freshly ground black pepper
1 tablespoon chopped red onion
¼ teaspoon chopped fresh garlic
1 teaspoon peeled and grated fresh gingerroot, plus a few slices, for garnish
¼ cup dry white wine
1 tablespoon fresh lemon juice
Rosemary sprigs, optional, for garnish

1. Place the oil in a large sauté pan over high heat until almost smoking hot.

2. Season both sides of the pork chops with salt and pepper and add to the hot pan.

3. Add the onion, garlic, and ginger and continue to sear the pork for about 2 minutes on each side to brown.

4. Turn the chops over, add the wine and lemon juice, and simmer, covered, until the liquid is reduced, about 6 minutes more, and remove from the heat. To serve, place the pork chops on 2 plates, top with the reduced liquid over all, and garnish with fresh ginger slices and rosemary sprigs, if desired. (If the liquid has all evaporated, add a couple of tablespoons of water and whisk it around to deglaze the pan.)

MAKE IT MEMORABLE

A simple Summer Squash Sauté (page 194) and some Cauliflower Rice Pilaf (page 199) are easy sides that can be made right alongside the pork chops on top of the stove.

HEALTHFUL HINTS

The boneless pork loin is already a lean protein, but an even lower fat alternative is to use the filet mignon of pork, pork tenderloin. When using pork tenderloin, just cut boneless chops in the same weight and fashion as described for the loin pork chops.

Herb-Roasted New York Strip Sirloin

All by itself, the New York strip sirloin roast commands the respect of those who are lucky enough to partake of its splendor! That's a mouthful, and so is this tantalizing and luscious cut of tender sirloin. It is simple enough to make and special enough to feed the whole gang on that holiday, Sunday family dinner, or any other important occasion. If you think you've had steak before, think again! This roast might cost a bit, but go ahead and treat yourself and your family once in a while. You deserve it!

Yield:	**8 servings; 10 ounces each**
Prep Time:	**15 minutes**
Cook Time:	**1 hour and 35 minutes**
Calories:	**440**
Total Fat:	**20 grams**
Saturated Fat:	**5 grams**
Carbohydrates:	**1 gram**
Net Carbohydrates:	**1 gram**
Fiber:	**0 gram**
Protein:	**60 grams**

5 pounds boneless strip sirloin roast
2 teaspoons kosher salt
½ teaspoon freshly ground black pepper
6 tablespoons fresh Herb Rub (page 90)

SPECIAL EQUIPMENT: medium roasting pan

1. Preheat the oven to 350°F. Grease a shallow roasting pan.

2. Trim any excess fat from the strip sirloin, leaving a thin-layered wide strip down the center of the top.

3. Season the roast with salt and pepper and then evenly rub the entire loin with the herb rub.

4. Place the sirloin in the shallow greased roasting pan and bake for 20 minutes. Then reduce the temperature to 300°F and continue roasting for about 1 hour and 15 minutes more, or until an instant-read thermometer stuck in the thickest part reads 140°F for a rare roast. Remove the roast from the oven and let rest for at least 10 minutes before slicing.

MAKE IT MEMORABLE

For a special occasion or just a great family meal, serve this roast with Cauliflower "Mac" and Cheese Casserole (page 203) and Roasted Vegetables (page 191).

HEALTHFUL HINTS

Slow cooking the roast at a low temperature allows the fats to flavor and tenderize the meat, but after cooking you can trim all the fat off the edges for the leanest possible meal.

Poultry

My feathered friends, let's talk turkey—and chicken, too! Seriously, is there a single cut of meat more versatile than the chicken breast? Low in fat, high in protein, zero carbs, and endless possibilities!

People tell me that they're tired of the same ol' chicken breast day in and day out and all I can say is, "Get one of my books!" Chicken isn't boring; chicken is what *you* make of it! With just a handful of ingredients, I invented **Easy Cheesy Chili Chicken** that left my whole family tongue-tied *and* delighted.

My sons are so crazy for **Gourmet Chicken Stir-Fry** that I don't think the wok ever makes it back into the cupboard. And why should it? Stir-fries are quick, easy, and always changing, depending on what vegetables we have stocked in our crisper drawer. As for me, I reinvented my old Chinese food favorite, **General Tso's Chicken,** to curb my takeout cravings. It's *all* of the flavor without *any* of the added sugars and starches!

But if you're still looking for a change of pace, Turkey Day certainly comes more than once a year in my house. I'll usually go for the fresh turkey breasts in lieu of the whole bird and roast them, then slice them up for lunch meat. For something a little more exciting, my **Turkey Fajita Wraps** are a wonderfully light indulgence.

Whatever your taste, the following poultry recipes certainly won't leave you crying *fowl.* Okay, that's a really old joke, but here's an even older one. Why did the chicken cross the road? To get to these recipes!

Kim's Stuffed Chicken Breasts with Lemony White Wine Sauce

This recipe is courtesy of Kim Keegan and Scott McGowan. Rachel and I were looking for a house to rent in Connecticut one afternoon, and we stopped to have a salad in my childhood hometown, Monroe, at a pizza place I used to frequent as a kid. It was still owned by the McGowans—the same family that owned it when I lived there forty years earlier!—and Scott, who is about my age, was running it. We were talking with Scott when a friend of his, Monroe volunteer firefighter Kim Keegan, overheard us mention low carb. She interrupted nicely and we talked with her for a long while, too! We gave her our now retired video, and eight months later, she's down over one hundred pounds! Well, she and Scott collaborated to develop some recipes, and this is just one of the dishes that helped Kim lose all the weight!

Yield:	2 servings
Prep Time:	30 minutes
Cook Time:	10 minutes
Calories:	740
Total Fat:	32 grams
Saturated Fat:	16 grams
Carbohydrates:	8 grams
Net Carbohydrates:	6 grams
Fiber:	2 grams
Protein:	91 grams

STUFFING

1 cup cooked fresh spinach, chopped and drained well
½ cup whole milk ricotta cheese
½ cup crumbled Gorgonzola cheese
4 slices cooked bacon, crumbled
Kosher salt and freshly ground black pepper to taste
1 large egg

SAUCE

½ cup dry white wine
½ cup chicken stock, no sugar added
1 tablespoon Dijon mustard
1 lemon, juiced
Kosher salt and freshly ground black pepper

CHICKEN

Two 8-ounce boneless, skinless chicken breast halves
Kosher salt and freshly ground black pepper
2 tablespoons vegetable oil
1 tablespoon chopped fresh Italian parsley, for garnish

1. Make the stuffing: In a bowl, combine the spinach, ricotta, Gorgonzola, and bacon and mix well. Season with salt and pepper. Add the egg, mix well, and set aside.

2. Make the sauce: Combine the wine and stock in a saucepan. Bring to a boil and reduce to a saucelike consistency. Whisk in the mustard, lemon juice, and season with salt and pepper to taste. Set aside.

3. Make the chicken: Place each chicken breast between 2 doubled-up sheets of plastic wrap, and pound until the chicken is an even ¼-inch thickness with tenderizing mallet or rolling pin.

4. Divide the stuffing between the breasts, mounding it along the center of each. Fold the bottom edge of each breast over the stuffing, fold in the sides, and roll forward until completely wrapped, to form a tightly rolled package. Secure each flap with a toothpick. Season the chicken all over with salt and pepper to taste.

5. Heat the oil in a large skillet over medium heat and add the chicken and cook, turning occasionally, until browned, about 2 minutes per side. Cover the skillet, turn the heat down to low, and cook until just cooked through, about 5 minutes more. Transfer the chicken to a cutting board and let rest for 5 minutes.

6. Meanwhile, pour the sauce into the same skillet over high heat and cook, stirring and scraping the bottom with a wooden spoon.

7. Slice the chicken into medallions, divide between 2 plates, and spoon some of the sauce over each. Sprinkle with the parsley. Serve immediately.

MAKE IT MEMORABLE

Cauliflower "Mac" and Cheese Casserole (page 203) goes well with this chicken breast dinner, and a Breadless Bread Pudding (page 230) can be made ahead.

HEALTHFUL HINTS

To lighten up this recipe, the whole milk ricotta may be replaced with low fat and the Gorgonzola may be cut down to ¼ cup or replaced entirely by ¼ cup roasted red pepper strips. You may also eliminate the sauce if you wish, saving both carbs and calories since there are plenty of flavors in this chicken all by its lonesome!

Family-Style Chicken

Family-style chicken was a comfort food of the highest order for both Rachel and me when we were kids in New England! It's still a holiday tradition for Rachel's family (and ours now, too) to go at least once a year to Wright's Farm, a family-style restaurant in Rhode Island. This is the place where they truly do make the best family-style chicken on the planet! Now, it doesn't have to be a holiday and you don't have to drive to R.I. to enjoy succulent chicken that falls right off the bones. You need only a few common ingredients and a couple of hours to relax as it cooks!

Yield:	**4 servings**
Prep Time:	**15 minutes**
Cook Time:	**2 hours**
Calories:	**250**
Total Fat:	**11 grams**
Saturated Fat:	**2.5 grams**
Carbohydrates:	**1 gram**
Net Carbohydrates:	**1 gram**
Fiber:	**0 gram**
Protein:	**35 grams**

Vegetable oil spray, as needed
1 (4-pound) chicken, cut into 8 serving pieces
1 teaspoon kosher salt
1 teaspoon paprika
½ teaspoon freshly ground black pepper
½ teaspoon poultry seasoning
½ teaspoon dried oregano
⅛ teaspoon garlic powder
4 bay leaves
Lemon zest, optional, for garnish
Chopped parsley, optional, for garnish

SPECIAL EQUIPMENT: medium roasting pan

1. Preheat the oven to 350°F. Lightly coat a roasting pan with vegetable oil spray.

2. Place the chicken pieces in the center of the pan and sprinkle each piece evenly with the ingredients.

3. Cover the pan tightly with aluminum foil and bake for 1 hour.

4. Remove the chicken from the oven and baste with the drippings. Continue baking uncovered until well browned, about 1 hour more, until the meat is falling off the bones.

5. Arrange the chicken on a platter and sprinkle with the garnishes, if desired, to serve family style!

MAKE IT MEMORABLE

Surround the serving platter with Roasted Vegetables (page 191). You can even throw the vegetables right in the pan with the chicken during the second hour of cooking.

HEALTHFUL HINTS

Fat can be reduced by taking the skin off the chicken, but wait until after cooking, since, believe it or not, fat from the skin only adds flavor to the chicken during cooking, with none of the fat calories being absorbed by the meat.

Herb-Roasted Chicken Breasts

Whenever chicken breast is on sale for $1.99 a pound, we stock up. And that's pretty often, making it a constant challenge to come up with new recipes to keep our meals interesting. This recipe came about because we had some leftover herb rub (made with leftover herbs, of course) I simply rubbed some on the chicken and baked it. All I can say is WOW! Everyone thought it was phenomenal and I think you will, too!

Yield:	**6 servings**
Prep Time:	**20 minutes**
Cook Time:	**35 minutes**
Calories:	**360**
Total Fat:	**10 grams**
Saturated Fat:	**2 grams**
Carbohydrates:	**.5 gram**
Net Carbohydrates:	**.5 gram**
Fiber:	**0 gram**
Protein:	**4 grams**

Vegetable oil spray, as needed
3 tablespoons fresh Herb Rub (page 90)
2½ pounds boneless, skinless chicken breasts, butterfly cut into separate fillets
Lemon slices, fresh herb sprig, for garnish

1. Preheat the oven to 400°F. Spray a sheet pan with vegetable oil.

2. Place the herb rub and chicken breast pieces into a bowl and toss until coated.

3. Place the coated fillets on the greased sheet pan and bake for about 35 minutes, or until when tested with an instant-read thermometer in the thickest piece the internal temperature reads at least 165°F. Serve garnished with a slice of lemon and a sprig of any one of the herbs used to make the rub.

MAKE IT MEMORABLE

Roasted Vegetables (page 191) are an easy side dish that can be baked in the oven right along with the chicken.

HEALTHFUL HINT

Try this recipe using other lean proteins such as pork tenderloin.

Easy Cheesy Chili Chicken

Jimi Volpe, my best friend for over thirty years—the person who taught me how to cook—was over at the house one night when we decided to cook something up. We were so hungry that we simply opened the refrigerator and starting pulling food out. Thirty minutes later we were eating this dish. Jimi said, "Mmmm . . . very easy and cheesy." Then, of course, I said, "That's what I'll call it!" It quickly became a favorite around here. But don't take our word for it; it's *so* easy, practically all you have to do to head for the great Southwest is to click your heels together and say the title three times fast!

2 tablespoons extra virgin olive oil
2 tablespoons chopped fresh cilantro leaves, plus a few whole leaves, for garnish
1 tablespoon chili powder
1 tablespoon ground cumin
2 teaspoons kosher salt
1 garlic clove, chopped
½ teaspoon freshly ground black pepper
⅛ teaspoon cayenne pepper

Yield:	4 servings; 8 ounces each
Prep Time:	10 minutes
Cook Time:	20 minutes
Calories:	455
Total Fat:	20 grams
Saturated Fat:	8 grams
Carbohydrates:	5 grams
Net Carbohydrates:	3 grams
Fiber:	2 grams
Protein:	70 grams

2 pounds boneless, skinless chicken breast (about 4 halves)
¼ cup julienned green bell pepper
2 tablespoons diced red onion
1 medium plum tomato, cored and diced (about ¼ cup)
4 ounces shredded Colby Jack cheese

1. Preheat the oven to 400°F. Line a sheet pan with aluminum foil.

2. Whisk together the oil, chopped cilantro, chili powder, cumin, salt, garlic, pepper, and cayenne in a bowl; add the chicken and toss to coat.

3. Transfer the chicken to the foil-lined baking sheet and arrange the green pepper, onion, and tomato over each. Roast until the largest piece is just cooked through, and an instant-read thermometer inserted in the thickest part reads 165°F, about 20 minutes.

4. Remove the chicken from the oven and immediately top with the cheese. Transfer the chicken to a platter or among 4 plates and garnish with fresh cilantro leaves. Serve as the cheese melts.

MAKE IT MEMORABLE

Refreshing Jicama Slaw (page 118) makes a perfect side for this dish, and a hotbed of Cauliflower Rice Pilaf (page 199) is in order (great for all that overflowing cheese)!

HEALTHFUL HINTS

This lean chicken is *so* spicy and good that it's easy to lighten up when it comes to the cheese. But don't go without cheese—simply use a little less, or a low-fat cheese, and still enjoy all the wonderful flavors this recipe dishes up!

Turkey Fajita Wraps

These lettuce wraps are great for anyone, especially if you are just starting out with *Stella Style*. We invented a bunch of these so we could enjoy our favorite foods and flavors without giving in to the white stuff it usually sits between. Make them for someone you love, and you'll be the star of the show! If you are maintaining your weight or incorporating whole grains, a true whole wheat wrap can also be used in this recipe (it's certainly a healthy option). As they say in the movies—it's a wrap!

Yield:	**6 servings**
Prep Time:	**20 minutes**
Cook Time:	**5 minutes**
Calories:	**210**
Total Fat:	**12 grams**
Saturated Fat:	**6 grams**
Carbohydrates:	**4 grams**
Net Carbohydrates:	**3 grams**
Fiber:	**1 gram**
Protein:	**19 grams**

2 tablespoons canola oil
1 small red onion, thinly sliced
1 red bell pepper, cored, seeded, and thinly sliced
1 green bell pepper, cored, seeded, and thinly sliced
1 garlic clove, minced
1 pound boneless, skinless turkey breast, cut into thin strips
½ tablespoon ground cumin
½ tablespoon chili powder
½ teaspoon kosher salt
¼ teaspoon freshly ground black pepper
2 dashes cayenne pepper
6 large red leaf lettuce leaves
2 tablespoons finely chopped cilantro leaves
4 ounces shredded Colby Jack, Monterey Jack, or Cheddar cheese
¼ cup sour cream
12 wooden toothpicks

1. Heat the oil in a large skillet over high heat. Add the onion, bell peppers, and garlic and cook, stirring, until slightly softened.

2. Add the turkey, cumin, chili powder, salt, pepper, and cayenne and cook, stirring, until cooked through, about 5 minutes.

3. Spoon a couple of tablespoons of the turkey mixture on the inside of a lettuce leaf, sprinkle with cilantro, top with a tablespoon of cheese, and a dollop of sour cream

and roll up like a burrito. Close with toothpicks. Repeat to make 6 wraps total. Serve immediately.

MAKE IT MEMORABLE

These wraps are great served with a side of Cool Cucumber Chipotle Chutney (page 92).

HEALTHFUL HINTS

You can lighten up this recipe by using low-fat cheese and low-fat sour cream, or replace them altogether with fresh avocado slices.

Gourmet Chicken Stir-Fry

This recipe requires a bit of shopping and preparing, but you have my word that the end result is more than worth the effort. This stir-fry reigns supreme in my house, and let me tell you—we eat a lot of stir-fry! It's Anthony's meal of choice. Sure, you can open your refrigerator and just start throwing random ingredients into a wok, but a little planning can go a long way! It certainly does here. The colors of all the vegetables alone are worth the price of admission, but it's the combination of flavors that will have you hooked.

Yield:	**6 servings**
Prep Time:	**15 minutes**
Cook Time:	**6 minutes**
Calories:	**270**
Total Fat:	**10 grams**
Saturated Fat:	**1.5 grams**
Carbohydrates:	**11 grams**
Net Carbohydrates:	**7 grams**
Fiber:	**4 grams**
Protein:	**35 grams**

2 tablespoons canola oil
1½ pounds boneless, skinless chicken breast, cut into thin strips
1 red bell pepper, cored, seeded, and julienned
1 yellow bell pepper, cored, seeded, and julienned
¼ cup thinly sliced red onion
1 cup half-moon sliced yellow squash
1 cup small broccoli florets
1 baby eggplant, cut into chunks
8 ounces firm tofu, cut into 1-inch chunks
1 garlic clove, minced
½ cup teriyaki sauce (check the label: no more than 2 grams sugar per serving)
2 cups sliced bok choy
1 cup fresh bean sprouts
¼ teaspoon freshly ground black pepper
¼ teaspoon kosher salt
½ cup snow peas
2 tablespoons sesame oil

1. Start by preparing and cutting all the vegetables and measuring your ingredients so that they are ready to go. Once you begin stir-frying, it goes very quickly.

2. In a wok or large skillet, heat the canola oil over high heat until almost smoking. Add the chicken breast strips and cook for 2 minutes just until they start to brown.

3. Add the bell peppers and onion while stirring constantly. While continuing to stir, add the squash, broccoli, eggplant, tofu, garlic, and teriyaki sauce and cook stirring constantly for 2 minutes.

4. Add the bok choy, sprouts, pepper, and salt and cook stirring until crisp-tender, about 2 minutes more.

5. Stir in the snow peas and sesame oil, remove from the heat and serve immediately divided among 6 plates or shallow bowls.

MAKE IT MEMORABLE

A simple shredded iceberg lettuce salad with Wasabe Ginger Vinaigrette (page 87) will start this meal off right, and a few of Rachel's Marvelous Macaroons (page 222) are a heavenly finish!

HEALTHFUL HINTS

If you are strictly watching your carbs, simply take more of the chicken than the vegetables when making your plate. (But you MUST still eat some of the vegetables!) And the teriyaki sauce (it does have some sugar) may be omitted and replaced with 2 tablespoons soy sauce for flavor.

General Tso's Chicken

We all love Chinese food, and who doesn't? My mother always chose Chinese restaurants when we went out to eat so I learned to love it early on. Unfortunately, nowadays, Chinese restaurants use quite a bit of sugar and cornstarch, so you do need to be careful, especially when it comes to those wonderful sauces! As in this recipe, I have learned to simply prepare Chinese food without the cornstarch and sugars—the rest is just great fresh food, guaranteed to bring good fortune!

Yield:	**4 servings**
Prep Time:	**15 minutes**
Inactive Prep Time:	**1 hour**
Cook Time:	**6 minutes**
Calories:	**360**
Total Fat:	**13 grams**
Saturated Fat:	**2.5 grams**
Carbohydrates:	**3 grams**
Net Carbohydrates:	**2 grams**
Fiber:	**2 grams**
Protein:	**53 grams**

MARINADE

1½ tablespoons soy sauce
1½ tablespoons rice wine vinegar
1 tablespoon sesame oil
2 tablespoons fresh orange zest or 1 tablespoon dried peel (Zest is the very outer orange peel without any white attached. Use a zesting tool or potato peeler, and cut into very thin strips.)
1 tablespoon peeled and grated fresh ginger
1 tablespoon sugar substitute (recommended: Splenda)
1 garlic clove, minced
¼ teaspoon chili paste
¼ teaspoon freshly ground black pepper

1½ pounds boneless, skinless chicken breast, cut into thin 2-inch-long strips
2 tablespoons canola oil
2 tablespoons diced red bell pepper
⅓ cup sliced green onion

SPECIAL EQUIPMENT: gallon-sized sealable plastic bag; wok

1. Whisk the marinade ingredients together in a bowl and transfer to the plastic bag with the chicken strips. Marinate the chicken in the refrigerator for 1 hour.

2. When ready to cook, remove the chicken from the bag and save the marinade.

3. In a wok or large skillet, heat the canola oil over high heat until almost smoking. Add the chicken breast strips and cook for 2 minutes just until they start to brown.

4. Add the bell pepper, sliced green onion, and reserved marinade and continue to cook for about 4 more minutes while stirring constantly, until the sauce is reduced and the chicken is fully cooked. Remove from the heat and serve immediately divided among 4 plates or shallow bowls.

MAKE IT MEMORABLE

Start your trip to the Far East with Bacon-Wrapped Teriyaki Scallops (page 76), followed by the general's chicken atop Cauliflower Rice Pilaf (page 199). And you can bring it all home with a few Chocolate Almond Finger Cookies (page 224).

HEALTHFUL HINTS

A low sodium soy sauce may be used and all the marinade ingredients may be cut in half to lighten up this recipe. The sugar substitute may also be omitted, if desired.

Chicken Saltimbocca

I enjoy classic Italian food; it's a part of my heritage that I could never do without, and, thankfully, I don't have to! Most Italian meals, aside from the occasional bread crumbs or pasta, are naturally low in carbs and great if you are just starting out on low carb. I remember when I first started; I couldn't believe that I could eat the foods that I grew up on and still lose weight. Well, take my word for it, losing weight *can* be fun, and you *can* eat the great meals you grew up on, too! So get cooking—you have to eat to lose weight, and this recipe is a delicious place to start!

Yield:	4 servings
Prep Time:	20 minutes
Cook Time:	15 minutes
Calories:	320
Total Fat:	13 grams
Saturated Fat:	3 grams
Carbohydrates:	6 grams
Net Carbohydrates:	6 grams
Fiber:	0 gram
Protein:	41 grams

1 cup cooked spinach, chopped and drained well (may use frozen)
1 tablespoon olive oil
2 tablespoons grated Parmesan cheese
2 tablespoons diced roasted red pepper
1 garlic clove, minced
¼ teaspoon kosher salt
⅛ teaspoon freshly ground black pepper

CHICKEN

1 pound boneless, skinless chicken breast (4 thin 4-ounce cutlets)
¼ teaspoon kosher salt
⅛ teaspoon freshly ground black pepper
8 fresh sage leaves, plus 4 leaves, optional, for garnish
2 ounces (4 slices) prosciutto
4 wooden toothpicks
2 tablespoons vegetable oil
1 cup chicken stock, no sugar added
2 tablespoons fresh lemon juice, plus 2 lemon slices, optional, for garnish
Kosher salt and freshly ground black pepper to taste, if needed
1 tablespoon chopped fresh Italian parsley

1. In a bowl, combine the spinach, olive oil, Parmesan, roasted pepper, garlic, salt, and pepper and set aside.

2. Make the chicken: Place the 4 chicken cutlets between 2 doubled-up sheets of plastic wrap and pound with a tenderizing mallet or rolling pin until the chicken has an even ¼-inch thickness.

3. Season the pounded chicken breasts on both sides with salt and pepper and lay flat on the counter. Top each of the 4 cutlets with 2 fresh sage leaves, a slice of prosciutto, and equal amounts of the seasoned spinach.

4. Fold the bottom edge of each cutlet over the spinach, roll forward like a burrito, and secure with a toothpick.

5. Heat the oil in a large skillet over medium heat and add the chicken and cook, turning occasionally until browned, about 2 minutes per side. Add the chicken stock and lemon juice while stirring and scraping the bottom with a wooden spoon to loosen and incorporate all the flavors from the pan.

6. Bring to a boil, then reduce the heat to low, and cover the skillet. Simmer for about 6 minutes until the chicken is fully cooked. Transfer the chicken to a cutting board.

7. Turn the heat to high and continue to cook the liquid for about 5 more minutes, until reduced to about ½ cup. Remove the sauce from the heat, season with salt and pepper to taste if needed, and stir in the parsley. Serve 2 rolls on each plate. Spoon the sauce over each roll and garnish with lemon slices and fresh sage leaves, if desired.

MAKE IT MEMORABLE

Italian Marinated Vegetables (page 205) are a cool start to this hot and flavorful Italian meal. But don't get frozen in your tracks; chill out later with a Honeydew and Blackberry Granita (page 246)!

HEALTHFUL HINTS

This recipe may be lightened up by omitting the Parmesan cheese and using low-fat turkey bacon in place of the prosciutto.

Curried Chicken Thighs

I've always been a big fan of chicken thighs. Maybe it's just a personal preference, but I think the meat is more rich and flavorful than chicken breast. With a little work in the kitchen, you can save a bundle. We buy those 10-pound bags of chicken leg quarters that go on sale all the time for less than sixty cents a pound and separate the thighs from the legs. The legs go in a pot for making chicken salad, and we save the broth as soup! Use the thighs to make this recipe, and you have three very big meals for less than six dollars!

Yield:	4 servings
Prep Time:	15 minutes
Inactive Prep Time:	3 hours
Cook Time:	20 minutes
Calories:	260
Total Fat:	15 grams
Saturated Fat:	3.5 grams
Carbohydrates:	1 gram
Net Carbohydrates:	1 gram
Fiber:	0 gram
Protein:	30 grams

1 tablespoon extra virgin olive oil
2 tablespoons curry powder
1 tablespoon sugar substitute (recommended: Splenda)
1½ teaspoons kosher salt
¼ teaspoon freshly ground black pepper
1 garlic clove, chopped
1½ pounds boneless, skinless chicken thighs (about 8 pieces)
Fresh parsley or rosemary, optional, for garnish

SPECIAL EQUIPMENT: gallon-sized sealable plastic bag

1. Mix all the ingredients together in a bowl and rub evenly over all the chicken pieces.

2. Transfer the chicken to the plastic bag or a covered container and refrigerate for at least 2 hours and up to overnight.

3. When you're ready to cook, build a charcoal fire or preheat the gas grill.

4. Remove the chicken from the marinade. Grill the thighs, turning twice, until browned and cooked through, about 5 minutes per side. (The chicken should read 165°F when tested with an instant-read thermometer in the thickest part and there should be no pink at all.) Transfer the chicken to a platter and garnish with parsley or rosemary, if desired.

MAKE IT MEMORABLE

Summer Squash Salsa (page 99) is the perfect condiment for this spicy chicken. The whole meal can be rounded out with a Summer Squash Sauté (page 194)!

HEALTHFUL HINTS

You can lighten up this recipe by using boneless, skinless chicken breast in place of the thighs. If you choose, the sugar substitute may be left out.

Grilled Basil–Marinated Chicken

Keeping it simple in the kitchen is no small matter. It was important in the restaurants so that we could get the food out on time, and it's even more important at home. Who has time to cook anymore? By keeping it simple, you do! We *can* keep our healthy eating goals in line, and nothing could be easier than this chicken! Throw the ingredients in a bag in the morning, and when you get home, just fire up the grill. You'll be eating in minutes!

1 tablespoon extra virgin olive oil
1 tablespoon red wine vinegar
1 tablespoon chopped basil leaves, plus 4 sprigs, for garnish
1 tablespoon finely chopped red onion
2 teaspoons kosher salt
1 teaspoon whole black peppercorns
1 garlic clove, chopped
4 boneless, skinless chicken breast halves (about 1½ pounds)

SPECIAL EQUIPMENT: gallon-sized sealable plastic bag

Yield:	**4 servings**
Prep Time:	**15 minutes**
Inactive Prep Time:	**3 hours**
Cook Time:	**16 minutes**
Calories:	**220**
Total Fat:	**7 grams**
Saturated Fat:	**1.5 grams**
Carbohydrates:	**1 gram**
Net Carbohydrates:	**1 gram**
Fiber:	**0 gram**
Protein:	**34 grams**

1. Whisk together the oil, vinegar, basil, onion, salt, peppercorns, and garlic in a bowl.

2. Transfer the marinade to the plastic bag with the chicken and shake to combine. Refrigerate for at least 3 hours and up to overnight.

3. When ready to cook, build a charcoal fire or preheat a gas grill.

4. Remove the chicken from the marinade. Grill the chicken, turning once, until browned and just cooked through, about 4 minutes per side. (The chicken should read 165°F when tested with an instant-read thermometer and there should be no pink.) Transfer the chicken to a platter and garnish with the basil sprigs.

MAKE IT MEMORABLE

For an easy anytime outdoor dinner, start with some Jicama Slaw (page 118), which can be made ahead, and serve up a few Wild Mushroom Brochettes (page 196) right off the grill with the chicken! Wow your guests with Balsamic-Grilled Strawberries and Cream (page 238) for dessert!

HEALTHFUL HINT

It's hard to make this dish lighter, but you can replace the olive oil with fresh lemon juice to lighten it up a bit.

Fish and Seafood

There's plenty of fish in the sea, they say. There are even more ways that they can be prepared!

Seafood is the ultimate lean protein. The little fat that fish does have is loaded with omega-3 fatty acids that your body needs! Rachel swears by salmon, and eats it at least once a week for healthier looking skin. Even I was surprised by how much of a difference it makes! Omega-3's can even *lower* your risk of heart disease. Now *that's* food that you can use. Oh, and it tastes great, too! But don't take my word for it—just try a fillet of my **Chili-Rubbed Salmon** or **Roasted Pecan and Herb-Crusted Salmon.**

Tell me you're making **Monkfish Kebabs** and **Fried Ipswich Clams** as appetizers, and I'll be at your place by five!

You can play a little low-carb gourmet with delicious **Tilapia and Prawn Mousse Roulades** or a reinvented favorite of mine, **Spaghetti Squash with Clams Provençal Sauce.**

Just remember that when purchasing seafood, fresh is best! The fresher, the better. Not sure what is and isn't fresh? Trust your nose. Look for a subtle ocean smell that isn't overpowering.

Me, I catch my own to ensure optimum freshness. I'm a chef by day and fisherman by night. Out on the open sea, the wind in my face—I'm just kidding!

But seriously, are you making those **Monkfish Kebabs**? I'm getting hungry!

Blackened Salmon (or Chicken Breast)

I cannot begin to tell you all the uses for blackened salmon or chicken breast. There are just way too many options—and it's *so* easy and quick to make! I suggest making extra, and individually wrapping the leftovers. Great for the microwave or for grab-and-go gourmet meals! Make sure to turn your overhead exhaust fan on before starting to cook.

Yield:	**2 servings**
Prep Time:	**5 minutes**
Cook Time:	**10 minutes**
Calories:	**310**
Total Fat:	**15 grams**
Saturated Fat:	**2 grams**
Carbohydrates:	**2 grams**
Net Carbohydrates:	**1 gram**
Fiber:	**1 gram**
Protein:	**39 grams**

2 (6-ounce) skinless, boneless salmon fillets or 2 (8-ounce) skinless, boneless chicken breast halves, pounded thin
3 tablespoons Blackening Spice (recipe follows)
2 tablespoons canola oil
1 lemon, cut into 8 wedges

1. Coat the salmon or chicken fillets with about 1½ tablespoons of the blackening spice.

2. Add the oil to a large cast-iron skillet and place over high heat until almost smoking hot.

3. Place the salmon fillet or chicken breast gently in the skillet and sear for about 3 minutes on one side and then flip over and turn the heat down to medium. Cook the salmon until it's slightly pink in the center, about 2 minutes more; or cook the chicken until cooked through, 3 to 4 minutes more. Garnish with lemon wedges and serve as an entrée with your favorite vegetables!

BLACKENING SPICE

5 tablespoons kosher salt
5 tablespoons paprika
1 tablespoon dried thyme
1 tablespoon freshly ground black pepper
1 tablespoon garlic powder
½ teaspoon cayenne pepper
½ teaspoon ground white pepper

Mix all the ingredients well and store in a sealed container or spice canister.

MAKE IT MEMORABLE

Use over your favorite salad, such as our Blackened Salmon Salad Niçoise (page 105).

HEALTHFUL HINT

Using flavorful spices such as the blackening spice recipe to season everything from vegetables to meats allows for less use of fats such as butter while still tasting great.

Chili-Rubbed Baked Salmon

Salmon is loaded with cholesterol-reducing omega-3 fatty acids and potassium—and it can actually help make your skin look younger! Really! Rachel has me trained to eat it at least two or three times a week when I have a TV appearance. But the truth is, I love salmon most for the flavor, and how versatile, quick, and easy it is to make. When choosing salmon, wild is a real treat, but, we usually buy farm-raised because it's always on sale somewhere (one-third the price and still quite good).

Yield:	**4 servings**
Prep Time:	**10 minutes**
Cook Time:	**15 minutes**
Calories:	**350**
Total Fat:	**20 grams**
Saturated Fat:	**3 grams**
Carbohydrates:	**2 grams**
Net Carbohydrates:	**1 gram**
Fiber:	**1 gram**
Protein:	**39 grams**

Vegetable oil cooking spray
2 tablespoons olive oil
2 tablespoons lemon juice, freshly squeezed (1 lemon)
2 tablespoons chopped red onion
¼ teaspoon chopped fresh garlic
1 tablespoon chili powder
1 teaspoon ground cumin
½ teaspoon kosher salt
¼ teaspoon freshly ground black pepper
⅛ teaspoon cayenne pepper (2 dashes)
1½ pounds boneless, skinless salmon fillet, cut into 2 thick fillets, center cut recommended (end pieces are not the best for this recipe)

1. Preheat the oven to 375°F. Spray a sheet pan with vegetable oil spray and set aside.

2. To make the rub for the salmon, place all the ingredients, except the salmon, into a medium bowl and mix well.

3. Add the salmon to the bowl and gently coat each fillet with the rub.

4. Place the coated fillets on the greased sheet pan, top with any remaining rub that can be scraped from the bowl, and bake for approximately 15 minutes. (The thickness of the salmon fillets may vary; thin pieces will cook faster.)

5. Remove the cooked salmon from the oven and serve.

MAKE IT MEMORABLE

Top each salmon fillet with Cool Cucumber Chipotle Chutney (page 92) and serve with Baked Zucchini Fries (page 198). Use any leftovers to make a great seafood salad the next day!

Roasted Pecan and Herb-Crusted Salmon

Ever since Rachel found out about the health benefits of salmon, I've been under the gun to keep coming up with new and exciting ways to prepare it! Rachel literally brings salmon home from the market at least twice a week, more often when we're going to be on television. She always says that salmon is great for the complexion *and* my arthritis. I don't know a lot about all that, but I do know that I like it. Once you've tried this recipe, I know you will, too!

Yield:	4 servings
Prep Time:	15 minutes
Cook Time:	15 minutes
Calories:	700
Total Fat:	46 grams
Saturated Fat:	9 grams
Carbohydrates:	10 grams
Net Carbohydrates:	6.5 grams
Fiber:	3.5 grams
Protein:	77 grams

VEGETABLE MIXTURE

1 small fennel bulb, cored and thinly sliced (reserve tops or fronds)
2 plum tomatoes, cored and cut in half lengthwise
½ cup julienned yellow bell pepper
½ cup julienned green bell pepper
½ cup sliced red onion
2 tablespoons extra virgin olive oil
½ teaspoon kosher salt
⅛ teaspoon garlic powder
⅛ teaspoon freshly ground black pepper

SALMON

2 tablespoons chopped fennel fronds (all stems or stalks removed)
2 tablespoons chopped fresh basil leaves
1½ tablespoons Dijon mustard
½ teaspoon kosher salt
⅛ teaspoon freshly ground black pepper
4 (8-ounce) boneless, skinless salmon fillets
2 ounces dry vermouth or white wine
2 tablespoons fresh lemon juice
2 tablespoons unsalted butter, melted
½ cup coarsely chopped pecans
1 lemon, cut into wedges, optional, for garnish

1. Preheat the oven to 400°F.

2. To make the vegetable mixture: Combine all of the ingredients in a shallow roasting pan and toss to mix. Spread the mixture out to form a bed for the salmon.

3. To make the salmon: In a small bowl, mix the fennel fronds, basil, mustard, salt, and pepper. Rub each salmon fillet with the mixture and arrange the fillets over the top of the vegetables and drizzle with the vermouth and lemon juice.

4. Combine the melted butter and pecans in a small bowl and top each fillet with it.

5. Roast the salmon until just cooked through and the vegetables are tender, 15 to 17 minutes. Serve on 4 plates with each fillet on top of the vegetables, just as it was cooked, and garnish with lemon wedges, if desired.

MAKE IT MEMORABLE

The veggies are built in with this recipe, but a great starter for this dish is a delicious Cream of Asparagus Soup (page 119). Top off this satisfying meal in style with a refreshing Honeydew and Blackberry Granita (page 246).

HEALTHFUL HINTS

Salmon has plenty of natural good fats; you may still lighten up this recipe by replacing the butter with a trans-fat-free margarine or extra virgin olive oil.

Thai Scallop and Prawn Stir-Fry

We'll cook anything in a wok in the Stella household! How else can you get *so* many nutrients in a one-pan meal? This colorful array of stir-fried vitamin-filled vegetables is incredibly versatile; Anthony might load his up with tofu while Christian uses lean chicken breast. Rachel and I are seafood lovers, so when it comes to our stir-fry, it only makes sense to put scallops and shrimp in our trusty wok. And not only does it make sense, it makes for another Stella family favorite that is sure to please!

Yield:	**6 servings**
Prep Time:	**15 minutes**
Cook Time:	**6 minutes**
Calories:	**240**
Total Fat:	**9 grams**
Saturated Fat:	**1 gram**
Carbohydrates:	**0 grams**
Net Carbohydrates:	**6 grams**
Fiber:	**2 grams**
Protein:	**29 grams**

2 tablespoons canola oil
1 pound sea scallops, whole (if very large, cut in half)
½ pound (about 36 to a pound) medium raw shrimp, peeled and deveined
¼ cup thinly sliced red onion
1 cup half-moon sliced yellow squash
1 cup small broccoli florets
1 cup sliced button mushrooms
½ cup julienne sliced bamboo shoots
2 garlic cloves, minced
1 cup chicken broth, low sodium and no sugar
2 cups sliced bok choy
1 cup fresh bean sprouts
¼ teaspoon freshly ground black pepper
¼ teaspoon kosher salt
½ cup snow peas
¼ cup sliced scallions
1 teaspoon red curry paste (available at Asian food markets)
2 tablespoons sesame oil
2 tablespoon fresh lime juice
6 sprigs any fresh herb, optional, for garnish
½ cup toasted peanuts, optional, for garnish

1. Start by preparing and cutting all the vegetables and measuring your ingredients so that they are ready to go. Once you begin stir-frying, it goes very quickly.

2. In a wok or large skillet, heat the canola oil over high heat until almost smoking. Add the scallops and shrimp and cook, tossing, just for 1 minute, remove, and reserve.

3. To the same hot wok, add the onion, squash, broccoli, mushrooms, bamboo shoots, and garlic and cook stirring constantly for 2 minutes.

4. Add the reserved scallops and shrimp along with the chicken broth and the remaining ingredients and cook on high for about 3 minutes more to reduce the sauce. (If there is too much liquid when the stir-fry is done, pour off the broth, reduce in a pan over high heat, and mix back into the stir-fry to serve.) Serve hot, divided among 6 plates or shallow bowls, garnished with any fresh herb and sprinkled with toasted peanuts, if desired.

MAKE IT MEMORABLE

This all-in-one meal doesn't need a thing before or along with it to make it complete, but afterward you may want to sit back and relax with a dish of Frozen Custard Ice Cream (page 242).

HEALTHFUL HINTS

If you are watching your carbs strictly, simply take more of the shrimp and scallops than the vegetables when making your plate, and include a small sampling of the many vegetables.

Monkfish Kebabs

The first time I used monkfish in the kitchen was at Windows on the Green in the Pier 66 Hotel in Fort Lauderdale, Florida, around 1981. It was a weird and ugly-looking fish—and thank goodness someone else knew how to fillet it, because I wouldn't have known where to start! I hear that the name actually comes from the poor monks who were given this delicacy by local fishermen because it was *so* ugly that it was considered useless! Lucky for the monks, it tastes as rich as lobster and sweet as scallops! Nowadays, it comes nice and trimmed, ready and easy to use. Try it, you'll like it!

Yield:	**4 servings; 2 skewers each**
Prep Time:	**15 minutes**
Cook Time:	**6 minutes**
Inactive Cook Time:	**30 minutes**
Calories:	**310**
Total Fat:	**12 grams**
Saturated Fat:	**2.5 grams**
Carbohydrates:	**5 grams**
Net Carbohydrates:	**3 grams**
Fiber:	**2 grams**
Protein:	**44 grams**

8 (8-inch) bamboo skewers
2 tablespoons extra virgin olive oil
2 tablespoons fresh lemon juice
1 tablespoon chopped fresh cilantro leaves, plus 4 sprigs, for garnish
1 teaspoon ground cumin
1 teaspoon kosher salt
½ teaspoon freshly ground black pepper
½ teaspoon minced fresh garlic
2 pounds fresh monkfish, cut into 1½-inch cubes (may use grouper or swordfish)
1 red bell pepper, seeded and cut into 1½-inch squares
1 green bell pepper, seeded and cut into 1½-inch squares
8 ounces whole small button mushrooms
1 lemon, cut into wedges, optional, for garnish

SPECIAL EQUIPMENT: gallon-sized sealable plastic bag; grill or grill pan

1. Soak 8 bamboo skewers in water for 30 minutes to 1 hour. (This will keep them from burning later.)

2. Whisk together the oil, lemon juice, cilantro, cumin, salt, pepper, and garlic in a bowl.

3. Transfer the marinade to the plastic bag with the monkfish cubes and shake to combine. Refrigerate for at least 30 minutes and up to 2 hours.

4. Preheat a grill or grill pan to high.

5. Remove the fish cubes from the marinade and the skewers from the water, and thread 3 pieces onto each skewer, alternating with red and green bell peppers and mushrooms, ending with a mushroom on top.

6. Place the skewers on the edges of the grill with the longest part of the stick hanging off the edge away from the fire. Stay close by and turn the sticks by hand to keep from burning. Skewers are done in just 2 to 3 minutes on each side. Serve 2 skewers per plate and garnish with sprigs of fresh cilantro and lemon wedges, if desired.

MAKE IT MEMORABLE

You can serve these kebabs with rich and creamy Mornay Sauce (page 96) or with refreshing cold Summer Squash Salsa (page 99). Either way, they're great atop Cauliflower Rice Pilaf (page 199)!

HEALTHFUL HINT

You may eliminate the oil in the recipe to lighten it up a bit. Just use an old chef's trick and put vegetable oil on a cloth towel and swab the grill rack just before using the grill to prevent sticking.

Fried Ipswich Clams

They call these *whole belly* clams in Woonsocket, Rhode Island, where Rachel grew up. A true comfort food for her—and now, for me too—we enjoyed many a heaping plate of these sweet and tender delights whenever we visited Rachel's parents. We don't do white flour these days, but we've found that soy flour makes an ideal deep-fried breading alternative. The flavor and textures just work perfectly! This recipe is *so* easy and quick and I just *know* that you will also really dig these clams!

Yield:	6 servings
Prep Time:	15 minutes
Cook Time:	2 minutes
Calories:	210
Total Fat:	10 grams
Saturated Fat:	2 grams
Carbohydrates:	10 grams
Net Carbohydrates:	6 grams
Fiber:	4 grams
Protein:	22 grams

3 to 6 cups vegetable oil (more or less, depending on pot size)
3 eggs
¼ cup water

BREADING
2⅓ cups soy flour
2 teaspoons kosher salt
1 teaspoon freshly ground black pepper
1 teaspoon garlic powder
1 teaspoon poultry seasoning

2 cups shelled raw Ipswich clams, drained well (raw shelled "whole belly" Ipswich clams can be purchased at larger seafood markets fresh or frozen in a small plastic tub and are called "Selects")

Lemon wedges, optional for garnish

SPECIAL EQUIPMENT: portable deep-fryer

1. Fill and preheat a portable deep fryer to 350°F or place a heavy pot over medium-high heat with at least an inch of vegetable oil. Heat the oil to 350°F; it is important to monitor and maintain the temperature, or the soy flour breading and your oil will burn. (Never overfill the fryer or pot with oil. You must leave room for it to bubble up when the clams are added.)

2. In a medium bowl, mix the eggs and water to make an egg wash.

3. In a large bowl, mix the breading ingredients together.

4. Dip a handful of the drained raw clams into the breading and shake the bowl to coat, then place the clams in the egg wash, then back into the breading, and shake the bowl vigorously again to coat the clams well.

5. Pat off any excess breading and carefully place the clams in the hot oil in batches, as necessary. Fry until golden brown and crisp, 1 to 2 minutes. (Be careful! Stand at arm's length while frying and make sure not to overcook; the whole belly clams can explode in the oil and splatter.) Remove and drain on paper towels. Serve immediately garnished with lemon wedges, if desired.

MAKE IT MEMORABLE

Serve these clams atop a bed of Baked Zucchini Fries (page 198), and for the perfect dip, you must try the Totally Tartar Sauce (page 101)!

HEALTHFUL HINTS

The clams are already wet, so to lighten up this recipe you may simply skip the egg wash altogether, bread them once lightly, and fry. Unfortunately, baking is not an alternative for this fried recipe as it would be with chicken.

Spaghetti Squash with Clams Provençal Sauce

By now, you know that I love spaghetti squash *almost* as much as I love my family. And my affection comes with a good reason: It's a wonder vegetable bestowed upon us from high above. A fresh alternative to pasta in every single way, it's loaded with enough fiber to make it worth its weight in gold! (Maybe that explains its wonderful golden yellow color!) The way I see it, if I can indulge in one of my favorite comfort foods—such as linguini with clam sauce—and get a heapin' dose of vitamins, minerals, and fiber without thinking; if I can eat something like this and lose weight; I should be able to scream SPAGHETTI SQUASH from the top of a mountain at the top of my lungs. And so I will: ***SPAAAGHETTIII SQUAAASH!!!***

Yield:	**6 servings**
Prep Time:	**20 minutes**
Cook Time:	**30 minutes**
Calories:	**150**
Total Fat:	**11 grams**
Saturated Fat:	**2 grams**
Carbohydrates:	**7 grams**
Net Carbohydrates:	**5 grams**
Fiber:	**2 grams**
Protein:	**8 grams**

4 cups cooked spaghetti squash (about ½ medium spaghetti squash)
Clams Provençal Sauce (recipe follows)

This recipe is for half of the squash. Double the recipe to use all of it.

1. Slice the squash in half lengthwise. Scoop out the seeds with a spoon as you would do with a pumpkin.

2. Completely submerge both cleaned squash halves in boiling water and cook for 20 to 25 minutes, or until the inside is tender and pulls apart in strands when scraped with a fork. (It is better to undercook if you are not sure.)

3. Remove, drain, and cool with cold water or an ice bath to stop the cooking. Then use a fork to scrape the cooked squash out of its skin, fluffing and separating the squash into spaghetti-like strands as you do so. Discard the skins.

4. Reheat 4 cups of the squash strands by dipping with a strainer in boiling water just before serving.

5. Top with Clams Provençal Sauce.

CLAMS PROVENÇAL SAUCE
¼ cup extra virgin olive oil
2 fresh garlic cloves, minced
2 cups minced clams with liquid (do not drain)
1 tablespoon chopped fresh basil leaves
1 teaspoon chopped fresh oregano (may use ½ teaspoon dried)
¼ teaspoon freshly ground black pepper
¼ cup freshly grated Parmesan cheese
2 plum tomatoes, diced
Fresh basil leaves, optional, for garnish
¼ cup black olives, pitted and sliced, optional, for garnish

1. Add the olive oil and garlic to a medium saucepan over medium-high heat and cook for just a minute.

2. Add the clams, basil, oregano, and pepper and simmer for 5 minutes more. Remove from the heat and stir in the cheese.

3. Pour the sauce over or toss with the hot spaghetti squash, divide among 6 dishes, and sprinkle the diced tomatoes over each. Garnish with fresh basil leaves and sliced black olives, if desired.

MAKE IT MEMORABLE

Shaved Zucchini Parmesan Salad (page 116) makes a nice start to a *Stella Style* Italian meal, especially if you have a nightcap of Panna Cotta and Cranberry Martinis (page 244)!

HEALTHFUL HINTS

Instead of adding the cheese to the sauce, lightly sprinkle half as much of the Parmesan cheese over the top before serving. You may omit the olive oil completely and simply simmer the herbs in the clams and broth, if you wish. Just before serving, you may add 1 tablespoon trans-fat-free margarine to add richness to the sauce if you have omitted the olive oil.

Baked Stuffed Shrimp Mornay

When it comes to different ways to make shrimp, Forrest Gump has nothing on me! This is a classic oldie-but-goodie from my French Continental cuisine days. Everyone raved about this dish when I made it, but I was so focused on serving others that I never took time to sit down and eat healthy good foods like this for myself. I was too busy eating fast food! When I did start taking the time to enjoy my meals, the pounds dropped off. People ask me all the time how I was able to lose the weight and stick with it, and all I can say over and over is, by eating wonderful satisfying meals like this!

Yield:	6 servings; 4 stuffed shrimp each
Prep Time:	30 minutes
Cook Time:	10 minutes
Calories:	380
Total Fat:	25 grams
Saturated Fat:	15 grams
Carbohydrates:	2 grams
Net Carbohydrates:	2 grams
Fiber:	0 gram
Protein:	30 grams

Vegetable oil spray

CRAB STUFFING

8 ounces cream cheese, softened, at room temperature

8 ounces lump crabmeat, or any real crabmeat will do (do *not* use artificial crab or "surimi" products; they have sugar. Just do like I do and buy a couple of king crab legs and take out the meat. It's cheaper in the long run and really good!)

⅓ cup grated Parmesan cheese

1 tablespoon fresh chopped parsley, plus 4 sprigs, optional, for garnish

1 teaspoon poultry seasoning

¼ teaspoon freshly ground black pepper

⅛ teaspoon fresh minced garlic (may use garlic powder)

⅛ teaspoon kosher salt

1 pound raw shrimp (21 to 25 pieces per pound tiger prawns, with the tail left on; if you do not want to be short, ask for exactly 24 shrimp, with a couple of extra for good measure)

2 tablespoons melted unsalted butter

1 ounce dry white wine, Chablis or Chardonnay

1 teaspoon fresh lemon juice

¼ teaspoon kosher salt

⅛ teaspoon freshly ground black pepper

6 tablespoons Mornay Sauce (page 96), more or less as desired

1 lemon, cut into 8 wedges, optional, for garnish

1. Preheat the oven to 375°F and coat a sheet pan with vegetable oil spray.

2. In a large bowl, mix all the crab stuffing ingredients until blended.

3. Leaving the tails on, peel and devein the shrimp, cutting down the back where the vein was, cutting it almost in half lengthwise but not quite.

4. Lay the shrimp close together and flat on the coated sheet pan, cut side down, and place a rounded teaspoon of the crab stuffing in the center of each. Wrap the tail up over the stuffing and press it slightly into the stuffing so it will hold its shape.

5. Drizzle the shrimp with a mixture of the melted butter, wine, and lemon juice and season lightly with salt and pepper. Bake for about 10 minutes, or until the shrimp are tender and just cooked.

6. Serve 4 stuffed shrimp to a plate. Drape with Mornay Sauce and garnish with sprigs of parsley and lemon wedges, if desired.

MAKE IT MEMORABLE

Melon and Prosciutto Bites (page 81) are just the right start for this rich gourmet dinner. A simple steamed asparagus, broccoli, or cauliflower goes perfectly with the sauce, too!

HEALTHFUL HINTS

To lighten up the fats in this recipe, low-fat cream cheese or Neufchâtel cheese may be used and the Parmesan cheese may be omitted. A trans-fat-free margarine or olive oil may be used in place of the butter, and if you prefer not to use wine, low-sodium chicken stock may be substituted.

Tilapia and Prawn Mousse Roulades

As a chef in the eighties, I helped promote the aquaculture program with the Florida Department of Natural Resources and Seafood Marketing Bureau. The bureau still operates today and helps promote small independent aquaculture businesses, such as oyster and clam farmers on the Indian River and farm-raised catfish pond operators in the Panhandle. Around 1984, these farmers gave me a new breed of farm-raised fish to try; it was fresh out of *clean* water, had a very mild flavor, a firm texture, and very few, if any, bones. It was the perfect fish to use for all my fillet of sole or flounder recipes and was called tilapia. Twenty plus years later, the secret is out: tilapia rocks! Thank you, Florida aquaculture farmers!

Yield:	**4 servings**
Prep Time:	**25 minutes**
Cook Time:	**10 to 12 minutes**
Calories:	**440**
Total Fat:	**31 grams**
Saturated Fat:	**17 grams**
Carbohydrates:	**3 grams**
Net Carbohydrates:	**3 grams**
Fiber:	**0 gram**
Protein:	**36 grams**

1 pound peeled and deveined raw shrimp, any size (tiger prawns are best)
1 cup heavy cream
¼ teaspoon kosher salt
⅛ teaspoon freshly ground black pepper
⅛ teaspoon ground nutmeg
1 tablespoon diced roasted red pepper
1 tablespoon chopped fresh parsley
2 tablespoons unsalted butter
¾ pound tilapia fillets, about 4 medium fillets cut in half down the center lengthwise to make 8 long pieces
2 tablespoons fresh lemon juice
2 ounces dry white wine, Chablis or Chardonnay
Kosher salt and freshly ground black pepper, to taste
4 sprigs fresh basil, optional, for garnish
1 lemon, cut into 8 wedges, optional, for garnish

SPECIAL EQUIPMENT: food processor

1. Preheat the oven to 375°F. Coat a sheet pan generously with butter.

2. Dice one-quarter of the peeled raw shrimp and reserve. Place the remaining shrimp, cream, ¼ teaspoon salt, ⅛ teaspoon pepper, and nutmeg in the food processor and blend on high for about 30 seconds until thick and creamy. Transfer to a bowl and mix in the reserved diced shrimp, red pepper, and parsley.

3. Working over the sheet pan, place a heaping tablespoon of the mousse on each tilapia fillet half, quickly wrap the fillet in a circle around the mousse, and place upright close together on the sheet pan. (The mousse should hold the tilapia fillet in place like glue.)

4. Drizzle the roulades with lemon juice and wine and season lightly with salt and pepper. Bake for about 10 minutes, until the mousse in the center rises and browns. (If you are not sure, stick a toothpick in the center. If it comes out clean, they're done.) Serve 2 roulades to a plate, garnished with fresh basil sprigs and 2 wedges of lemon, if desired.

MAKE IT MEMORABLE

Nothing could be more delicious and decadent than Foolproof Hollandaise Sauce (page 94) or Low-Fat Hollandaise Sauce (page 95), draped over the top of these delectable seafood roulades! And make room on the plate for the perfect side: Spinach, Roasted Peppers, and Artichoke Sauté (page 192).

HEALTHFUL HINTS

To lighten up the fats in this recipe, soy milk may be used in place of the cream and trans-fat-free margarine or olive oil may be used in place of the butter. If you prefer not to use wine, low-sodium chicken stock may be substituted.

Kristy's Recipe for Success

I didn't have any spectacular reason for being overweight. I can't exactly blame having a baby or a traumatic event. The only thing I can blame is boredom. Boredom and Little Debbie!

My mother essentially raised two kids on her own and spent more time worrying about us eating than *what* we were eating. I don't know the exact day I became overweight, but I guess I started gaining weight when I was five. The first thing I ever prepared for myself was boxed macaroni and cheese, and I pretty much lived on that until I was in college. It was cheap, easy, and went well with my Little Debbie snacks. It wasn't like my mom didn't care, though. She took me to doctors and encouraged me to try diets. I had probably tried every diet on the planet, but they never seemed to work.

It took moving two hundred miles away from home to motivate me to try again. My brother had always been pretty skinny and one day I just asked him about his workout routine. He vaguely mentioned cutting carbs, and I couldn't believe what I was hearing. I checked Dr. Atkins' book out of the school library and started reading. Years of low-fat conditioning had me almost laughing at this man, but I figured I'd give it a shot. Not only for my health but for what remained of my self-esteem.

Within a week, I had lost a dress size. I was falling out of my jeans, week after week, rushing to the thrift store to get temporary replacements because I was losing the weight so fast. I literally looked in the mirror and couldn't help but stare. Where did I go?

Everyone is different and sometimes you have to try the most unlikely idea to see success. After losing about one hundred pounds, my success has encouraged people around me, even strangers, to try again!

I went from a large teenage girl who could barely walk around the block to a twenty-three-year-old woman who can run four miles every morning. The key to success isn't *fat* or *meat,* it's about eating RIGHT and eating until you're full on the RIGHT THINGS. Not shakes, not bars, not fads, not working out twelve times a week. Knowing the Stellas has been a wonderful experience. The support and advice found on their show and Web forum have been invaluable to me and my family. We've been through such similar situations that it's nice to know we're not alone.

Vegetables

When I first started eating low carb, I was shocked to hear so many people labeling it as a meat-and-egg-free-for-all that frowned upon vegetables. My refrigerator certainly wasn't devoid of vegetables! In fact, quite the opposite.

Low-carb, high-fiber veggies are crucial to being *Stella Style* successful. In fact, they're one of the main reasons I say that you should *forget counting carbs.* Some people would rather cut back on their vegetables in order to "afford" a processed product with the extra carbs they've saved. But it's not about the number of carbs, it's about the *quality*—and you won't find any that are any more beneficial than a fiber and vitamin-packed vegetable such as broccoli. In fact, a vegetable that is full of fiber may actually bring down an entire meal's effect on your blood sugar. That's right, eating more carbs from veggies aids in the digestion, rather than the absorption, of other carbs that you're ingesting with them.

So for once, you can eat fries and feel good about it afterward—**Baked Zucchini Fries,** that is! Speaking of starchy favorites, my **Cauliflower Rice Pilaf** has all the taste of traditional rice pilaf, without the high-carb count. Give it a try! You won't be disappointed, and you'll also be doing something good for yourself.

A platter of **Grilled Portabellas, Peppers, and Squash** is the perfect accompaniment to just about any meal, and an even better party food. Why serve raw veggies when there's a perfectly good grill in the backyard?

Anyway you cook 'em, make sure you eat your veggies—and make sure you eat them often. Can I say that enough? Never! I'd say it again right here, but I'll just let the recipes do the talking instead. I say eat them because they're so darn good for you. What will they have to say? Probably that you should eat them often because they *taste* so darn good!

Green Beans Casserole

Holidays are when we really crave a tableful of classic comfort food, and this casserole fits the bill perfectly! Fresh green beans and mushrooms replace canned, and onion straws (without breading) are a terrific topper. Whether you're trying to eat healthier foods or to lose weight, here's proof that you don't have to give up the foods you grew up with. Get cookin' and then get comfortable—you're in for an enjoyable ride all the way to the finish line!

Yield:	**6 servings**
Prep Time:	**15 minutes**
Cook Time:	**17 minutes**
Calories:	**90**
Total Fat:	**4.5 grams**
Saturated Fat:	**2.5 grams**
Carbohydrates:	**7.5 grams**
Net Carbohydrates:	**4 grams**
Fiber:	**3.5 grams**
Protein:	**4 grams**

ONION STRAWS

½ cup very thinly sliced onion
2 tablespoons grated Parmesan cheese
⅛ teaspoon freshly ground black pepper
⅛ teaspoon garlic powder

CASSEROLE

1 pound green beans, ends trimmed
1 tablespoon vegetable or canola oil
½ cup very thinly sliced white onion
8 ounces button mushrooms, cleaned and sliced
1½ teaspoons kosher salt
⅛ teaspoon garlic powder
⅛ teaspoon freshly ground black pepper
½ cup chicken broth, no sugar, low sodium
1 teaspoon chopped fresh thyme, plus a few sprigs, for garnish
½ cup sour cream

SPECIAL EQUIPMENT: 10-inch glass pie pan

1. Preheat the oven to 350°F.

2. Make the Onion Straws: Combine all the ingredients in a small bowl, toss to mix, and arrange in a single layer on a baking sheet. Set aside.

3. Make the Casserole: Bring a small pot of water to boil and season lightly with salt.

Boil the green beans until tender, but still crispy, about 5 minutes. Drain and chill the beans in an ice water bath or under cold running water. Drain again and transfer to a bowl.

4. Heat the oil in a large skillet over medium-high heat. Add the onion, mushrooms, salt, garlic, and pepper and cook, stirring, about 2 minutes.

5. Add the chicken broth and thyme and cook until almost all the liquid has evaporated, 3 to 4 minutes.

6. Transfer the mushroom mixture to the bowl of green beans, add the sour cream, and toss to combine.

7. Pour the green bean mixture into the pie pan. Bake the casserole and onion straws on separate racks until the straws are well browned and crispy (almost burnt, otherwise they will be soggy), 15 to 17 minutes. Top the casserole with the straws, and serve garnished with thyme sprigs.

MAKE IT MEMORABLE

For that very special meal, go all out and serve this comfort food classic alongside Herb-Roasted New York Strip Sirloin (page 147) and serve up some of Rachel's Pumpkin Pound Cake (page 229) for dessert!

HEALTHFUL HINTS

You can easily lighten this recipe by using low-fat sour cream and baking the onion straws without the Parmesan cheese.

Grilled Portabellas, Peppers, and Squash

I love grilling because it's: quick, easy, fun, relaxing, healthy, satisfying, different, flavorful, and usually takes place outside, away from distractions like phones and e-mails! (deep breath) . . . And almost anything you can grill is good for you! Throwing on a colorful assortment of veggies on the grill along with your protein makes for easy cookin'. As a bonus, when you're cooking with color, you know you're eating healthy!

Yield:	6 servings
Prep Time:	10 minutes
Cook Time:	10 minutes
Calories:	80
Total Fat:	5 grams
Saturated Fat:	1 gram
Carbohydrates:	7 grams
Net Carbohydrates:	4 grams
Fiber:	3 grams
Protein:	1 gram

2 portabella mushroom caps, stemmed
1 red bell pepper, cored, seeded, and quartered
1 medium yellow squash, halved lengthwise
1 medium zucchini, halved lengthwise
1 medium red onion, cut into ½-inch-thick slices
½ teaspoon kosher salt
¼ teaspoon freshly ground black pepper
2 tablespoons extra virgin olive oil
2 garlic cloves, minced

1. Build a charcoal fire or preheat a gas grill or indoor grill pan.

2. Place all of the vegetables on a baking sheet, season with salt and pepper, and toss with the olive oil and garlic. (Be careful that the onion slices do not fall apart.)

3. Place the vegetables, cut side down, on the grill. Cook for 4 to 5 minutes on each side until tender and nicely marked by the grill. Remove from the grill and serve each person a small assortment of each veggie!

MAKE IT MEMORABLE

These veggies go perfect with our Pork Souvlaki (page 124) with Easy Tzatziki Sauce (page 93), and they cook on the grill together in the same amount of time, 10 minutes!

HEALTHFUL HINTS

Almost all vegetables are great grilled. We grill everything from eggplant to asparagus and tomatoes to scallions. Try your favorite and always pick different color vegetables.

Roasted Vegetables

Here it comes again . . . "When you're cooking with color, you're cooking healthy!" That's my motto and I'm sticking to it! I've been cooking with color since my French Continental cuisine days of the late seventies, when we used beautifully colored food to decorate the plates. I've never stopped decorating plates with colorful foods, but today I understand that eating different colors and varieties of vegetables (like this dish has) is a surefire, simple way to assure that you are getting the most vitamins and nutrients from your food! Now go make something pretty!

Yield:	**6 servings**
Prep Time:	**10 minutes**
Cook Time:	**35 to 40 minutes**
Calories:	**90**
Total Fat:	**4.5 grams**
Saturated Fat:	**1 gram**
Carbohydrates:	**10 grams**
Net Carbohydrates:	**7 grams**
Fiber:	**3 grams**
Protein:	**3 grams**

Vegetable oil spray
3 celery ribs, cut into thirds
2 medium yellow squash, halved crosswise
2 medium zucchini, halved crosswise
1 medium yellow onion, quartered (about 1 cup)
1 red bell pepper, cored, seeded, and quartered
1 garlic clove, minced
2 tablespoons olive oil
1½ teaspoons kosher salt
1 teaspoon dried oregano
1 teaspoon paprika
¼ teaspoon freshly ground black pepper
⅛ teaspoon garlic powder

SPECIAL EQUIPMENT: roasting pan

1. Preheat the oven to 350°F and spray a roasting pan with vegetable oil.

2. Toss all of the ingredients including the cut vegetables in a large bowl.

3. Arrange the vegetables in the roasting pan and bake for 35 to 40 minutes until well done. Arrange on a decorative platter to serve.

MAKE IT MEMORABLE

These vegetables are perfect to serve with Family-Style Chicken (page 152) since they can be cooked together in the same pan! I like to have a simple iceberg lettuce salad to complete the meal.

HEALTHFUL HINT

To save a few carbs, you can omit the yellow onion, cutting down on natural sugars.

Spinach, Roasted Peppers, and Artichoke Sauté

Fresh or frozen, spinach is a versatile vegetable that you should keep on hand for a no-brainer of a great side! It cooks in a few minutes and can be different every time you have it. For me, it depends on my mood and what's in the refrigerator. From Mediterranean sauté to ricotta and spinach sauté extraordinaire, you're limited only by your imagination! Spinach: It's not just for Popeye anymore!

¼ cup (½ stick) unsalted butter
4 ounces prosciutto di Parma, diced (may use baked ham or bacon)
2 tablespoons diced red onion
1 small garlic clove, minced
1 (6-ounce) jar roasted red pepper strips, drained
1 (6-ounce) jar marinated artichoke hearts, drained and quartered
1 (1-pound) bag frozen spinach, thawed, chopped, and drained well

Kosher salt to taste
⅛ teaspoon freshly ground black pepper
1 tablespoon freshly squeezed lemon juice (about ¼ lemon)

Yield:	6 servings
Prep Time:	10 minutes
Cook Time:	5 minutes
Calories:	165
Total Fat:	10 grams
Saturated Fat:	5 grams
Carbohydrates:	6 grams
Net Carbohydrates:	3 grams
Fiber:	3 grams
Protein:	5 grams

1. Melt the butter in a large pan over medium-high heat. Add the prosciutto, onion, garlic, roasted red pepper strips, and artichokes and cook, stirring, until tender, about 2 minutes.

2. Add the spinach and cook, stirring, until hot, about 3 minutes. Remove from the heat and season with salt and pepper.

3. Drizzle the lemon juice over everything and serve immediately.

MAKE IT MEMORABLE

This sauté is the perfect side for Chicken Saltimbocca (page 162). And preparing Panna Cotta and Cranberry Martinis (page 244) ahead will make you a rock star for the evening!

HEALTHFUL HINTS

Easily lighten this recipe by replacing the butter with trans-fat-free margarine or olive oil. The Parma ham can be left out altogether or replaced with walnuts, or with chopped cooked leftover chicken breast or turkey for healthier fats.

Summer Squash Sauté

I like easy, and this vegetable side dish is about as simple as it can ever get in cooking. It has color, flavor, and is seasonally refreshing. We always keep squash and zucchini on hand for just these reasons—and this streamlined Summer Squash Sauté is the perfect last-minute accompaniment for almost any entrée.

Yield:	2 servings
Prep Time:	10 minutes
Cook Time:	3 minutes
Calories:	100
Total Fat:	7 grams
Saturated Fat:	1 gram
Carbohydrates:	8 grams
Net Carbohydrates:	5 grams
Fiber:	3 grams
Protein:	2 grams

1 tablespoon olive oil
¼ cup sliced red onion
1 small yellow squash, cut into long ¼-inch-thick slices on the diagonal
1 small zucchini, cut into long ¼-inch-thick slices on the diagonal
1 garlic clove, finely chopped
½ teaspoon kosher salt
⅛ teaspoon freshly ground black pepper
3 cherry tomatoes, halved
1 tablespoon thinly sliced basil leaves

1. Heat the oil in a large skillet over medium-high heat. Add the onion, yellow squash, zucchini, garlic, salt, and pepper and cook, stirring occasionally, until lightly browned and crisp-tender, about 2 minutes.

2. Add the tomatoes and basil and cook, stirring, until tender, about 1 minute more. Serve immediately.

MAKE IT MEMORABLE

This dish makes a great side for Kim's Stuffed Chicken Breasts with Lemony White Wine Sauce (page 150).

HEALTHFUL HINT

For once I am left speechless—it just doesn't get any healthier than this! Enjoy this side dish without guilt!

Braised Texas Cabbage

Rachel and I were in San Antonio, Texas, for the first time recently, and we actually stayed right across the street from the Alamo. We got to experience Texas-style food firsthand, like side salads big enough to set up camp in. Then there was the spicy hot tang to everything on the menus, much like this cabbage that we had while we were there. I can't remember exactly where—but I do remember the Alamo!

Yield:	**6 servings**
Prep Time:	**10 minutes**
Cook Time:	**5 minutes**
Calories:	**90**
Total Fat:	**4.5 grams**
Saturated Fat:	**3 grams**
Carbohydrates:	**9 grams**
Net Carbohydrates:	**6 grams**
Fiber:	**3 grams**
Protein:	**3 grams**

2 tablespoons unsalted butter
½ red onion, thinly sliced
2 garlic cloves, minced
6 cups cabbage, coarsely chopped
¾ cup low-sodium beef broth
½ tablespoon chili powder
1 teaspoon ground cumin
½ teaspoon Chipotle Tabasco Sauce, optional (may use ⅛ teaspoon cayenne pepper)
¼ teaspoon kosher salt
⅛ teaspoon freshly ground black pepper

1. Melt the butter in a large pan over medium-high heat. Add the onion, garlic, and cabbage and cook, stirring, until tender, about 2 minutes.

2. Add the beef broth and the rest of the seasonings and cook a few minutes more, stirring constantly, until the liquid reduces by half. Serve hot.

MAKE IT MEMORABLE

Get ready for a hot night when you serve this cabbage with Chili-Rubbed Baked Salmon (page 170). Just make sure you have plenty of White Wine Sangria (page 213) on hand to put out any fires!

HEALTHFUL HINT

You can lighten up this recipe by replacing the butter with trans-fat-free margarine or olive oil.

Wild Mushroom Brochettes

Whether you're throwing steak, chicken, or salmon on the grill, mushrooms make the perfect accompaniment every time! I have always loved mushrooms from sautéed to fried and everything in between, but this grilled assortment is one of my favorites. It's easy to make, can be assembled in minutes, and cooks even faster. Give them a try and easily turn an otherwise ordinary dinner into a gourmet masterpiece!

Yield:	**6 servings**
Prep Time:	**15 minutes**
Cook Time:	**3 minutes**
Calories:	**40**
Total Fat:	**2.5 grams**
Saturated Fat:	**0 gram**
Carbohydrates:	**3 grams**
Net Carbohydrates:	**2 grams**
Fiber:	**1 gram**
Protein:	**2 grams**

30 (8-inch) bamboo skewers
1 large or 2 medium portabella caps, cut into 6½-inch-wide strips
¼ pound shiitake mushrooms, the larger the better
¼ pound oyster mushrooms (choose 6 nice clusters and treat them very gently or they will fall apart)
1 tablespoon olive oil
1 teaspoon fresh lemon juice
2 garlic cloves, minced
½ teaspoon kosher salt
⅛ teaspoon freshly ground black pepper
1 teaspoon freshly chopped parsley, optional, for garnish

1. Soak the bamboo skewers in water to keep them from burning later. Build a charcoal fire or preheat a gas grill or indoor grill pan to medium-high.

2. Gently wipe all the mushrooms clean with a damp cloth and place them on a baking sheet.

3. Mix the oil, lemon juice, and seasonings in a small bowl and drizzle over all the mushrooms to coat well.

4. Thread the mushrooms on the skewers. Begin with a portabella strip, pushing it about two-thirds of the way down toward the bottom of the skewer. Then carefully thread a delicate oyster mushroom cluster, followed by a large shiitake cap to finish it off, leaving an inch or so at the top. (If you have extra mushrooms, just make more!)

5. Place the brochettes on the edges of the grill, with the longest part of the stick hanging off the edge away from the fire. Stay close and turn the sticks by hand once to keep from burning. Brochettes are done in just 2 to 3 minutes. (If a mushroom falls off the skewer, just put it back on after cooking. And if a skewer burns up, simply place the grilled mushrooms on a new skewer to serve.) Serve hot off the grill sprinkled with fresh chopped parsley, if desired.

MAKE IT MEMORABLE

I like to serve these brochettes leaning up against a nice juicy steak like Ernie's Greco-Roman Rib Eyes (page 134), or next to some thick slices of Herb-Roasted New York Strip Sirloin (page 147).

HEALTHFUL HINTS

You can cut down the olive oil to 1 teaspoon to lighten up this recipe, but just before placing the brochettes on the grill you must swab your grill grate with vegetable oil on a cloth to prevent sticking.

Baked Zucchini Fries

If we can turn plain old white potatoes into golden, beloved french fries, then is it so far fetched to imagine that we could accomplish similar results with a zucchini? Well, maybe just a little, but these new fries are a great-tasting healthy alternative. Once you start serving them in place of regular fries, you're on your way to changing your eating habits for the better!

Yield:	**8 servings; about 4 ounces each**
Prep Time:	**10 minutes**
Cook Time:	**15 minutes**
Calories:	**15**
Total Fat:	**0 gram**
Saturated Fat:	**0 gram**
Carbohydrates:	**3 grams**
Net Carbohydrates:	**2 grams**
Fiber:	**1 gram**
Protein:	**1 gram**

3 zucchini, about 4 cups
Vegetable oil spray
2 teaspoons chili powder
1 teaspoon kosher salt
½ teaspoon garlic powder
¼ teaspoon freshly ground black pepper
⅛ teaspoon cayenne pepper, optional, if you like spicy

1. Preheat the oven to 500°F.

2. Trim the ends off the zucchini and cut them lengthwise into ¼-inch-thick slices. Then cut those slices into 3-inch-long fries, place flat on a nonstick sheet pan, and spray them and the pan liberally with vegetable oil spray.

3. Place all the seasonings in a small bowl, mix well, and sprinkle evenly over all the fries. Bake for about 15 minutes until well browned. Serve immediately. (If you place the zucchini fries on a heatproof wire rack or screen within the sheet pan, they will crisp up better.)

MAKE IT MEMORABLE

Enjoy your fries traditionally with some Quick and Easy Ketchup (page 99), and with your favorite burger from our Boredom-Bashing Burger Ideas (page 135)!

HEALTHFUL HINT

The salt in this recipe may be reduced or replaced with a no-salt seasoning.

Cauliflower Rice Pilaf

Who says you have to use rice to make rice pilaf? Well, maybe the name does, but that didn't stop me from trying to use cauliflower instead! This recipe works perfectly wherever you would serve rice, from stir-fries to my favorite, with bacon bits and melting Cheddar cheese on top! Go ahead and serve it as a side, or make a meal out of it; you know you can't go overboard with carbs or guilt with this satisfying, healthy cravings buster!

Yield:	4 servings
Prep Time:	15 minutes
Cook Time:	12 minutes
Calories:	50
Total Fat:	4.5 grams
Saturated Fat:	2 grams
Carbohydrates:	2 grams
Net Carbohydrates:	1 gram
Fiber:	1 gram
Protein:	1 gram

2 cups raw cauliflower, shredded with a cheese grater
1 tablespoon unsalted butter
1 tablespoon olive oil
2 tablespoons chopped yellow onion
¼ teaspoon minced fresh garlic
1 cup low-sodium chicken broth, no sugar added
1 teaspoon chopped fresh parsley
2 bay leaves
½ teaspoon turmeric
½ teaspoon kosher salt
¼ teaspoon freshly ground black pepper

1. Grate the fresh cauliflower head as you would cheese, using the largest holes of a cheese grater. A food processor with a grating blade is easiest for this.

2. Heat the butter and oil in a large skillet over medium-high heat. Add the onion, garlic, and shredded cauliflower and cook for 2 minutes while stirring.

3. Add the chicken broth and seasonings and simmer for about 9 minutes until tender, stirring occasionally. Serve hot!

MAKE IT MEMORABLE

This is a great side for almost any meal, but it is exceptional when served with General Tso's Chicken (page 160) or with Gourmet Chicken Stir-Fry (page 158).

HEALTHFUL HINTS

The butter may be replaced with trans-fat-free margarine or all olive oil to lighten up this recipe.

Vegetarian Entrées

- BBQ Baked Soybeans
- Cauliflower "Mac" and Cheese Casserole
- Italian Marinated Vegetables
- Eggplant Rolatini Casserole
- Cauliflower Hash Browns

No, that's not a misprint. More and more, I'm running into people who are living proof that vegetarians can successfully live a low-carb lifestyle.

It's not easy, unless, of course, you know what you're looking for! It *can* be made simpler, however, with just a bit of creativity. Just think of all the great veggies, nuts, seeds, dairy, and low-carb fruits that we already know are *Stella Style* essentials.

In fact, some of these vegetarian entrées are my most inventive recipes yet! My **BBQ Baked Soybeans, Cauliflower "Mac" and Cheese Casserole,** and **Cauliflower Hash Browns** are fresh reinventions of their high-carb cousins that make perfect sides—or, they can be enjoyed all by their lonesome! For something a little more hearty, try my **Eggplant Rolatini Casserole.** It tastes so good you may *want* seconds, but I dare you to still be hungry after a plateful!

If you're worried about getting enough protein, tofu or textured vegetable and soy can make sure you get all you need. Most meat alternatives are low in carbs *and* high in fiber, so how can you go wrong?

Many of the recipes in this book can be altered to include vegetarian protein with just one simple substitution, but the recipes in this section won't require any substitutions. They were vegetarian from day one, even if I didn't realize it until compiling them for this book, because I write recipes with only one goal in mind—making them taste great!

BBQ Baked Soybeans

This is one of Rachel's newest creations and it's definitely a Weiner! The soybeans lend themselves perfectly to this quick and healthy alternative to the traditional version, something we have not had in years! I asked Rachel how these can be done in just 6 minutes, and she said that the soybeans are fully cooked already, so there's no messing with soaking. They were even better the next day when the flavors had time to soak into the beans, so they're perfect for making ahead. Batter up; it's time for hot dogs and beans again!

Yield:	**6 servings**
Prep Time:	**10 minutes**
Cook Time:	**6 minutes**
Calories:	**60**
Total Fat:	**1 gram**
Saturated Fat:	**0 gram**
Carbohydrates:	**7 grams**
Net Carbohydrates:	**4 grams**
Fiber:	**3 grams**
Protein:	**6 grams**

½ cup Quick and Easy Ketchup (page 99)
⅛ teaspoon liquid smoke (available in a small bottle in the spice or condiment isles)
¼ teaspoon ground dry mustard
¼ teaspoon garlic powder
¼ teaspoon onion powder
½ teaspoon kosher salt
¼ teaspoon freshly ground black pepper
1 tablespoon sugar substitute (recommended: Splenda)
1 (15-oz) can black soybeans, rinsed and drained (we use Eden brand found at health food stores and in some supermarkets)

1. Add all the ingredients but the beans to a saucepan over medium-high heat and cook while stirring for just a minute to blend.

2. Finish by adding the beans and cooking while stirring for another 5 minutes until heated through, and serve in a ceramic crock for flair!

MAKE IT MEMORABLE

Serve alongside grilled or pan-seared all beef hot dogs (we like Nathan's or Sabrette brand) and some Jicama Slaw (page 118). Make it decadent by adding some cooked bacon!

HEALTHFUL HINTS

Black soybeans are filled with fiber and make a great anytime side dish when simply sautéed in olive oil with a single minced garlic clove, salt, and pepper.

Cauliflower "Mac" and Cheese Casserole

Christian's favorite comfort food growing up was macaroni and cheese, and not the good stuff either. We're talking the three-for-a-dollar brand that is about as nutritious and flavorful as the boxes it came in! Trading useless processed foods for healthier fresh food alternatives like this cauliflower casserole was the key to successful weight loss for Christian and our whole family. This is a perfect side dish, and also a great dish to make in advance and have on hand for an anytime meal or snack!

Yield:	**8 servings**
Prep Time:	**15 minutes**
Cook Time:	**20 minutes**
Calories:	**190**
Total Fat:	**15 grams**
Saturated Fat:	**9 grams**
Carbohydrates:	**7 grams**
Net Carbohydrates:	**4 grams**
Fiber:	**3 grams**
Protein:	**7 grams**

Kosher salt, as needed, plus ½ teaspoon
Vegetable oil spray
1 large head cauliflower, cut into small florets
¾ cup heavy cream (may use sugar-free soy milk)
2 ounces cream cheese, cut into small pieces (may use low-fat cream cheese)
1½ teaspoons Dijon mustard
1½ cups shredded sharp Cheddar cheese, plus ½ cup for topping the casserole
¼ teaspoon freshly ground black pepper
⅛ teaspoon garlic powder

EQUIPMENT: 8-by-8-inch baking dish

1. Preheat the oven to 375°F. Bring a large pot of water to a boil. Season the water with salt. Spray the baking dish with vegetable oil spray.

2. Cook the cauliflower in the boiling water until crisp-tender, about 5 minutes.

3. Drain well and pat between several layers of paper towels to dry. Transfer the cauliflower to the baking dish and set aside.

4. Bring the cream to a simmer in a small saucepan and whisk in the cream cheese and mustard until smooth.

5. Stir in the 1½ cups of cheese, salt, pepper, and garlic powder and whisk just until the cheese melts, 1 to 2 minutes. Remove from the heat, pour over the cauliflower, and stir to combine.

6. Top with the remaining ½ cup cheese and bake until browned and bubbly hot, about 15 minutes, and serve.

MAKE IT MEMORABLE

Add in some leftover cooked chicken, chunked baked ham, or even crab and shrimp for a hearty all in one meal!

HEALTHFUL HINTS

Besides using unsweetened soy milk in place of heavy cream or low-fat cheese in place of regular, you may even cut the cream and all the cheese amounts in half. This will make less sauce and take a bit less time to bake, but will still have all the great flavor! (You must also cut the Dijon mustard amount in half, but not the seasonings.)

Italian Marinated Vegetables

When [illegible] and I first started out on our low-carb journey years ago, we became personal chefs, calling ourselves "The Low Carb Chefs." We duplicated for our clients what we had done for ourselves by shopping, bringing fresh foods to their homes, and cooking all their meals for the week right there in their own kitchens! There were always plenty of veggies involved: all kinds, all colors, and always a bit of each left over, too. From olives to broccoli, it all went into the marinated vegetables. Funny enough, it turned out to be one of the most requested dishes!

Yield:	**12 servings; 6 ounces each**
Prep Time:	**15 minutes**
Cook Time:	**2 minutes**
Calories:	**150**
Total Fat:	**13 grams**
Saturated Fat:	**1 gram**
Carbohydrates:	**5 grams**
Net Carbohydrates:	**4 grams**
Fiber:	**1 gram**
Protein:	**3 grams**

VEGETABLES

¼ cup freshly squeezed lemon juice
1 tablespoon kosher salt
1 pound broccoli rabe, trimmed
1 cup small cauliflower florets
8 ounces button mushrooms (cleaned and cut in half if too large)
1 cup sliced zucchini, cut in half-moons
1 cup sliced yellow squash, cut in half-moons
½ cup roasted red pepper strips
½ cup marinated, quartered artichoke hearts
½ cup oil-cured black olives, pitted

ITALIAN MARINADE

¼ cup red wine vinegar
2 tablespoons freshly squeezed lemon juice
1 tablespoon Dijon mustard
2 teaspoons kosher salt
½ teaspoon freshly ground black pepper
1 garlic clove, chopped
⅓ cup extra virgin olive oil
½ cup canola oil
1 tablespoon thinly sliced fresh basil, plus whole leaves, for garnish
1 lemon, cut into wedges, optional, for garnish

SPECIAL EQUIPMENT: large stockpot with submersible pasta basket

1. Make the vegetables: Fill the stockpot with water and bring to a boil. Stir in the lemon juice and salt.

2. Fill the pasta basket with the broccoli rabe, cauliflower, mushrooms, zucchini, and squash. Submerge in the boiling water and cook, covered, for 2 minutes. Remove the basket and refresh the vegetables under cold running water; drain well.

3. Transfer the vegetables to a bowl and mix with the red pepper strips, artichokes, and olives.

4. In a blender, combine the vinegar, lemon juice, mustard, salt, pepper, and garlic. Mix on medium until completely blended.

5. While the motor is running, slowly pour in the oils in a steady stream to make a smooth dressing.

6. Pour the dressing over the vegetables. Add the basil and toss well. Chill for at least 2 hours before serving. Arrange on a decorative platter garnished with fresh basil and lemon wedges, if desired.

MAKE IT MEMORABLE

These delicious vegetables are great as an anytime snack or serve them as the lead into a main course of Chicken Saltimbocca (page 162), with a side of Spinach, Roasted Peppers, and Artichoke Sauté (page 192).

HEALTHFUL HINTS

To lighten up this recipe eliminate the Dijon mustard and all the canola oil, using only the ⅓ cup extra virgin olive oil. To make this work, you must also increase the amount of lemon juice to 3 tablespoons and the vinegar to ⅓ cup, creating an acid-based marinade that works just fine!

Eggplant Rolatini Casserole

The first time my mother made eggplant rolatini, I was hooked! I already loved eggplant, but this dish was a heavenly cross between my two favorites, eggplant Parmesan and lasagna! I'll never stop making those traditional Italian foods I grew up with and love *so* dearly, and why would I? The ingredients in this recipe are naturally low carb; the only thing I've changed is to season the egg wash while leaving out the bread crumbs altogether.

Yield:	12 servings
Prep Time:	25 minutes
Cook Time:	37 minutes
Calories:	240
Total Fat:	15 grams
Saturated Fat:	7 grams
Carbohydrates:	8 grams
Net Carbohydrates:	5 grams
Fiber:	3 grams
Protein:	18 grams

EGGPLANT

3 large eggs
2 tablespoons grated Parmesan cheese
1 tablespoon water
1 teaspoon kosher salt
½ teaspoon dried oregano
⅛ teaspoon garlic powder
2 medium eggplant

TOMATO SAUCE

1 tablespoon extra virgin olive oil
2 tablespoons diced red onion
2 garlic cloves, chopped
1 (14-ounce) can diced tomatoes, no sugar added
1 (8-ounce) can tomato sauce, no sugar added
½ teaspoon dried basil
¼ teaspoon garlic powder
½ teaspoon dried oregano
⅛ teaspoon kosher salt
⅛ teaspoon freshly ground black pepper

CHEESE FILLING

15 ounces whole milk ricotta cheese
8 ounces shredded mozzarella cheese
½ cup grated Parmesan cheese
¼ cup diced roasted red pepper
1 tablespoon chopped flat-leaf parsley
1 tablespoon chopped fresh oregano

1 garlic clove, minced
¼ teaspoon freshly ground black pepper
1 large egg

TOPPING
4 ounces shredded mozzarella cheese
1 tablespoon olive oil
½ teaspoon dried oregano
Leaves from 1 bunch of basil, torn into pieces, optional, for garnish

SPECIAL EQUIPMENT: 9-by-13-inch baking dish with sides

1. Spray vegetable oil on the baking sheet. Preheat the oven to 400°F.

2. Whisk together the eggs, Parmesan, water, salt, oregano, and garlic powder in a bowl.

3. Trim the ends off each eggplant and, using a potato peeler, peel off 2 large swaths of skin on two sides. Cut each eggplant lengthwise into 6 slices about ½ inch thick. (If you end up with more than 12 slices, just pick out the best ones.)

4. Dip each slice into the egg mixture and transfer to the baking sheet. (If the baking sheet seems crowded, divide the slices among 2 baking sheets.) Pour any remaining egg mixture over the eggplant and bake until lightly browned, about 12 minutes. Let cool slightly before carefully loosening each slice from the pan with a flat spatula.

5. Turn the oven down to 350°F. Meanwhile, make the tomato sauce: Heat the oil in a saucepan over medium heat. Add the onion and garlic and cook, stirring, until soft and translucent.

6. Add the remaining ingredients and cook, stirring, for 2 minutes more.

7. Make the cheese filling: Mix all of the ingredients together in a bowl.

8. To assemble the rolatini: Place 2 tablespoons of the cheese filling in the center of each eggplant slice and roll them up and place in a single layer, seam side down, in the baking dish.

9. Pour the tomato sauce over the top, cover the rolatini with the topping ingredients, and bake for 25 minutes until the cheese starts to brown on top and the filling starts to ooze out of the rolls. Remove and serve garnished with the basil, if desired.

MAKE IT MEMORABLE

Start this classic Italian family meal off right with a uniquely different Shaved Zucchini Parmesan Salad (page 116), and top the dinner off with a light and refreshing dessert of Fresh Berries and Sabayon (page 240).

HEALTHFUL HINTS

To lighten up this recipe, you may use part-skim ricotta cheese and low-fat mozzarella cheese. Another healthy way to lower fats: halve the filling recipe and add 1½ cups of fresh or frozen chopped vegetables such as broccoli, spinach, zucchini, yellow squash, or mushrooms to replace the lost volume.

Cauliflower Hash Browns

We have cauliflower in the house all the time, and so we're always finding new uses for it. We've used it in place of potatoes for my mother's egg potato salad—and even to make mashed "potatoes"—but this recipe really takes the prize! I made it from leftovers one morning and it tasted so good, I now cook it as a dinner vegetable! That means you can use last night's leftover cauliflower to make these breakfast hash browns, for a simple, satisfying morning meal!

1 large egg
1 teaspoon paprika
½ teaspoon kosher salt
¼ teaspoon freshly ground black pepper
¼ teaspoon garlic powder
2 tablespoons chopped cooked bacon (about 4 pieces)

Yield:	4 servings; 2 pieces each
Prep Time:	15 minutes
Cook Time:	5 minutes
Calories:	80
Total Fat:	7 grams
Saturated Fat:	1.5 grams
Carbohydrates:	3 grams
Net Carbohydrates:	2 grams
Fiber:	1 gram
Protein:	5 grams

2 tablespoons chopped yellow onion
1 tablespoon chopped green bell pepper
1½ cups cooked cauliflower, shredded (use the large hole side of a cheese grater)
2 tablespoons vegetable oil

1. Add all the ingredients except the cauliflower and oil to a bowl and mix well.

2. Gently fold in the cooked shredded cauliflower with a fork.

3. Place about a teaspoon of the oil in a small nonstick sauté pan over medium heat. Drop a heaping tablespoon of the cauliflower mix in the pan—one at a time—and cook for about 2 minutes on each side until both sides are golden brown. Repeat until all the mixture is used. Serve hot.

MAKE IT MEMORABLE

These hash browns go perfectly with any breakfast, such as Hot Ham and Cheese Egg Roll (page 34), or with something special such as Rachel's Birthday Omelet (page 38). And for a simple way to start your day, just top these hash browns with a fried egg.

HEALTHFUL HINTS

The bacon may be substituted with turkey bacon or left out to lighten up this recipe. The oil may be replaced with trans-fat-free margarine for cooking the hash browns.

Beverages

Spiked Tea

White Wine Sangria

Frozen Margaritas

Anthony's Berry Good Smoothies

Fresh Fruit Slushees

The Danny Cocktail

Now you can have your fruit—and drink it, too! My **Fresh Fruit Slushees** and **Anthony's Berry Good Smoothies** have no refined sugars. By using whole fruit instead of extracting just the juice, you save on calories and get to keep the fiber.

When I weighed 467 pounds, the liquids I drank were far from a concern. We'd even buy those gallon jugs of artificially colored, artificially flavored grape "drink." We called it juice. We honestly didn't know that it was just high-fructose corn syrup and water—tons of empty, useless calories.

My eating habits were so bad that what I drank was barely a blip on the radar. I never stopped to think about the calories in a glass of orange juice or the sugars in a can of soda. That stuff adds up, especially for a man as large as I was. I could easily drink an entire carton of fruit juice *and* a two-liter bottle of soda in one day. I was probably consuming my recommended calories for the day just in beverages!

For some, the *best* change you can possibly make is the switch to sugar-free drinks. You'll instantly have more freedom with your food choices because you've cleared so many calories out of your diet.

Also deserving all the mention it gets is plain, regular, fresh water. From the tap or the bottle, we should all be drinking six to eight glasses of water a day. It's a no-brainer and I know you may be tired of hearing about it! But it's such an easy, important step toward success that it's worth talking about again and again.

Still, when you've been drinking water all day and you need to unwind, why not kick back with my low-carb **Spiked Tea** or a refreshing **White Wine Sangria**?

Stella Style is all about making healthier choices and that doesn't stop at the fork! Thankfully, there is now an abundance of sugar-free choices to quench your thirst.

Cheers!

Spiked Tea

In my grocery store, they keep the malt and "novelty" alcoholic beverages in a refrigerated section between the cheeses and fresh meat. It seems that this beverage section is slowly swallowing more and more of my fresh food! Every week, there's a new bottled drink on the market—and they're *loaded* with extra sugar and carbs! This recipe is a twist on a popular favorite that I've seen everywhere recently. The twist is—it's actually low carb!

Yield:	**4 servings**
Prep Time:	**10 minutes**
Calories:	**20**
Total Fat:	**0 gram**
Saturated Fat:	**0 gram**
Carbohydrates:	**1 gram**
Net Carbohydrates:	**1 gram**
Fiber:	**0 gram**
Protein:	**0 gram**

1 cup fresh brewed green tea (may use any fresh brewed tea)
1 ounce gin or vodka
1 tablespoon fresh lime juice
1 tablespoon fresh lemon juice
2 packets sugar substitute (recommended: Splenda)
1 lime, cut into wedges, optional, for garnish

Mix all the ingredients together in a cocktail shaker and serve poured over ice and garnished with a lime wedge on the rim of the glass, if desired.

SPECIAL EQUIPMENT: cocktail shaker

MAKE IT MEMORABLE

I would tell you to go heavy on the alcohol, but then you might not remember much of anything!

HEALTHFUL HINTS

I joke about overindulging, but keep in mind that alcohol can inhibit weight loss. So enjoy drinks like this in moderation, especially if you notice your weight loss slowing!

White Wine Sangria

Rachel and I prefer a cool white wine when it's warm out, so I took a Mexican favorite and dressed it up to fit our tastes—and our lifestyle! I'm drinking a glass of this sangria as I am writing this on one of the hottest days in Connecticut history. So maybe it's the sangria talking, or maybe it's all this sun, but I can almost hear a mariachi band coming from my neighbor's backyard!

Yield:	**8 servings**
Prep Time:	**10 minutes**
Calories:	**45**
Total Fat:	**0 gram**
Saturated Fat:	**0 gram**
Carbohydrates:	**2 grams**
Net Carbohydrates:	**2 grams**
Fiber:	**0 gram**
Protein:	**0 gram**

2 cups dry Chardonnay, Chablis, or Pinot Grigio wine
2 cups club soda or seltzer water (you may also substitute diet lemon lime soda)
¼ cup fresh lime juice
¼ cup fresh lemon juice
4 packets sugar substitute (recommended: Splenda)
1 lemon, sliced into circles
1 lime, sliced into circles

SPECIAL EQUIPMENT: punch bowl

Mix all the ingredients together in a punch bowl. Serve immediately poured into glasses over ice.

MAKE IT MEMORABLE

Kick off your next fiesta with an Iceberg Prairie Salad with Smoky Green Chile Ranch Dressing (page 111), Turkey Fajita Wraps (page 156), and you know what to wash it all down with . . . Sangria Blanca, Por Favor!

HEALTHFUL HINTS

Keep in mind that alcohol can inhibit weight loss. So enjoy drinks like this in moderation, especially if your weight loss slows!

Frozen Margaritas

I was throwing ingredients into a blender to make lemon-lime slushees and it hit me: what I was blending up was obviously low carb—and so is tequila! I always keep a bottle of tequila in the house to cook with, honestly. So into the blender went some of that tequila and these margaritas were born! They're as good as the real thing with one small difference. No sugar highs—or subsequent lows.

Yield:	**4 servings**
Prep Time:	**5 minutes**
Calories:	**80**
Total Fat:	**0 gram**
Saturated Fat:	**0 gram**
Carbohydrates:	**3 grams**
Net Carbohydrates:	**3 grams**
Fiber:	**0 gram**
Protein:	**0 gram**

2 cups ice cubes
¼ cup sugar substitute, more or less to taste (recommended: Splenda)
¾ cup water
4 ounces tequila, more or less to your partytude (attitude)
Juice from 2 lemons
Juice from 2 limes
Lemon slices, for garnish
Lime slices, for garnish
Coarse margarita-style salt, as needed

EQUIPMENT: blender; 4 old-fashioned glasses

1. Make the margaritas: Place all the ingredients in a blender, except the lemon and lime slices and coarse salt, and blend on high until smooth, 1 to 2 minutes.

2. Run a lemon slice around the rims of the glasses to dampen them; then dip them in a small plate of salt to coat.

3. Pour the margaritas into the prepared glasses and garnish with lemon and lime slices.

MAKE IT MEMORABLE

I last made these drinks for a family gathering to soothe the heat from the Jamaican BBQ Ribs (page 126) that I was cookin' up. With Rachel's now famous BBQ Baked Soybeans (page 202) and Jicama Slaw (page 118), it was the perfect backyard party!

HEALTHFUL HINTS

The sugar substitute can be left out, making a sour drink—different but still great. And if you're watching your sodium, definitely skip the salted rim (I do).

Anthony's Berry Good Smoothies

My sons should be soy milk spokesmen! Whenever they have anyone over, the blender comes out and these smoothies are coming right up. The combination of soy milk and vanilla extract makes for a rich and creamy taste reminiscent of vanilla ice cream. You should see our guests' mouths drop when we tell them that it's not ice cream but soy milk. Or when we explain that they're actually *good* for you!

Yield:	**3 servings**
Prep Time:	**2 minutes**
Calories:	**70**
Total Fat:	**2 grams**
Saturated Fat:	**0 gram**
Carbohydrates:	**8 grams**
Net Carbohydrates:	**5 grams**
Fiber:	**3 grams**
Protein:	**4 grams**

½ cup frozen strawberries
¼ cup frozen raspberries
¼ cup frozen blueberries
1 cup soy milk, no sugar added
¼ cup sugar substitute (recommended: Splenda)
¼ teaspoon vanilla extract, no sugar added

SPECIAL EQUIPMENT: blender

Place all the ingredients in a blender and blend on high until smooth, 1 to 2 minutes.

MAKE IT MEMORABLE

Use 1 cup of strawberries and omit the other berries for a smoothie that tastes just like a strawberry milk shake!

HEALTHFUL HINT

If the berries are sweet, you can omit the sugar substitute.

Fresh Fruit Slushees

Late at night, you can hear the engines roar—and I mean the loud motor on my new blender that tells me Anthony has now burned out yet another one! It's my fault I guess, since we always keep berries and melon in the refrigerator (we know it's his favorite dessert or snack). This refreshing recipe is my favorite so far as it's absolutely perfect on a hot day, but it's also fun to mix it up from time to time with different fruit combinations—like cantaloupe and honeydew, raspberries, blackberries, and blueberries. What's your favorite?

Yield:	**4 servings; 8 ounces each**
Prep Time:	**5 minutes**
Calories:	**20**
Total Fat:	**0 gram**
Saturated Fat:	**0 gram**
Carbohydrates:	**4.5 grams**
Net Carbohydrates:	**3.5 grams**
Fiber:	**1 gram**
Protein:	**0 gram**

½ cup fresh strawberries
¼ cup fresh blueberries
1 lime, juiced
¾ cup water
2 cups ice cubes
¼ cup sugar substitute, more or less to taste (recommended: Splenda)
Lime slices, optional, for garnish
4 whole strawberries, optional, for garnish

SPECIAL EQUIPMENT: blender

Place all the ingredients in a blender, except the garnishes, cover tightly, and blend on high for 1 to 2 minutes, or until smooth. Use the pulse button or turn the blender on and off to help chop the ice evenly. Serve immediately poured into 4 glasses, and garnish with fresh lime slices and a strawberry on the edge of the glass, if desired.

MAKE IT MEMORABLE

Just a bit of rum will make this recipe really memorable. (No flavored rums, please.) If you like, you can add a small amount of soy milk or heavy cream, turning this slushee into a yummy milk shake.

HEALTHFUL HINTS

If the berries are very sweet, you may choose to omit the sugar substitute. And if you're not that concerned with natural sugars, a small amount of honey tastes great, too.

The Danny Cocktail

I was at a local restaurant and bar in Westport, Connecticut, called Dunvilles, when I noticed the bartender pouring Fresca into a glass of ice. It looked *so* refreshing—it was 95 in the shade outside, and I hadn't had a Fresca in so long that I had almost forgotten how much I liked it. So, naturally, I asked for one. Steve, the bartender, politely told me that it was the only can, and that it was for making a very special and *secret* drink: The Danny Cocktail. Well, the secret's out now! Steve and I suggest that anyone who wants this drink at Dunvilles (or anywhere else) should BYOCOF: Bring your own can of Fresca!

Yield:	1 serving
Prep Time:	5 minutes
Calories:	130
Total Fat:	0 gram
Saturated Fat:	0 gram
Carbohydrates:	0 gram
Net Carbohydrates:	0 gram
Fiber:	0 gram
Protein:	0 gram

2 ounces vodka
⅓ cup club soda
⅓ cup Fresca brand diet soda
1 lime, cut into wedges, optional, for garnish

Pour the ingredients in a glass over ice and serve garnished with a lime wedge on the rim.

MAKE IT MEMORABLE

Need a reason to try this drink? Have a football party and toast to your friends with a spicy Buffalo Shrimp Cocktail (page 70) and some Bueno Jalapeños (page 72).

HEALTHFUL HINTS

Alcohol, although zero carbohydrates, has been known to slow weight loss on a low-carb lifestyle. If you think alcohol is to blame for a slowdown, it just might be. Everything in moderation is the key! Oh, and do *not* operate heavy cooking equipment while drinking!

Dinah's Recipe for Success

I was thin, relatively speaking, most all my life. I married twenty-four years ago at the age of twenty-three, and it seemed my weight started creeping up as soon as I signed the marriage license. Almost five years later, I had our first son and six years later, along came our second son. The baby weight never left. In 1998, I lost my thirty-two-year-old baby brother and depression became a daily part of my life.

So did pain, both mental and physical. My back hurt, my knees hurt, my feet hurt. Okay, I guess everything hurt. Three years ago, I was diagnosed with fibromyalgia, so I had a name to go with the pain. Fibro isn't curable, but it is manageable.

In May 2003, I went home and saw that my sister had lost about twenty-five pounds following the Atkins plan. She looked great, and she inspired me to investigate this way of life. The more I read about low carb, the more I realized that I was sensitive to carbohydrates and it could very well be the reason I was having so many health problems.

On May 12, 2003, I began my journey. I had roughly 123 pounds to lose to get to where I think I'll be most comfortable. It seemed like such a formidable task! In the first month I lost eighteen pounds. I felt SO much better! I didn't have the sluggishness, the shortness of breath, and chronic fatigue. I had ENERGY!

I've never eaten so well in my life, and now, with *Stella Style,* I've been told I've never *cooked* better in my life! I love to cook; experimenting with different recipes and learning how to modify the way I cook has become my favorite hobby. I have never EVER felt deprived and I eat until I'm full. I am keeping my carb intake to around 20 to 35 per day, and as of today I am down eighty pounds!

My LC journey isn't over; as a matter of fact it has just begun! I still have roughly sixty pounds to go. But I do know one thing. This is my new life, and I won't ever live my old life again. I feel like I have been reborn at forty-seven years young!

Desserts

All right! You've made it this far—and that means it's time for dessert! You've been waiting for me to say that, haven't you?

When my family first started low carb, we were clueless as to how to satisfy a sweet tooth. Truth is, much of our cravings for sweets disappeared two weeks into our new lifestyle. We had broken our addiction to sugar and we'd never felt better! But that doesn't mean that we didn't still get the occasional urge for, say, *chocolate* or sweet *baked goods.*

It was going to take all the creativity we could muster! Thankfully, Rachel was a commercial baker and has a great baking sense that she applies to naturally low-carb ingredients. Almond flour, pumpkin, and coconut are key elements of incredible desserts such as her moist and memorable **Pumpkin Pound Cake** or her too-good-to-be-true **Marvelous Macaroons.**

By now, you may have dropped the book and gone to find a baking pan, but wait! There's amazingly rich **Tiramisù for You**! It sounds so good that you may not even be reading this right now. Meaning that I can probably just use the rest of this space to talk about anything I want. But hey—now I've made *myself* hungry for dessert! What I wouldn't do for some **Chocolate Pecan Truffles.** If only there was a way to make them low carb. Well, there is—and it's coming right up!

Even though no refined sugars go into my recipes, on *Stella Style,* no sugar craving goes unanswered! So get out those dessert plates and forks. That is, if these decadent treats can even make it to the table!

BITES

SLICES

SPOONFULS

Bites

Chocolate Pecan Truffles

All I can say is . . . WOW! Sometimes we just blow ourselves away! Made from pure *real* chocolate, without the white stuff, these truffles are just what you need to "Curb the Urge"! As real as they get, but you can enjoy them without the guilt! Ready, set . . . chocolate!

Yield:	**8 servings; 2 pieces each**
Prep Time:	**20 minutes**
Cook Time:	**5 minutes**
Chill Time:	**2 hours**
Calories:	**90**
Total Fat:	**9 grams**
Saturated Fat:	**4.5 grams**
Carbohydrates:	**4 grams**
Net Carbohydrates:	**3 grams**
Fiber:	**1 gram**
Protein:	**1 gram**

1 ounce unsweetened chocolate, chopped (we use Bakers' brand)
½ cup plus 1 tablespoon sugar substitute (recommended: Splenda)
3 tablespoons heavy cream (may use butter)
1 teaspoon instant coffee granules, optional
½ teaspoon vanilla extract, no sugar added
2 tablespoons unsalted butter
¼ cup chopped pecans
2 tablespoons unsweetened cocoa powder

SPECIAL EQUIPMENT: melon baller

1. Place the unsweetened chocolate in a heatproof bowl to melt over a pan of simmering water. (Be careful that the water does not boil rapidly, or the chocolate could burn.)

2. Whisk in ½ cup sugar substitute, then add the cream, instant coffee, if desired, and vanilla and blend thoroughly.

3. Remove the bowl from the heat, whisk in the butter until well blended, and then stir in the chopped pecans. Put the mix in a shallow bowl or dish and refrigerate for 1½ hours until completely set.

4. Add the cocoa powder and 1 tablespoon sugar substitute to a small bowl and mix together well.

5. Once the chocolate pecan mixture has chilled sufficiently, remove it and scrape the melon baller across the top, dipped in hot water each time, to make chocolate balls (approximately 1 inch round).

6. Place each ball in the cocoa mix and shake the bowl to coat well. Repeat until done, about 16 balls, and lay them in a single layer in a wax paper–coated container with lid. Refrigerate for at least 30 minutes more before enjoying!

MAKE IT MEMORABLE

These truffles may be saved for up to 1 week refrigerated or for several months frozen.

HEALTHFUL HINTS

The heavy cream and butter in this recipe can be replaced by a light trans-fat-free margarine and the pecans can be substituted with chopped almonds to reduce the fats.

Rachel's Marvelous Macaroons

This was a fun recipe to test and get right. Ordinarily, it takes a few tries, but for some reason we had to make this recipe . . . oh, about fifteen times. I just couldn't get enough of these macaroons, and I mean that literally! It's as if we have gremlins or something. Every time Rachel made a batch, by the time I got to the kitchen to test them, they were gone! My best advice is to stay in the kitchen for the 15 minutes it takes them to cool. (I tried it and wound up eating almost all of them myself while they were still hot!)

Yield:	**8 servings; 2 per serving**
Prep Time:	**15 minutes**
Cook Time:	**20 minutes**
Calories:	**80**
Total Fat:	**7 grams**
Saturated Fat:	**4 grams**
Carbohydrates:	**4 grams**
Net Carbohydrates:	**2 grams**
Fiber:	**2 grams**
Protein:	**2 grams**

¼ cup blanched Almond Flour (page 85) (blanched almond flour is made from raw almonds with the brown hulls removed; regular almond flour will turn the macaroons brown)
½ teaspoon baking soda
⅛ teaspoon salt
3 egg whites
1½ teaspoons vanilla extract, no sugar added
½ teaspoon coconut extract, no sugar added
¼ teaspoon pure almond extract
⅓ cup plus 1 tablespoon sugar substitute (recommended: Splenda)
1½ teaspoons unsalted butter or trans-fat-free margarine, softened, at room temperature
1⅓ tightly packed cups shredded unsweetened coconut (use fresh or unsweetened shredded; can be found at health food stores)

SPECIAL EQUIPMENT, OPTIONAL: 1-ounce ice cream scoop; parchment paper or silicone mat–lined cookie sheet (we prefer the silicone mat; it works great!)

1. Place the baking rack in the center of the oven and preheat the oven to 350°F.

2. In a small bowl, whisk together the almond flour, baking soda, and salt and set aside.

3. In a medium bowl, whisk together the egg whites and extracts until foamy, then stir in the sugar substitute and butter until well blended.

4. Add the mixed dry ingredients to the egg mixture and fold in the coconut until everything is combined.

5. Wet your fingers and form 16 equal balls of the mix, about 4 teaspoons each, or use a 1-ounce ice cream scoop tightly packed with the mix.

6. Place the macaroons on the lined sheet pan and bake for approximately 15 minutes, until they start to turn golden brown all over.

7. Remove the macaroons from the oven and let cool completely, about 15 minutes, before serving.

Refrigerate any leftovers in a covered container. (Macaroons will soften greatly after being covered and refrigerated.)

MAKE IT MEMORABLE

Serve as a decadent dessert by cutting the macaroons in half, drizzling with rum, and topping with fresh whipped cream.

HEALTHFUL HINTS

Lighten up this recipe by using alternative ingredients such as a trans-fat-free margarine in place of the butter (it even comes in a lactose-free version these days). Although macaroons are normally very sweet, you may cut down on the sugar substitute to ¼ cup and not compromise the flavor!

Chocolate Almond Finger Cookies

When Rachel first made these, I didn't know what to think about them. After I ate about ten of them, I still could not get a handle on what exactly it was that I liked about them. They have a taste that's all their own! I could tell I really liked them, though, because I ate way too many and couldn't stop, a problem that everyone in the house had with these! So here they are, with no description offered other than—be careful! For some reason, they can be addictive . . .

Yield:	**10 servings; 5 cookies each**
Prep Time:	**15 minutes**
Cook Time:	**12 minutes**
Calories:	**170**
Total Fat:	**16 grams**
Saturated Fat:	**7 grams**
Carbohydrates:	**5 grams**
Net Carbohydrates:	**3 grams**
Fiber:	**2 grams**
Protein:	**4 grams**

8 tablespoons (1 stick) unsalted butter, softened
½ cup sugar substitute (recommended: Splenda)
2 large egg whites
2 tablespoons unsweetened cocoa powder
1½ cups Almond Flour (page 85)

SPECIAL EQUIPMENT: electric mixer; pastry bag fitted with a ½-inch plain tip

1. Preheat the oven to 350°F and line 2 cookie sheet pans with parchment paper.

2. In the bowl of an electric mixer, beat the softened butter on medium speed for about 2 minutes, then add the sugar substitute and beat for another minute until the mix is well blended and turns white.

3. Add the egg whites and beat until smooth.

4. Remove from the mixer and use a rubber spatula to mix in the cocoa powder and almond flour until well blended.

5. Scrape the mix into a pastry bag and pipe out 2-inch-long finger cookies on the lined sheet pans, leaving a couple of inches of space in between each one. Makes about 50 finger cookies. (You may use the pastry bag without a tip if you do not have one large enough, or you may use a teaspoon to make the cookies.)

6. Bake for about 12 minutes and then remove and cool on racks. The cookies are best served immediately once fully cooled, but they can also be stored on the counter in a covered container or plastic zip-lock bag for up to 3 days. (When stored, they lose their crispness.)

MAKE IT MEMORABLE

Line a martini or margarita glass with 3 finger cookies and add Fresh Berries and Sabayon (page 240) for a dessert you or your guests won't soon forget!

HEALTHFUL HINTS

To lighten up this recipe, the butter may be replaced with trans-fat-free margarine, and the sugar substitute may be reduced to ¼ cup for a bittersweet treat.

Baked Meringue Cookies

I remember the baked meringue candies they had when I was a kid; they came in different shapes and melted in your mouth. And who could ever forget the infamous *Peeps* at Eastertime? Before I started low carb, I never would have thought of baking my own meringues, yet they are sooo easy I could have made them with my eyes closed. Sometimes the simplest things can be the best things, and these classic baked meringue cookies are the proof! Don't do without *or* let the sugar cravings get you down—just make these fluffy delights and keep a bag of them on hand!

Yield:	**12 servings; 4 cookies each**
Prep Time:	**15 minutes**
Cook Time:	**45 minutes**
Calories:	**10**
Total Fat:	**0 gram**
Saturated Fat:	**0 gram**
Carbohydrates:	**1 gram**
Net Carbohydrates:	**1 gram**
Fiber:	**0 gram**
Protein:	**2 grams**

Vegetable oil spray
6 large egg whites
1 teaspoon vanilla extract, no sugar added
¼ teaspoon cream of tartar
⅓ cup sugar substitute (recommended: Splenda)
1 tablespoon unsweetened cocoa powder, optional, if want chocolate meringues

SPECIAL EQUIPMENT: electric mixer

1. Preheat the oven to 350°F and spray 2 cookie sheet pans with vegetable oil.

2. Add the egg whites to a mixing bowl and beat on high speed for about 1 minute until frothy. Then add the remaining ingredients and continue beating until soft peaks form.

3. To make the meringues, use heaping tablespoons of the mixture laid in rows on the sprayed sheet pans, leaving a couple of inches of space in between each one. The recipe makes about 48 meringue cookies.

4. Bake for 40 to 45 minutes until browned, then remove from the cookie sheets, and cool on racks. These cookies are best served fully cooled. They may be stored on the counter in a covered container or plastic zip-lock bag for up to 1 week.

MAKE IT MEMORABLE

Pop these easy dessert snacks in a zip-lock baggie for on-the-go snacks or brown baggin' it at lunchtime! At parties, a tray piled high makes a tasty and attractive replacement for cookies or cakes.

HEALTHFUL HINT

These little cookies are wonderful all around—just look at those nutritional counts! Enjoy them as is.

Cinnamon Crisps

Don't give in to cravings—with only 6 ingredients and 15 minutes, you can have a great tasting crunchy sweet treat that's sure to cure the sugar blues! I think these crisps taste like honey-cinnamon flavored graham crackers! I especially like them with an espresso at about four in the afternoon. Rachel loves them with spiced green tea. The kids just love them with everything! But best of all, since they are made with healthy fats, loaded with fiber and sugar free, they can be eaten with all of the enjoyment, and none of the guilt!

Yield:	**8 servings; 3 crisps each**
Prep Time:	**20 minutes**
Cook Time:	**15 minutes**
Calories:	**70**
Total Fat:	**6 grams**
Saturated Fat:	**0 gram**
Carbohydrates:	**3 grams**
Net Carbohydrates:	**2 grams**
Fiber:	**1 gram**
Protein:	**3 grams**

1 cup Almond Flour (page 85)
¼ cup sugar substitute (recommended: Splenda)
1 egg white
⅛ teaspoon salt
½ teaspoon ground cinnamon
½ teaspoon vanilla extract, no sugar added
1 teaspoon sugar substitute, for top (recommended: Splenda)
⅛ teaspoon ground cinnamon, for top

1. Preheat the oven to 350°F and line a sheet pan with parchment paper.

2. Add all the ingredients, except the last two, to a bowl and mix well with a wooden spoon.

3. Using two teaspoons, one to scrape the mixture off of the other, place 24 spoonfuls in 4 rows of 6 spaced evenly apart on the sheet pan. Then press each spoonful down slightly to make the crisps more flat in shape and about 1 inch square and ¼ inch thick.

4. Sprinkle each crisp evenly with a mixture of 1 teaspoon sugar substitute and ⅛ teaspoon cinnamon and bake for 15 minutes or until crispy. Cool and serve or store on the counter in a covered container for up to 3 days.

MAKE IT MEMORABLE

These crisps are great by themselves as an anytime cravings buster, but they can be a real treat that kids love (we're all kids at heart!) served with a Fresh Raspberry Fruit Dip (page 58).

HEALTHFUL HINTS

If you have not given up sugar entirely, you may use brown sugar in place of the sugar substitute for a healthier alternative to white sugar. But if you are trying to lose weight by eating low carb, you should avoid all sugars until you reach your desired weight.

Slices

Pumpkin Pound Cake

This pound cake is nutty from the almonds and rich and dense from the pumpkin without a drop of flour or cream! It makes a perfect quick start in the morning or a slow-savoring finish to a Sunday family meal. It's always a hit during the holidays—Rachel and I wrap it, pan and all, in colored cellophane, and bring it to family and friends when we visit. *They* get a gift and *we're* guaranteed a no-sugar dessert at the end of the day!

Vegetable oil spray, as needed
2 tablespoons wheat bran
2½ cups Almond Flour (page 85)
1½ cups sugar substitute (recommended: Splenda)
1½ teaspoons baking powder
1½ teaspoons pumpkin pie spice
¼ teaspoon salt
7 large eggs
1½ cups canned pure pumpkin (not pumpkin pie filling)
1½ teaspoons vanilla extract (no sugar added)

Yield:	**12 servings**
Prep Time:	**15 minutes**
Cook Time:	**1½ hours**
Calories:	**180**
Total Fat:	**13 grams**
Saturated Fat:	**1.5 grams**
Carbohydrates:	**11 grams**
Net Carbohydrates:	**8 grams**
Fiber:	**4 grams**
Protein:	**8 grams**

EQUIPMENT: 9-by-5-inch loaf pan

1. Preheat the oven to 300°F.

2. Heavily spray the loaf pan with vegetable oil spray and sprinkle with the wheat bran, shaking the pan to coat on all sides; this will prevent sticking.

3. In a bowl whisk together the almond flour, sugar substitute, baking powder, pumpkin pie spice, and salt.

4. In another bowl, beat the eggs and then whisk in the pumpkin and vanilla. Combine the dry and wet ingredients and stir until combined.

5. Pour the batter into the prepared pan. Bake until golden brown and a toothpick comes out clean when stuck in the center, about 1½ hours. Cool completely before removing from the pan. Slice into 6 thick slices and cut each slice in half to make 12 portions. Serve warm or cold.

MAKE IT MEMORABLE

Serve alongside traditional favorites like roast turkey and ham, or griddle in the morning and top with a thin slice of cream cheese.

HEALTHFUL HINTS

You may use egg whites or Eggbeaters in place of the whole eggs and the sugar substitute may be reduced by as much as half for a less sweet but still great cake!

Breadless Bread Pudding

When I first met Rachel twenty-five years ago, she worked in a commercial bakery and would always tell me stories about how things were made. One thing I remember was how they made bread pudding and why. She said they would make it when they had lots of leftover and stale donuts, because that way they could resell the merchandise with a brand-new expiration date. Well, *we don't need no stinkin' bread*—and the proof is really in this pudding!

Yield:	**9 servings**
Prep Time:	**10 minutes**
Cook Time:	**1½ hours**
Chill Time:	**3 hours**
Calories:	**170**
Total Fat:	**15 grams**
Saturated Fat:	**9 grams**
Carbohydrates:	**3 grams**
Net Carbohydrates:	**3 grams**
Fiber:	**0 gram**
Protein:	**6 grams**

4 large eggs
1 cup heavy cream
1 cup whole milk ricotta cheese
½ cup sugar substitute (recommended: Splenda)
2 teaspoons vanilla extract, no sugar added
½ teaspoon ground cinnamon, plus a bit more, optional, for garnish

SPECIAL EQUIPMENT: hand-held or tabletop mixer; 8-by-8-inch baking pan

1. Preheat the oven to 325°F. Spray the baking pan with vegetable oil.

2. Add all the ingredients to a mixing bowl and beat on high with a mixer for about 2 minutes until well blended.

3. Pour the mix into the sprayed baking pan and bake for about 1½ hours until well browned. Cool on the counter and then refrigerate for at least 3 hours. To serve, cut the pudding into 9 squares and garnish each with a dash of ground cinnamon, if desired.

MAKE IT MEMORABLE

This pudding can be a classic finish for a comfort food dinner of Family-Style Chicken (page 152). Add a few fresh blueberries or strawberries on top for an out of this world dessert!

HEALTHFUL HINTS

You may lighten up this recipe by using soy milk in place of the heavy cream and low-fat ricotta cheese in place of the whole milk ricotta. The sugar substitute may be reduced by half for a less sweet version that's still great.

Tiramisù for You

Tiramisù is a recipe that just sounds good—everyone loves it, even before they see it! I tell you this so that you'll know that this phenomenal dessert is worth the considerable effort it requires to make. It's not difficult; I've broken down the many simple steps into substeps to make it easier. The only thing you'll need to fear is that anyone who tries it will be begging you to make it every day! So I suggest you go ahead right now and make this Tiramisù for *You!*

Yield:	**8 servings**
Prep Time:	**1 hour**
Cook Time:	**27 minutes**
Chill Time:	**8 hours to overnight**
Calories:	**380**
Total Fat:	**37 grams**
Saturated Fat:	**18 grams**
Carbohydrates:	**8 grams**
Net Carbohydrates:	**6 grams**
Fiber:	**2 grams**
Protein:	**8 grams**

LADYFINGERS

½ cup (1 stick) unsalted butter, softened
¾ cup sugar substitute (recommended: Splenda)
1¼ cups Almond Flour (page 85)
1 large egg
1 teaspoon vanilla extract, no sugar added
½ teaspoon pure almond extract
¼ teaspoon cream of tartar
¼ teaspoon baking soda

MASCARPONE FILLING

½ cup heavy cream
1 tablespoon sugar substitute (recommended: Splenda)
8 ounces mascarpone cheese
4 ounces cream cheese, softened
1½ teaspoons vanilla extract, no sugar added
1 egg yolk

MOCHA GLAZE AND DUSTING

½ cup boiling water
1 tablespoon instant coffee granules
1 teaspoon sugar substitute, plus 1 tablespoon (recommended: Splenda)
1 tablespoon unsweetened cocoa powder

8 fresh strawberries, optional, for garnish

SPECIAL EQUIPMENT: electric mixer; 8-by-8-inch baking pan well sprayed with vegetable oil; an 8-by-4-inch loaf pan

1. Preheat the oven to 350°F.

2. Make the Ladyfingers: In the bowl of an electric mixer, beat the softened butter on medium speed for about 2 minutes, then add the sugar substitute and beat for another minute until well blended and the mix turns white.

3. Remove the bowl from the mixer and using a wooden spoon mix in the almond flour and remaining ladyfinger ingredients until smooth.

4. Pour the mix into the well-sprayed 8-by-8-inch baking pan and tap the pan flat on the counter a few times to spread the mix evenly. Bake for about 17 minutes until golden brown, then remove and cool on a rack.

5. When cooled, remove the cooked cake layer by first loosening it and then quickly flipping the pan over onto a sheet pan. Cut the cake into 12 even pieces to make the ladyfingers and place them back in the oven to bake for an additional 8 to 10 minutes until well done and somewhat crispy around the edges. Remove and cool.

1. Make the Mascarpone Filling: In the bowl of an electric mixer, beat the heavy cream with the sugar substitute on high until peaks form. Remove the whipped cream from the bowl and set it aside (no need to clean the bowl or beaters).

2. In the same mixer bowl, beat the mascarpone cheese, softened cream cheese, vanilla, and egg yolk on high speed for 1 to 2 minutes until light and fluffy.

3. Remove the bowl from the mixer and fold in the whipped cream to finish and reserve.

1. Make the Mocha Glaze and Dusting: Add the instant coffee and 1 teaspoon sugar substitute to the boiling water and stir to dissolve.

2. To make the dusting, mix together 1 tablespoon sugar substitute with the cocoa powder in a small bowl.

1. Put It All Together: Place 6 of the ladyfingers in the bottom of the 8-by-4-inch loaf pan and drizzle with half of the mocha glaze.

2. Next spoon in half of the filling, spread evenly, and sprinkle with half of the dusting mixture. Repeat the steps for a second layer and chill covered for at least 8 hours or overnight. To serve, cut into 8 equal slices and garnish with fresh strawberries, if desired.

MAKE IT MEMORABLE

Start your meal of the century with Herb Boursin Cheese Spread (page 59) and fresh vegetable crudités. Then bring out the French-Style Mussels (page 78), followed by Herbed Filet Mignon and Red Wine Mushrooms (page 141), a fitting lead to the grand finale of Tiramisù for You!

HEALTHFUL HINTS

To lighten up this recipe, low-fat cream cheese may be used and the mascarpone cheese may be replaced with Neufchâtel cheese. Also, the heavy cream may be omitted altogether, making for a filling with a heavier texture that's lighter in fats!

Lemon Meringue Pie

This is a must-try recipe! The pie looks and tastes fantastic. You have to try it! Yes, I am building you up once again. This pie is more work than most of the recipes in this book, but it's not impossible and can be great fun, too! It's a lot like putting a puzzle together, and when you are done, the results will WOW you. I love bringing a labor of love to the table. Everyone says, "Wow," and it makes my efforts all worthwhile! When life hands you lemons . . . make lemon meringue pie!

Yield:	**8 servings**
Prep Time:	**45 minutes**
Cook Time:	**25 minutes**
Chill Time:	**2 hours**
Calories:	**160**
Total Fat:	**11 grams**
Saturated Fat:	**3 grams**
Carbohydrates:	**9 grams**
Net Carbohydrates:	**8 grams**
Fiber:	**1 gram**
Protein:	**7 grams**

CRUST

Vegetable oil spray
1 egg white
1 cup Almond Flour (page 85)
¼ cup sugar substitute (recommended: Splenda)
⅛ teaspoon salt
2 tablespoons butter, softened

MERINGUE

6 large egg whites
½ teaspoon cream of tartar
¼ cup sugar substitute (recommended: Splenda)
1 teaspoon vanilla extract, no sugar added

FILLING

5 egg yolks, at room temperature (save the whites for the meringue, and you will still need 1 more)
1½ cups water
1 cup sugar substitute (recommended: Splenda)
1 tablespoon grated lemon peel
½ cup fresh lemon juice
¼ teaspoon salt
1 envelope unflavored gelatin (recommended: Knox brand)
¼ cup cold water

SPECIAL EQUIPMENT: electric mixer; one 9-inch pie pan

1. Preheat the oven to 325°F. Spray the pie pan generously with vegetable oil.

2. Make the Crust: In a medium bowl, whisk the egg white with a fork until frothy and add the remaining crust ingredients. Mix until well blended and doughlike.

3. Place the dough in the center of the pie pan and cover loosely with plastic wrap. Press down through the plastic to spread the dough evenly to cover the entire inside of the pan. (Make sure to coat the sides all the way to the top.) Discard the plastic wrap and replace it with a round piece of parchment paper. (Trim the edges afterward if needed.) Set aside and prepare the meringue.

1. Make and Bake the Meringue: Add the egg whites to a mixing bowl and beat on high speed for about 1 minute until frothy. Then add the remaining meringue ingredients and continue beating until soft peaks form.

2. Scoop the meringue into the piecrust right on top of the parchment pape and spread it out, mounding in the center. (The paper and meringue will be lifted off the crust after baking so the pie may be filled later.) Bake the crust and meringue together for 25 to 30 minutes until the meringue is golden brown. Remove from the oven and let cool until ready to fill.

1. Prepare an ice water bath with an insert bowl.

2. Make the Filling and Pie: In a saucepan over medium heat, whisk together the egg yolks, 1½ cups water, sugar substitute, lemon peel, lemon juice, and salt. Cook while stirring slowly and constantly with a wooden spoon for about 15 minutes being careful not to let the filling boil.

3. Just before the filling is done, dissolve the gelatin in ¼ cup cold water and let sit for 1 minute, then quickly whisk it into the hot filling.

4. Immediately remove the filling from the heat and pour it into the bowl resting in the ice water bath to cool.

5. Once cooled, pour the filling into the cooked piecrust.

6. Carefully remove the parchment paper from the baked meringue and place the meringue on top of the filled pie to finish. Refrigerate uncovered for at least 2 hours before serving.

MAKE IT MEMORABLE

Take this pie along to family gatherings or serve it at home after an easygoing dinner of Family-Style Chicken (page 152)!

HEALTHFUL HINT

The butter in this recipe can be replaced with a trans-fat-free margarine.

Spoonfuls

Balsamic-Grilled Strawberries and Cream

I love to grill (if I've said it once, I've said it a million times) and so I thought, why stop with dessert? It takes very little effort to throw some luscious strawberries on the grill, but you'll still seem like a superhero. This is an easy alternative and a great gourmet twist on a classic dessert!

Yield:	**4 servings**
Prep Time:	**10 minutes**
Cook Time:	**2 minutes**
Calories:	**160**
Total Fat:	**14 grams**
Saturated Fat:	**6 grams**
Carbohydrates:	**6.5 grams**
Net Carbohydrates:	**5.5 grams**
Fiber:	**1 gram**
Protein:	**2 grams**

Fresh Whipped Cream (recipe follows)
8 large whole strawberries or 1 pint any size (For best display results, organic strawberries with long stems still attached are recommended.)
1 tablespoon balsamic vinegar
1 tablespoon sugar substitute (recommended: Splenda)
1 ounce toasted sliced almonds

SPECIAL EQUIPMENT: grill or grill pan; 4 champagne glasses; electric mixer

1. Preheat an outdoor grill or indoor grill pan to high.

2. Prepare the whipped cream as directed.

3. In a bowl, coat the strawberries with the balsamic vinegar and sugar substitute.

4. Place the strawberries on the hot grill to mark for 2 to 3 minutes. Remove from the heat and serve by placing a few warm grilled berries, stems up, in a champagne glass with a couple of tablespoons of fresh whipped cream carefully draped over them. Make sure the grill marks on the berries are still showing!

5 Sprinkle with toasted almonds.

FRESH WHIPPED CREAM
½ cup heavy cream
2 tablespoons sugar substitute (recommended: Splenda)
½ teaspoon vanilla extract, no sugar added

With an electric mixer on high, whip the heavy cream in a bowl just until frothy. Add the sugar substitute and vanilla and continue to whip on high until soft peaks form. Be careful not to overwhip, or the cream will break.

MAKE IT MEMORABLE

Place a half slice of our Pumpkin Pound Cake (page 229) in the bottom of the champagne glass and then top with the grilled strawberries and cream! Or add other berries such as raspberries and blueberries to make a filling and attractive dessert.

HEALTHFUL HINTS

In place of the fresh whipped cream, try topping the berries with a tablespoon of regular or low-fat sour cream sweetened with less than 1 packet of Splenda sugar substitute. Other fruits such as fresh peach and plum halves work well with this recipe, but strawberries have the least carbs, so they're best for those just getting started.

Fresh Berries and Sabayon

This delicate and rich dessert sauce is the kissin' cousin of the decadent hollandaise sauce, which is mostly used for vegetables and meats. But while they're made in almost the same exact way, sabayon's end result is far different. Just a little sabayon goes a long way to satisfy a sweet tooth by turning healthy, fresh berries into a dessert fit for a king (or a queen, of course)!

Yield:	**6 servings**
Prep Time:	**20 minutes**
Cook Time:	**6 minutes**
Calories:	**90**
Total Fat:	**2 grams**
Saturated Fat:	**0 gram**
Carbohydrates:	**13 grams**
Net Carbohydrates:	**9 grams**
Fiber:	**4 grams**
Protein:	**3 grams**

2 large eggs, separated
¼ cup sugar substitute, plus 1 tablespoon (recommended: Splenda)
¼ teaspoon grated lemon rind
½ cup dry white wine
1 pint fresh strawberries, cleaned and sliced
1 pint fresh blueberries
1 pint fresh raspberries
6 sprigs fresh mint, optional, for garnish

SPECIAL EQUIPMENT: electric mixer; 6 champagne glasses

1. Place a pot of water on medium heat to simmer, and ready an ice bath.

2. Add the egg whites to a mixing bowl and beat on high speed for about 1 minute until frothy, then add 1 tablespoon sugar substitute and continue beating until soft peaks form. Set aside.

3. Place a stainless steel bowl over the pot of simmering water and whisk in the egg yolks, ¼ cup sugar substitute, lemon, and white wine. Continue whisking the mixture over the simmering water until the volume of the sauce more than triples. Remove and immediately place the bowl over an ice bath and continue mixing until the sauce is cooled.

4. While the sauce chills over the ice bath, place equal amounts of the berries in each of 6 champagne glasses.

5. Fold the whipped egg whites into the chilled sauce and spoon a couple of tablespoons over the top of the berries. (Sabayon, much like hollandaise, is a delicate fresh sauce and should be made and used as needed. It is not a sauce that can be stored.)

MAKE IT MEMORABLE

If you are feeling like going overboard, go for it! It won't hurt a bit to try this recipe on top of some Frozen Custard Ice Cream (page 242) or atop Breadless Bread Pudding (page 230). It's all good!

HEALTHFUL HINTS

A small amount of berries and rich sabayon sauce can go a long way to satisfying cravings. So if you want to save on calories and fats, simply cut down on the portion and especially the amount of sauce used.

Frozen Custard Ice Cream

At first glance, this recipe seems very simple, and it can be; that is, if you believe that patience pays. With only four ingredients, you can make an outrageous dessert like a French pastry chef—as long as you are up for the challenge of standing in front of the stove for 25 minutes straight. I tell you this because if you try and rush this, you will be eating scrambled eggs instead of a heavenly French cream dessert! So get out the radio or CD player, get your ingredients ready, and try to meditate as you stir!

Yield:	**6 servings; about 4 ounces each**
Prep Time:	**10 minutes**
Cook Time:	**25 minutes**
Chill Time:	**2 hours**
Calories:	**150**
Total Fat:	**13 grams**
Saturated Fat:	**7 grams**
Carbohydrates:	**5 grams**
Net Carbohydrates:	**5 grams**
Fiber:	**0 gram**
Protein:	**4 grams**

2 cups half-and-half
1 teaspoon vanilla extract, no sugar added
4 egg yolks
⅓ cup sugar substitute (recommended: Splenda)
6 strawberries, cut into fans, optional, for garnish
6 sprigs fresh mint, optional, for garnish

SPECIAL EQUIPMENT: 6 champagne glasses

1. Prepare an ice water bath with an insert bowl.

2. In a heavy saucepan, scald 1 cup of the half-and-half and mix in the vanilla.

3. In a mixing bowl, beat the egg yolks with the nonheated remaining cup of half-and-half and blend in the sugar substitute. Then slowly whisk in the very hot half-and-half and pour everything back into the saucepan.

4. Place the saucepan back on the stove and reduce the heat to medium. Cook while stirring slowly and constantly with a wooden spoon for about 25 minutes until the sauce thickens enough to coat the back of a spoon, being careful not to ever let the sauce boil. (If the sauce gets too hot, just remove the saucepan from the stove for a minute and turn down the heat a bit before resuming cooking.)

5. When done, immediately remove from the heat and pour the sauce into a bowl resting in an ice water bath to cool the custard quickly.

6. Pour the cooled custard into 6 champagne glasses and freeze as ice cream or serve refrigerated as parfaits. Garnish each with a strawberry fan and a sprig of fresh mint before serving, if desired. (If the frozen ice cream is too hard to eat, thaw for a couple minutes before serving.)

MAKE IT MEMORABLE

This frozen delight makes the perfect ending to a comfort filled family meal of Steph's Chuck Pot Roast (page 143) and a Green Beans Casserole (page 188). For variety, simply add your favorite nuts—pecans or macadamias—or any fresh berries, for a great new flavor!

HEALTHFUL HINT

For those taking the Calorie Burner approach to *Stella Style,* you may lighten this recipe by replacing the half-and-half with skim milk.

Panna Cotta and Cranberry Martinis

This dessert recipe is great for when you're planning ahead, as it can be made up to two days in advance. Although it may look to be a bit involved, once you read through it, you will see it is quite easy. Those who have had problems with custards in the past may also appreciate the fact that panna cotta is thickened with a gelatin rather than eggs, making this recipe a snap! So why not snap to it? Even without the gin, this is one of my favorite martinis!

Yield:	**6 servings**
Prep Time:	**20 minutes**
Cook Time:	**7 minutes**
Chill Time:	**2 hours**
Calories:	**190**
Total Fat:	**14 grams**
Saturated Fat:	**9 grams**
Carbohydrates:	**11 grams**
Net Carbohydrates:	**10 grams**
Fiber:	**1 gram**
Protein:	**4 grams**

CRANBERRY RELISH
½ cup sugar substitute (recommended: Splenda)
½ cup water
6 ounces fresh or frozen cranberries
½ teaspoon orange zest

PANNA COTTA
2 tablespoons cold water
2 teaspoons unflavored gelatin
2 cups half-and-half
⅓ cup sugar substitute (recommended: Splenda)
1½ teaspoons vanilla extract, no sugar added
⅔ cup sour cream

¼ cup toasted sliced almonds, optional, for garnish

SPECIAL EQUIPMENT: 6 martini glasses

1. Make the Cranberry Relish: Combine the sugar substitute and water in a saucepan and bring to a boil.

2. Add the cranberries and orange zest and bring back to a boil. Then reduce the heat and simmer for about 7 minutes, stirring occasionally.

3. Remove from the heat, cool, and cover. Refrigerate for 30 minutes until well chilled before assembling the dessert. (Putting the relish in the freezer to chill can speed things up, but be careful not to freeze.)

1. Make the Panna Cotta: Add the cold water to a small bowl; pour in the gelatin and let sit for about 5 minutes to dissolve fully.

2. Heat the half-and-half, sugar substitute, and vanilla in a saucepan over medium heat while stirring constantly until almost boiling, but not quite.

3. Remove from the heat, stir in the dissolved gelatin and let cool for 15 minutes before mixing in the sour cream.

1. Put It All Together: Place a heaping tablespoon of chilled cranberry relish in the bottom of each of 6 martini glasses and then fill each glass evenly with the panna cotta mix. Refrigerate, covered, for 1 hour and then finish by topping each with another spoonful of cranberry relish and refrigerate for another hour. Serve garnished with toasted sliced almonds on top, if desired.

MAKE IT MEMORABLE

For that special occasion, enjoy Clams Parmesan (page 79) for starters, followed by Chicken Saltimbocca (page 162), and end with this unforgettable Panna Cotta and Cranberry Martinis powerhouse!

HEALTHFUL HINTS

To lighten up this recipe, use soy milk in place of the half-and-half and low-fat sour cream or plain yogurt to make the panna cotta. The cranberry relish may be replaced with a couple of tablespoons of fresh berries such as blueberries, raspberries, or strawberries!

Honeydew and Blackberry Granita

Granitas are an easy way to make a sorbet or sherbet. (Easy because you don't have to make simple syrup that requires tons of sugar and cooking, and you don't need any type of ice cream machine either.) All you need is fresh fruit, a freezer, and a little time to patiently caress this healthy and refreshing dessert to the finish line. You just can't lose with fresh fruit!

Yield:	**8 servings**
Prep Time:	**20 minutes**
Chill Time:	**3 hours**
Calories:	**60**
Total Fat:	**0 gram**
Saturated Fat:	**0 gram**
Carbohydrates:	**13 grams**
Net Carbohydrates:	**10 grams**
Fiber:	**3 grams**
Protein:	**1 gram**

1 honeydew melon, about 4 pounds
4 tablespoons sugar substitute (recommended: Splenda)
1 teaspoon fresh lemon juice
1 teaspoon fresh lime juice
1 pint fresh blackberries (may use raspberries)
1 ounce white wine (recommended: Pinot Grigio)
1 tablespoon lime zest, optional, for garnish

SPECIAL EQUIPMENT: food processor; 8-by-10-inch glass baking dish

1. Cut the melon in half and use a spoon to scoop out the seeds and discard. Then scoop out the fruit and place in the food processor.

2. Add 3 tablespoons sugar substitute and the lemon and lime juices to the fruit and puree in the food processor on high.

3. Pour the puree into the 8-by-10-inch glass baking dish so the liquid is about 1 inch deep. Freeze for 30 minutes and remove and use a fork to break up the ice with a scraping motion as it forms. Place back in the freezer and repeat this process every 30 minutes for about 3 hours until the ice is solid enough to hold its shape. (If the mix freezes too hard simply chop it with a knife or in your food processor for a few seconds.)

4. Mix the berries with the wine and the remaining 1 tablespoon sugar substitute and smash just a few of them with a fork. Place a couple of tablespoons of the granita in a shallow wineglass, top with a spoonful of the macerated berries, and serve garnished with a pinch of lime zest, if desired. Repeat . . .

MAKE IT MEMORABLE

This frozen treat will cool you off at a picnic, especially if you're serving Jamaican BBQ Ribs (page 126) or spicy Grilled Marinated Flank Steak (page 137)! And why not try making a cantaloupe granita and layering it with the honeydew for an outrageously different dessert!

HEALTHFUL HINTS

If the melon is sweet, you may eliminate the sugar substitute for a less sweet but still great flavor. If you do without the sweetener, I recommend not using the lemon or lime juices as they add an extra tart flavor.

Index